CAN
RUSSIA
COMPETE?

CAN RUSSIA COMPETE?

RAJ M. DESAI
ITZHAK GOLDBERG

editors

BROOKINGS INSTITUTION PRESS
Washington, D.C.

Can Russia Compete? may be ordered from:
Brookings Institution Press, 1775 Massachusetts Avenue, N.W.
Washington, D.C. 20036
Telephone: 1-800/537-5487 or 410/516-6956
E-mail: hfscustserv@press.jhu.edu; www.brookings.edu.

Library of Congress Cataloging-in-Publication data
Can Russia compete? / Raj M. Desai and Itzhak Goldberg, editors.
    p.   cm.
  Includes bibliographical references and index.
  Summary: "Looks at Russian government's push toward a knowledge-based economy,
particularly in the manufacturing sector. Quantifies and benchmarks sector's relative
strengths, identifying opportunities to increase Russian productivity and competitiveness.
Examines underlying firm-level determinants of knowledge absorption, competitiveness,
and productivity, with an eye to improving workers' skill levels and the investment
climate"—Provided by publisher.
  ISBN 978-0-8157-1831-4 (pbk. : alk. paper)
  1. Russia (Federation)—Economic policy—1991– 2. Competition—Russia
(Federation) I. Desai, Raj M., 1966– II. Goldberg, Itzhak, 1947– III. Title.

HC340.12.C35 2008
330.947—dc22   2008019821

9 8 7 6 5 4 3 2 1
The paper used in this publication meets minimum requirements of the
American National Standard for Information Sciences—Permanence of Paper
for Printed Library Materials: ANSI Z39.48-1992.

Typeset in Minion

Composition by Circle Graphics

Printed by R. R. Donnelley
Harrisonburg, Virginia

Contents

Foreword

Consider Russia's economic transformation in the past ten years. In 1999, Russia's economy was essentially bankrupt; it was leaking foreign exchange reserves; it was heavily indebted to the International Monetary Fund and highly dependent on financial assistance from the West; and it had been shrinking at about 6 percent a year since the breakup of the USSR. Today, Russia's stock of foreign reserves—which it has been accumulating at an average rate of almost 50 percent a *year*—now stands at about 25 percent of its total GDP. Russia holds one of the largest current account surpluses in the world, and it is one of the largest financiers of the U.S. current account deficit. And its economy has been growing at almost 7 percent since 1999. The average Russian citizen is almost twice as rich as he or she was in the depths of the post-Soviet recession.

Russia has come a long way in the last decade. But the good times that Russia's economy has enjoyed have been driven by a series of idiosyncratic factors that have been—and still could be—mostly fleeting. After the 1998 crisis, the collapse of the ruble led to the expansion of exports and import-competing sectors. Falling GDP created spare production capacity in Russian industry that could later be brought into production at lower cost. As these early benefits began to be offset by an increasing real exchange rate and rising production, oil and gas prices started their steep climb. The Russian oil and gas sector—less than 40 percent of exports in 1998—make up about 64 percent of Russia's exports today, earning the Russian economy more than $230 billion in revenue, or about $1,600 a year for every citizen.

That level of resource wealth is staggering, but oil and gas exports alone will not make Russia a permanently wealthy country. Despite Russia's efforts to stabilize oil and gas revenues through its stabilization fund, volatility due to unpredictable changes in oil and gas prices (along with the continuing appreciation of the real exchange rate) can easily undermine non-energy investment and inhibit the emergence of a vibrant private sector outside of the oil and gas sectors. Natural resource wealth often creates powerful incentives to capture and control the power and wealth that resource abundance provides. But more important, oil and gas wealth can divert both investment and attention away from building the economy that Russia will need to compete in the twenty-first century.

Competition in the new global economic environment is getting increasingly intense—a process that has been under way for some time. As this book makes clear, only a business environment that creates incentives for firms to invest productively, create jobs, and expand can deliver competitiveness and prosperity. In the past, China, India, and other emerging economies would compete solely on the basis of their low-skill, low-wage activities, slowly working their way up the value-added ladder. In the current environment, however, nations can quickly enter international markets by absorbing technologies, production processes, and management practices from around the world.

This volume—the result of collaboration between the World Bank and the Brookings Institution—argues that global competition has created a number of challenges for Russia, some of which Russia is ill-suited to meet unless its economic policies change. Globalization has dramatically increased the importance of productivity as a source of sustainable prosperity. Technology diffusion, skill acquisition, and the absorption of knowledge have become vital sources of economic growth and wealth. The results of knowledge and technology creation can contribute most to growth when they spread throughout the economy and are absorbed by a variety of economic agents, such as entrepreneurs, researchers, and firms of all sizes.

But Russia's labor productivity, although slightly ahead of that of Russia's neighbors in the Commonwealth of Independent States (CIS), ranks behind the productivity of most of Central Europe, all of the advanced industrialized countries, and countries such as Brazil and South Africa. Russia's "total factor productivity," the share of productivity not directly explained by the quantities of labor or capital used in production, also ranks much lower than that of the advanced economies that Russia aspires to emulate. At the same time, rapid technological change and growing skill intensity in many activities has increased the value of workers' skills and education.

Innovative activity is a crucial source of productivity growth, especially for middle-income countries that have already reached moderate levels of prosperity. Before the 1990s, Russia was widely regarded as a bastion of scientific knowledge. Russia's education system is well-developed, and the country boasts one of the highest percentages of university-educated individuals in the world. It also has large numbers of scientists and researchers per capita, and its spending on research development ranks highly. In other words, Russia's potential to innovate continues to be greater than that of most other countries at comparable levels of income.

But despite the considerable human and financial resources devoted to science and technology, Russia ranks low on most indicators of innovative output—patents, scientific papers, and so forth. Although the national research and development institutions created under its formerly centrally planned economy focused largely on the defense sector, they still remain important to Russia's innovation system; however, they have yet to create links with the international scientific community or with the private sector. At the enterprise level, there is less utilization of advanced technologies than in Indian or Chinese firms. Unlocking this scientific and technological potential and linking it with a more dynamic private sector must become a central part of Russia's economic strategy.

Russian authorities have been keenly aware of these challenges and on numerous occasions have expressed a desire to diversify the economy. The Russian Ministry of Economic Development and Trade, in particular, has enacted a series of administrative reforms since 2000, reducing red tape and barriers to business start-up and operations. But on other fronts, Russian authorities have often failed to follow through on some necessary steps.

Smaller and medium-sized Russian companies that have grown under strong competitive pressures and that are needed to diversify the economy, for example, are being penalized by the current policy regime. Many of these firms are targets of bribes, unauthorized inspections, regulatory harassment, and other forms of rent extraction. Moreover, the greater discretion over the economy that has resulted from the concentration of authority in the executive branch of government has often led to inconsistently enforced or interpreted regulations and to a high degree of uncertainty about the longer-term direction of Russia's economic policy.

The Russian government's 2006–2008 Mid-Term Program emphasized policy directions aimed at unleashing an "innovation economy." Vladimir Putin's "Russia 2020" speech, delivered at the State Council meeting in February 2008, emphasized a path of "innovative development" for the economy. And Russia's new president, Dmitry Medvedev, has also stressed the need for economic diversification through innovation. Several initiatives proposed in these statements are laudable—better protection and enforcement of intellectual property rights, increases in funding for basic scientific research, and greater investments in human capital. But the programs also emphasize more state control over the national "innovation system" through government-owned venture capital funds, government-owned development banking, and other forms of state intervention in the high-tech and knowledge sectors.

That Russia faces a choice may be a truism. It could continue along its path toward becoming a "rentier economy" whose prosperity is largely based on natural resources. Natural resource–led growth would continue as Russia pursued greater state intervention in economic life while tolerating large innovation gaps, deficiencies in worker skills, and associated weaknesses in the policy environment. Along this path, Russia would not build a competitive manufacturing base from which it could join global markets.

Or Russia can choose the path identified by Raj Desai, Itzhak Goldberg, and their colleagues in this volume—to make competitiveness the defining goal of its economic policy. Russia would maintain its commitment to sound macroeconomic management but address the weaknesses in the investment climate that have limited the country's productivity and innovative potential. It would improve its national research and development institutions, its firm-level incentives to absorb advanced global technologies and offer worker training, and a policy environment that has limited the growth potential of its most dynamic firms. The result would be economy-wide value creation from improved firm-level productivity due to increased competition, trade flows, worker mobility, and foreign direct investment.

Can Russia Compete? complements ongoing work at both the World Bank and Brookings. For the past three years, the World Bank has sponsored a series of flagship events organized by its Europe and Central Asia Region department to promote knowledge-based economic growth in client countries as well as a series of investment climate assessments identifying the microeconomic and market impediments to growth. The World Bank also has sponsored several regional studies on innovation and on building knowledge-based economies. Meanwhile, at Brookings, international competitiveness and the drivers of growth in Brazil, India, China, and Russia—the BRIC countries—are part of an ongoing project within the Global Economy and Development Program. In addition, a study of the political and economic consequences of natural resource dependence in Russia is the subject a forthcoming book from Brookings Press.

We hope that the findings and proposals in this book will facilitate an exchange of ideas and foster dialogue among policymakers in Russia and in the Eastern European and CIS region as a whole on the implementation of policies to develop strong, knowledge-intensive economies that can boost competitiveness, improve the productivity of jobs, and ultimately raise the region's standard of living.

STROBE TALBOTT
President
Brookings Institution

FERNANDO MONTES-NEGRET
Director, Private and
Financial Sector Development
Europe and Central Asia Region
World Bank

Acknowledgments

This volume is based on work that began at the World Bank more than three years ago to produce a report on the Russian investment climate that would assess the constraints and opportunities facing the Russian Federation in its efforts to create a more diverse and innovative economy. We are, therefore, heavily indebted to those individuals at the World Bank who were initially responsible for shaping the issues and priorities of the report: Alfred Jay Watkins and Alexandra L. Drees-Gross, under whose leadership the first phases of the project were begun and who contributed to the development of the project's overall concept and strategy.

We express our deep gratitude for the support and collaboration of the Higher School of Economics (HSE), Moscow State University, which formulated and conducted the enterprise surveys in Russia under the direction of Professor Evgeny Yasin and Dr. Andrei Yakovlev, with the participation of Ksenia Gonchar and Viktoria Golikova. The authors benefited immeasurably from the presentation of preliminary findings at HSE and from extensive conversations with our HSE colleagues. We also benefited from additional presentations at the Global Institute's Annual Russia-China Conference in Moscow and from feedback from Igor Fedyukin, Sergei Guriev, Ksenia Yudaeva, and Ekaterina Zhuravskaya.

Vastly strengthening the arguments, evidence, and conclusions of this volume were the contributions—both substantive and collaborative—of a number of colleagues: Paloma Anos-Casero, Igor Artemiev, Irina Astrakhan, Gail

Buyske, Alexandru Cojocaru, Jacqueline Coolidge, Carl Dahlman, Irina Dezhina, Inderbir S. Dhingra, Olga Emelyanova, Rostislav Kapelyushnikov, Laura Lanteri, John Litwack, Anna Lukyanova, Jack Martens, Emanuel Salinas Muñoz, David Tarr, and Sergei Ulatov. At the World Bank, Smita Kuriakose, Laura Lanteri, and Jasna Vukoje deserve a special mention for their invaluable production support and their overall supervision of the report through initial editing and production. We also are thankful for the extensive comments we received from those who took the time to review earlier drafts of our manuscript: Gordon Betcherman, Mark Dutz, William Maloney, and Shahid Yusuf.

Each of us would like to thank Fernando Montes-Negret, director of the Finance and Private Sector Development Department of the Europe and Central Asia Region at the World Bank, for his strong support of this endeavor, for his extensive comments on previous drafts, and for his valuable insights and ideas. Kristalina Georgieva, former country director for Russia at the World Bank, also encouraged our efforts to extend the initial findings contained in earlier drafts of the report. More recently, Lael Brainard, vice president of the Global Economy and Development Program at Brookings, has been extremely supportive of our endeavor and of the collaboration between the World Bank and Brookings.

Christopher Kelaher, Janet Walker, and Susan Woolen at Brookings Press and Valentina Kalk of the World Bank Publisher's Office deserve special thanks for overseeing the cooperation between our institutions and for their guidance on numerous matters related to publication. Our manuscript was efficiently and skillfully edited by Eileen Hughes.

For readers who wish to pursue the issues raised in this book, to examine the ongoing work of our institutions on these matters, or to replicate any of the results presented, all enterprise survey data used herein are available at www.brookings.edu/global (Brookings Institution) and www.worldbank.org/eca (World Bank).

one
Introduction

RAJ M. DESAI AND ITZHAK GOLDBERG

The Russian economy has been growing at an average nominal rate of 6 percent annually for the past decade. Among the most important factors contributing to its expansion has been the skyrocketing cost of oil and gas. In 2000, when Vladimir Putin took office, the cost of oil was approximately $20 a barrel; at the end of his term, it was five times higher. During Putin's presidency, Russia earned about $1 trillion in oil and gas revenues. Meanwhile, the competitiveness of Russian enterprises has become increasingly fragile because of the appreciating ruble, climbing resource prices, and rising wages as well as the exhaustion of Russia's excess industrial capacity. And in the past few years, the chorus of voices (both inside and outside the country) raising concerns about the sustainability of the Russian economy's performance has become louder. Observers have called for Russian authorities to take measures to counterbalance the nation's increasing economic dependence on natural resources.

Economic diversification can cover a wide number of issues and involve many challenges, including entrepreneurship, foreign investment, regional development, and physical infrastructure. In Russia's case, it comes down to one thing: ensuring that the manufacturing sector can compete in the global economy.

Russian competitiveness will not depend on centralized, top-down efforts to pick winners but on broader policy measures designed both to improve the investment climate—which affects firms' incentives to invest productively and create jobs—and to develop a more competitive, knowledge-based economy. Russian authorities are seeking to address many of the country's most important developmental challenges. They are emphasizing policies aimed at unleashing an "innovation economy," through, among other things, greater government commitment to research and development, better protection and enforcement of intellectual property rights, the formation of industrial technology parks, and the establishment of venture capital funds. Theirs is an ambitious program, yet it includes some controversial areas of economic policy that have yielded mixed results in other parts of the world. In particular, a "new industrial policy" aims to stimulate diversification and "knowledge absorption"—firms' application of current global technologies to their production process—through direct state support to and intervention in specific sectors and firms. The government has proposed an array of familiar mechanisms to accomplish this: state-managed technology programs, state-run development banks, state-owned venture capital funds, and so on.

But to exploit the opportunities generated by a good investment climate, Russian firms do not need more state intervention and support. They need a workforce with the skills required to carry out higher-value-added tasks. They also need the organizational and managerial capacity and the technical competence to invest, innovate, and enter strategic supply chain arrangements with other firms. Increasing the incentives for the private sector to offer specialized training to more workers should be a priority, and human capital measures should be accompanied by additional incentives to encourage firms to invest in commercial research and development (R&D), to absorb knowledge, and to adapt production processes so that they can move closer to the global technology frontier.

Economic diversification will require reducing investment risks induced by national and regional policies and lowering barriers to entry for newer, more dynamic, and innovative firms, specifically by facilitating transfer of land from municipalities and from older, loss-making firms. It also will require greater inclusiveness in government decisionmaking, more transparency regarding government decisionmaking, and stable legislation at all levels of government.

This book quantifies and benchmarks the relative strengths of Russian manufacturing and identifies opportunities to increase its productivity and competitiveness. Drawing on new surveys of manufacturing firms of all sizes, the book sets out proposals to

—enhance the innovative potential of Russian firms

—upgrade the skills of the workforce

—develop a business-friendly climate characterized by lower administrative costs and greater policy certainty.

The pursuit of sound economic policies following the financial crisis of the late 1990s and the rise of international prices for key natural resource exports have become the leading engines for Russia's economic growth. The results are better current account and fiscal balances, higher domestic demand, moderate inflation, and rising export revenues. But continuing dependence on commodity exports will leave Russia hostage to unpredictable shocks in international prices. Boosting non-oil exports, however, will not be easy: industrial production has been dominated by energy exporters and by ferrous metals since 2001.

Meanwhile, Russian manufacturing firms have lower average productivity relative to labor costs than do manufacturing firms in comparable countries. Even though Russia's manufacturing value added per worker is about the same as China's and India's, its comparative disadvantage lies in its higher labor costs, which reflect shortages of skilled labor despite high enrollment at higher levels of education. Russia's inputs in terms of share of researchers in the population and aggregate outlays for R&D in GDP are comparable with those of Germany and South Korea and far ahead of those of Brazil, China, and India. But the high level of inputs does not translate into high value added per capita. Russia lags behind OECD and other large middle-income countries in R&D outputs; it also has a relatively low number of patents and scientific publications per capita.

This volume focuses on the challenges now facing enterprises in Russia, highlighting sources of productivity growth and competitiveness within enterprises, including technological progress (knowledge absorption and innovation), worker skills, and the investment climate. After the 1998 crisis, as gross domestic product rebounded, investment accelerated, and foreign direct investment increased dramatically, Russia's recovery surpassed expectations. The recovery was driven to a large extent by the devaluation of the real exchange rate, the availability of cheap domestic inputs, and excess capacity and labor hoarding. Thanks to those three factors, the last several years have witnessed balanced growth, with a structural shift toward the service sector (consistent with Russia's goal of joining the club of postindustrial nations). Yet, a closer look at national accounts reveals that much of that shift has produced relative price increases in (nontradable) services and full capacity utilization in industry—indicators more characteristic of a resource-dependent economy than of successful industrial diversification.

Productivity Patterns and the Sustainability of Russia's Economic Performance

In chapter 2, Schaffer and Kuznetsov examine how productivity in Russian manufacturing compares with that in other large economies, such as Brazil, China, India, and South Africa, and in other developed economies. They argue that although productivity in the Russian manufacturing sector has been rising, it has not kept pace with rising real wages in recent years, limiting the international competitiveness of manufacturing. Russia's productivity lags behind that of Brazil, South Africa, and new EU entrants such as Poland. When adjusted for labor costs, it also lags behind that of India and China. And because real wages are rising rapidly and the ruble is rapidly appreciating, the international competitiveness of Russian manufacturing is suffering. This book argues that diversified growth will depend on better human capital, knowledge absorption and diffusion, and a favorable policy environment for business.

Some of the relative decline in manufacturing competitiveness is due to the increase in real wages in recent years. According to Schaffer and Kuznetsov, real wages in manufacturing in Russia (deflated by the producer price index) have increased by 72 percent since 1999. In 2004 the current dollar monthly wage in industry was over $250, an increase of 67 percent in just two years and a remarkable 266 percent increase over the $75 per month wage in 1999. Under these conditions, international competition from countries with cheaper labor costs may become increasingly difficult for Russian manufacturers. Russia's manufacturing productivity is now about 40 percent of Brazil's and a third of South Africa's.

Labor productivity in Russia, measured by value added per employee, is higher than that in India and China, but low labor costs in those two countries put Russia at a competitive disadvantage. For each dollar of wages, a Russian worker produces about half the output of an Indian or Chinese worker. The low productivity in manufacturing would be of less concern if it were matched with lower wages. But China's wages in manufacturing are 30 percent lower than Russia's.

Improving Knowledge Absorption

Improving the capacity of firms to tap into the world technology pool is an important way to increase productivity. Trade flows, worker mobility, licensing of codified knowledge, and foreign direct investment are all conduits of knowledge absorption. But adoption also requires a favorable investment climate, a skilled workforce, and sufficient domestic R&D. Chapter 3, by Goldberg, Blanco-Armas, Goddard, and Kuriakose, explores what can be done to boost the absorptive and innovative capacity of Russian enterprises.

The complementarities between firm-specific absorptive capacity and R&D and innovation are supported by extensive theoretical and empirical work. Despite the large size of Russia's R&D effort (in both expenditures and personnel), manufacturing productivity has not benefited. Based on research "inputs," Russia's productivity should be among the world's highest—on par with Germany's and South Korea's. Instead, Russia's R&D activities fall short of their potential.

Goldberg and colleagues propose three major reforms to the institutional and regulatory regime that governs research and development in the Russian Federation. First, they recommend that incentives be strengthened to encourage researchers at public R&D institutes to engage in commercial innovation with and promote knowledge absorption in private companies—and to facilitate the spinning off of private research groups from R&D institutes.

Scientific research teams in the public system often sell R&D services, on an informal basis, to enterprises. Although that practice may facilitate the "spontaneous privatization" of the R&D industry, it also leads to conflicts of interest between researchers and institutes, to uncertainty over the ownership of technical results, and to political concerns that the state is not capturing the returns from its investment and the resulting intellectual property.

The government should consider creating incentives, the authors argue, for spinning off research groups. The objective should be to reduce the burden of public financing for R&D institutes, foster commercial knowledge absorption by firms, and reallocate basic research funding toward universities. It also is important to hasten the dissolution of R&D institutes and teams within R&D institutes that work on obsolete scientific and industrial problems.

Second, the authors indicate that the government should provide incentives for private firms to invest more in their capacity for absorption-driven productivity growth.

Matching grants can encourage public-private risk sharing and orient the selection of research projects toward commercial concerns. They can support new technologies and production processes, investments in soft technology by private firms, and access to information and communication technologies and ISO (International Organization for Standardization) certification. But matching grant programs face risks from ineffective allocation due to corruption, capture, or poorly designed targeting strategies. In a successful program, the funding and allocation mechanisms are immunized from interference by public officials, politicians, or private groups and authorities monitor and enforce the neutrality of targeting.

Finally, the authors strongly urge the Russian government to avoid establishing state-owned or state-managed venture capital programs. The Russian government has proposed a state venture capital initiative—a government-owned institution that would participate in existing venture funds and contribute to the creation of funds to finance new companies. The record of state-owned venture capital funds in other countries is poor, so caution is warranted. In the most successful cases, governments typically have seeded the venture capital industry by investing in privately managed funds. In such public-private partnerships, governments mitigate some of the risk in technology-oriented start-ups, and the venture capitalist provides commercial and managerial expertise. A seed capital program aimed at promoting knowledge absorption is likely to work best when a matching grants program provides critical funding at the earlier stages of technological development, with later support by private VCs.

Upgrading Worker Skills

No incentives to encourage innovation will have their intended effects unless the Russian workforce can acquire the skills needed to meet the challenges of the global marketplace. Turning to this critical issue, Tan, Gimpelson, and Savchenko argue in chapter 4 that the Russian workforce, though highly educated by international standards, lacks the modern skills that firms need to compete globally, a deficit that can be made up for through an effective combination of vocational and in-house training. Russian firms can no longer rely on state-funded schools to provide them with workers who possess the skills and qualifications necessary for global competition. More companies are relying on in-house training to upgrade the skills of their employees, but they tend to provide it to a small fraction of employees. The government can assist firms in overcoming the skill shortfall by boosting the incentives for in-house training and by engaging with appropriate private sector counterparts to reform and expand vocational training.

In 2001 Russia had one of the most highly educated workforces in the world. For the bulk of the population (ages twenty-five and older), the average citizen had 10.5 years of schooling, ahead of Brazil, India, China, South Africa, and other transition countries as well as Germany, Japan, and the

United Kingdom. Russia also had one of the highest shares of population holding a tertiary-level degree (more than 50 percent), more than in Canada and more than twice the share in other postsocialist countries. But despite that significant educational achievement, Russia faces problems with the quality of education, the deterioration of secondary education, and the absence of effective professional training.

More than a third of all managers reported deterioration in the quality of their workforce between 1996 and 2005. The low quality of newly hired workers (rather than the high quality of employees who left the firms) may have been responsible for the reported deterioration. Almost half the firms hired workers with lower-quality skills, while only 10 percent improved workforce quality by hiring workers with higher-quality skills.

Tan, Gimpelson, and Savchenko encourage greater use of employer-targeted incentives for in-service training. The proportion of employees who receive in-house training in Russian firms is among the lowest for countries with data available. The authors argue that the Russian government should consider putting in place employer-targeted training policies to remedy the underinvestment in in-service training.

—*Payroll-levy training funds.* Employers should be closely involved in the governance of levy funds. Policies should be designed to increase competition in training provision from all providers, both public and private, including employers. Levy funds should be strictly earmarked for training and not diverted to other government uses.

—*Matching grants.* Training levies do not work especially well for small and medium enterprises, which are unlikely to be served by targeted training programs. Encouraging training in smaller enterprises may require more proactive approaches to address systemic weaknesses in training, technological capability, and access to finance. Matching grants can help to develop a training culture but by themselves will not expand the training market.

Improving the Investment Climate

In chapter 5, the final chapter, Desai looks at the policy-induced constraints on business activity that hold Russian firms back from becoming dynamic and internationally competitive. He notes that the Russian investment climate is still characterized by significant policy and regulatory instability as well as a tendency to punish its most dynamic and innovative firms. Although progress has been made since 2001, corruption, anticompetitive practices limiting entry of new firms, and the quality of the legal system have continued to deteriorate. Well-connected firms tend to enjoy preferential treatment, including special privileges, tax breaks, investment credits, direct subsidies, guaranteed loans, and access to state property; moreover, special economic zones have been created on the sites of specific enterprises. Firms controlled by regional private owners as well as by foreign investors are most likely to receive preferential treatment, and such favoritism toward the most politically influential firms hurts less influential regional firms.

Many problems in investment climates around the world—the policy-induced costs and risks that firms face as well as the formal and informal barriers to competition—are driven by weaknesses in the institutions that govern the investment climate. Those weaknesses may allow administrative corruption to go unchecked or encourage powerful private firms to "buy" legislation, government decrees, and regulatory and judicial decisions. Strengthening the capacity and credibility of institutions may require improving the system of checks and balances, the restraints on administrative discretion, the ability of all levels of government to make and enforce laws, and transparency in business-government relations.

Adopting such reforms has proven to be costly and politically complicated across the region. But the experience from investment climate reforms around the world suggests another way: to adopt manageable and sustainable reforms that encourage openness, competition, and greater integration with global markets and at the same time complement reforms to the systems for innovation and worker training.

A set of credibility-enhancing reforms that, though seemingly disparate, could prompt deeper reforms by empowering and supporting the natural constituencies for openness, rule-based regulation, and innovation in the Russian economy includes the following:

—greater transparency and flexibility in the acquisition and disposition of land, empowering entrepreneurs and firms

—an improved intellectual property rights regime, empowering inventors and entrepreneurs

—more openness in policymaking through consultation, empowering business associations.

Desai puts forward four proposals to move the Russian economy in the direction of the suggested reforms. First, he supports greater privatization of municipally held land. While many regions and municipalities have mechanisms to privatize real estate, they are neither transparent nor fair. Regions that adopted legislation on land privatization ahead of the federal law (the Land Code) tended to be the leaders in land reform. In other words, the adoption of the Land Code may have clarified the basis for land transactions, but it did not always persuade unwilling regions to initiate land reform and privatize land. About 90 percent of the firms trying to purchase land failed to finish the procedure in half a year. The lack of competition in real estate markets contributes to the problem. Effective land privatization will require greater use of auctions and tenders for vacant land (not discretionary and opaque administrative procedures) and greater transparency in the processes involved.

Second, Desai outlines ways of improving the allocation and protection of intellectual property rights (IPRs). Two primary weaknesses remain in the regime governing intellectual property rights. First, the assignment of IPRs remains unclear. There is an ongoing debate on who controls IPRs—the inventor, the inventor's employer (research institute or enterprise, either state-owned or private), or the state, which may have paid R&D costs. Those uncertainties complicate collaboration between private firms and public institutes, inhibit technology transfer, impair the ability to spin off companies into independent and growing businesses, and create potential conflicts of interest for the institutes. Second, registered IPRs are weakly protected due to the inability or unwillingness of public authorities to police producers or importers of pirated goods and to prosecute violators—a particular concern for foreign investors and exporters facing copyright piracy or patent infringement by domestic producers or importers.

What is needed? A more detailed elaboration of the distribution of IPRs among inventors, research organizations, and the state. A current draft of the Civil Code allows research organizations to become owners of IPRs for technologies developed using government funds "provided that the procurement contracts do not specify otherwise." The research and business communities are rightly concerned that this open-ended provision would allow public authorities to continue to exercise ownership of subsequent IPRs and prevent closer cooperation between innovators and firms.

Third, Desai argues that the government should strengthen the consultative basis for regulatory decisions by being more inclusive and in particular by encouraging greater participation by business associations.

Although firms that face competitive pressures are subject to harsher investment climate constraints than those that do not, when the same firms are members of business associations, they find themselves more protected from investment climate obstacles than their counterparts that are not members. Informing market participants about new and forthcoming legal and regulatory changes and requesting comments during a formal consultation period can improve the quality and stability of regulations and encourage sector buy-in. The participation of business associations that represent smaller firms should be actively encouraged, and the government should develop adequate mechanisms to consult the community of entrepreneurs and business people in an inclusive manner, informing market participants well in advance of new proposed measures. Regulatory transparency and predictability are especially important for smaller domestic investors and for prospective foreign investors. In sum, there is power in numbers: through collective action, innovative firms can mitigate investment climate constraints.

Finally, Desai encourages the Russian government to adopt one or more periodic "regulatory review" mechanisms to ensure that the rules and statutes under which businesses operate are not rendered obsolete by technological change or by changes in other economic conditions. Several countries around the world have used similar mechanisms—ranging from full-fledged regulatory impact assessments for proposed regulatory changes to "guillotine-style" reviews that eliminate outdated rules.

Methodology and Structure

The book uses different types of available data, including data in the Doing Business Database (World Bank 2006a), the World Bank Enterprise Surveys, the Business Environment and Enterprise Performance Survey (BEEPS), and the Russian Competitiveness and Investment Climate Assessment Survey, a new survey of Russian enterprises commissioned for this book, which includes the Large and Medium Enterprise (LME) Survey and the Small Enterprise (SE) Survey (see box 1-1).

On the basis of those data, the book presents international comparisons and benchmarks to illustrate the challenges to creating a competitive Russian economy. Where appropriate, the information is complemented by results of econometric regression analyses that illustrate the relationships among different investments, firm-level capabilities and characteristics, and the wider investment climate. The use of a combination of international comparisons based on aggregate and microeconomic data, econometric results from firm-level data, and relevant case studies—rather than a single data source—should increase confidence in the book's conclusions and policy recommendations.

Box 1-1. Data Sources

Enterprise Surveys: Since 2002 the World Bank has undertaken its Enterprise Surveys (formerly known as the Productivity and Investment Climate Surveys) in more than seventy-six countries, covering more than 50,000 firms. The Enterprise Surveys capture firms' experience in a range of areas, including regulation, tax policy, labor relations, infrastructure services, technology, and training. The surveys attempt to identify and, whenever possible, quantify firms' obstacles in the investment climate. Since the basic methodology is consistent across countries, many areas of the surveys allow international comparisons.

The Russian Competitiveness and Investment Climate Assessment Survey: This survey included two enterprise surveys of Russian firms carried out specifically for the study on which this book is based. The first covered large and medium enterprises (LME Survey); the second covered small enterprises (SE Survey). These surveys were designed by the World Bank and undertaken in partnership with the Higher School of Economics in Russia and the Russian government. The LME Survey covered a stratified random sample of 1,000 medium and large firms; the SE Survey covered 300 small firms.

Business Environment and Enterprise Performance Survey (BEEPS): Developed jointly by the World Bank and the European Bank for Reconstruction and Development, this survey was carried out in 1999, 2002, and 2005, covering countries in Central and Eastern Europe and Central Asia. The 2005 BEEPS was also conducted in Portugal, Spain, Greece, Germany, Ireland, and South Korea. The BEEPS examines a wide range of interactions between firms and the state that affect the business environment. It is designed to generate comparable measurements of corruption, state capture, lobbying, and the quality of the business environment, which can then be related to specific firm characteristics and firm performance.

Systemwide data: For the benchmarking of different segments of the overall economy in Russia, the study draws on country-level information collected and disseminated by the World Bank through its World Development Indicators; trade data from UN COMTRADE; labor productivity data from the ILO; and information collected by other international organizations, such as the OECD.

two
Productivity

MARK SCHAFFER AND BORIS KUZNETSOV

In the fifteen years since the collapse of the Soviet Union, the institutions and structure of the Russian economy have changed greatly. Although much can be said about the inconsistency of the transition and the incompleteness of many structural reforms, there is little doubt that Russia has moved from a centrally planned economy to a genuine market economy. All three main goals of the economic reform initiated fifteen years ago have been largely achieved. Prices are liberalized. Privatization is more or less complete. And the economy is now at least as open to international competition as many other market economies.

Since the prolonged economic depression of the 1990s, culminating in the major financial crisis of 1998, Russia has been one of the fastest-growing of the large emerging markets. But there is a certain uneasiness about the sustainability of its growth, both inside the country and abroad. Why? Because Russia's economic welfare depends on world market prices for the natural resources and primary goods that account for the bulk of its exports—and productivity in many sectors of the economy is fairly low.

Productivity is crucially important to the Russian economy for at least two reasons. First, the combination of an aging work force and a declining labor supply makes labor productivity growth imperative for sustainable economic growth. Second, the increasing openness of the Russian economy, combined with the negative impact of the persistent real revaluations of the ruble, is increasing the competitive pressure on Russian producers, particularly in manufacturing, in both internal and external markets. The oil and gas sector has limited growth potential due to the continuing depletion of existing oil and gas fields and the consequent necessary move to more expensive drilling projects in undeveloped regions and the sea shelf. In any case, the energy sector, while a locomotive of economic development, will never be large enough to provide gainful employment for a labor force of more than 70 million or prosperity for a population of 140 million. That is why having productive and internationally competitive sectors, particularly in manufacturing, is one of the most serious challenges facing the Russian economy and government.

Total factor productivity (TFP) provides a standard framework for analyzing productivity and growth. In very simple terms, economic output can be generated by growth in factor inputs (capital and labor) and by increases in the productivity of those inputs. The difference between output growth and the part of it that can be attributed to measured TFP growth is growth in inputs. The gap is sometimes referred to as the "TFP residual" or "Solow residual," after Robert Solow, the Nobel Prize winner who introduced the concept fifty-odd years ago. The same framework can be used for comparing the productivity of firms, sectors, or countries. Thus, the difference in manufacturing value added across countries, after differences in the amounts of labor and capital in manufacturing have been accounted for, is a difference in TFP.

Abramovitz (1956) called the TFP residual "a measure of our ignorance." And indeed, a central focus of research in this area has been to measure the contribution to TFP of other factors such as technology, the quality of inputs, competition, the economic environment, and so on. There is now a vast amount of theoretical work and empirical evidence on this subject from many countries and periods at the aggregate, firm, and establishment level. This book focuses on three contributors to TFP generally agreed to be central to growth: innovation and absorption, labor skills, and the investment climate, each the subject of a chapter.

This chapter presents an overview of recent macroeconomic developments in the Russian economy, with a focus on productivity and exports. It benchmarks Russia's productivity and competitiveness across a range of emerging and developed market economies and then extends the benchmarking to explore Russia's record of R&D inputs and technology-intensive outputs, the level of training and the skills of the labor force, and the quality of the investment climate. Key stylized facts, puzzles, and policy issues are identified for exploration in subsequent chapters.

Recent Trends in the Russian Economy

During the transition of the last fifteen years the Russian economy has had three major sources of aggregate productivity:

—intersectoral structural changes, that is, the reallocation of resources among different sectors with different levels of productivity

—the dynamics of productivity within sectors due to reallocation of market shares among firms with different productivity levels

—the growth of productivity inside firms due to restructuring and the absorption of knowledge and technology.

The relative importance of the three factors differed across the period, with the contribution shifting from intersectoral reallocations in the pre-1998 crisis subperiod to intrafirm productivity growth in recent years.[1]

By 2005 real GDP reached almost 90 percent of the pre-reform level of 1990. But that fact conceals wide variations across sectors and regions. Value added in manufacturing was less than 70 percent of the Soviet maximum. The oil and gas sector reestablished its pre-reform level of output while services—trade, transport, communications, and finance—exceeded it. Those changes in the structure of GDP were accompanied by massive reallocations of inputs across sectors, particularly from manufacturing to such newer sectors as trade and services. The reallocation of labor, though motivated mostly by necessity (massive job destruction in traditional manufacturing), transferred resources from the shrinking sectors to the growing sectors (figures 2-1 and 2-2).

After the bottoming out of the "transformational recession" in the mid-1990s, productivity dynamics went in opposite directions. The fastest-growing sectors (oil and gas, market services) had the smallest increases in labor productivity, and the sectors with the deepest initial declines in output (manufacturing) saw the biggest subsequent increases in productivity. The explanation for that apparent paradox is that the downsizing that redistributed labor resources from declining to growing sectors also increased the productivity of the former.[2] In the first half of the transition, productivity growth in the Russian economy depended mostly on the competitive pressure on manufacturing, which had high productivity growth because of significant restructuring through downsizing and exits. Oil and gas and market services, facing less competitive pressure and more market opportunities, expanded employment along with output.

So, despite structural changes and resource reallocations in the 1990s, the Russian economy started to grow after eight years of economic decline, with

Figure 2-1. Structure of Employment, 1990[a]

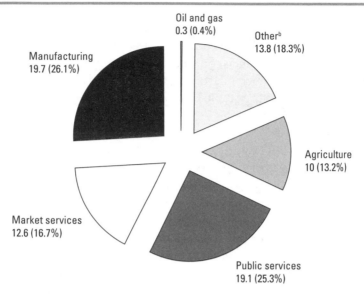

Sources: Goskomstat (1995) and ILO (2005).
a. Millions of workers and percent of labor force.
b. Including construction.

Figure 2-2. Structure of Employment, 2004[a]

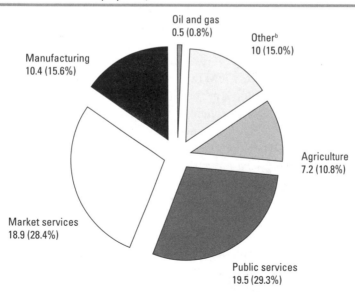

Sources: Rosstat (2006a); ILO (2005).
a. Millions of workers and percent of labor force.
b. Including construction.

overall labor productivity at about 70 percent of the 1990 level. The trigger for the growth that started in 1999 was the 1998 financial crisis and deep devaluation of the ruble. Imports became relatively expensive. Labor, energy, and some other material inputs became relatively cheap. And the competitiveness of Russian products, particularly in domestic markets, sharply increased as a result. In manufacturing, the growth of output led to higher capacity utilization for fixed capital and labor, which contributed to growing productivity.

Subsequent growth has been supported by increases in world market prices for Russia's key exports—oil, natural gas, and metals. The growth of export revenues, together with a conservative budget policy and higher contract and tax discipline, provided for macroeconomic stability and improvements in state finances, the banking system, and corporate finances. Additional revenues from higher production, higher efficiency, and export activities were distributed through the economy, resulting in steady growth in incomes and eventually in consumer demand—and to a lesser extent in the demand for investment goods. Growth of internal demand became the major driver of the Russian economy, fed by energy and metal exports. The fastest-growing sectors became retail trade, construction, real estate, and market services. Manufacturing also gained from the expansion in demand, though the effect was not as great or as prolonged as for non-tradables.

That internally oriented growth indicates the limited competitiveness of Russian manufacturing in world markets, despite annual growth of manufacturing productivity of 10 percent since 1998. While overall exports more than doubled between 1999 and 2004, it was mostly a result of the increases in oil and gas prices on the world market. The share of manufacturing in total exports remained very low. Even in the internal market, Russian producers of manufactured goods are beginning to lose market share. Since 2002 the volume of imports has grown much faster than that of exports despite the increases in export prices for Russian oil and gas. The appreciation of the real exchange rate explains that result to some extent, but it also can be explained by the inability of Russian industries to provide enough competitive consumer and investment goods to meet growing internal demand. The situation is aggravated by the fact that, in markets for both consumer and investment goods, increases in revenues, incomes, and imported goods lead not only to higher demand but also to higher standards of quality.

So although the current Russian trade balance looks extremely healthy, the trends are not favorable: export revenues depend exclusively on world market prices for natural resources, while import growth is a result of the relatively low competitiveness of manufacturing and will probably continue independent of exports. The competitiveness of the Russian economy and of manufacturing in particular cannot be achieved through a protectionist trade policy that closes the domestic market to international competition. Already a part of the global economy, Russia will be even more integrated after its accession to the WTO. For more balanced growth, Russia needs more diversified international trade, which can come from a more competitive and more productive manufacturing sector.

The Russian Economy and Manufacturing Productivity in the International Context

It is useful to benchmark Russia—its economic structure, competitiveness, and productivity—against other countries and groups of countries competing directly with Russian producers in the markets or for foreign direct investment (FDI) and against leading developed market economies at the world technological frontier.

GDP per capita at purchasing power parity (PPP) is a standard indicator of the aggregate productivity of a country and of its standard of living and level of development. Russia is one of the richer BRICS countries (Brazil, Russia, India, China, and South Africa), comparable to Poland, but its per capita GDP is less than half that of the developed countries, even a "new developed country" such as South Korea (table 2-1). Even with relatively high rates of growth, it will take decades for Russia to catch up with the leaders.

Russia is more industrialized than most of the BRICS countries. Its share of employment in agriculture is near South Korea's and declining quickly: since 1990, employment in agriculture has fallen by more than 20 percent. China and India, the last in the group to start the catching-up process, have the biggest shares of employment in agriculture; even China, with all its achievements in manufacturing and exports, is still a relatively poor and largely rural agricultural economy. A large, low-productivity agricultural sector is the main reason behind the relatively low per capita GDP of these countries. Russia, with a high share of services and industry, could be expected to have a higher level of GDP per capita.

The share of exports in GDP shows Russia to be an open economy, little different from the other more open countries in the group: its share is 35 percent, against 34 percent in China, 39 percent in Poland, 37 percent in South Korea, and 38 percent in Germany. Where Russia is different is in the structure of exports: more than half of exports are fuels, ores, and metals. Russia

Table 2-1. Basic Indicators for Selected Countries[a]

Indicator	Brazil	Russia	India	China	South Africa	Poland	South Korea	Spain	Germany
Population (millions)	184	144	1,080	1,296	46	38	48	43	83
GDP (US$ billions)	604.0	581.4	691.2	1,931.7	212.8	242.3	679.7	1,039.9	2,740.6
2004 GDP per capita in PPP (2000 US$)	7,531	9,101	2,885	5,419	10,286	11,924	18,840	23,019	26,013
Annual GDP growth 2000–04	2.2	6.1	6.2	9.4	3.2	2.9	4.6	3.1	0.7
Percent of employment in agriculture	19.8	10.0	56.7	44.1	10.3	18.4	8.8	5.7	2.5
	(2002)	(2003)	(2000)	(2002)	(2003)	(2003)	(2003)	(2003)	(2003)
Exports of goods and services (percent of GDP)	18.0	35.0	19.1	34.0	26.6	39.0	44.1	25.7	38.0
Imports of goods and services (percent of GDP)	13.4	22.3	22.5	31.4	27.1	41.0	39.7	29.3	33.1
Merchandise exports (percent of GDP)	16.0	31.6	10.9	30.7	21.6	30.9	37.3	17.2	33.3
Agricultural raw materials	0.6	1.0	0.1	0.2	0.5	0.4	0.3	0.2	0.3
Food	4.5	0.4	1.1	1.1	1.9	2.6	0.4	2.5	1.4
Fuel	0.7	15.8	0.9	0.7	2.0	1.7	1.5	0.6	0.6
Ores and metals	1.4	2.4	0.7	0.6	4.8	1.3	0.6	0.3	0.8
Manufactures	8.6	6.6	8.0	28.1	12.5	25.0	34.4	13.3	28.0
Unclassified[b]	5.3		0.1	0.1					2.3

Sources: World Bank (2006e) for population, GDP, GDP per capita, GDP growth, and exports; World Bank (2006e) for percent of employment in agriculture, except for the figure for India, which is from the Indian National Statistical Survey.

a. The BRICS group includes Brazil, Russia, India, China, and South Africa, which are considered by world financial markets to be a group of large emerging economies expected to grow rapidly in the medium to long term and to compete for international investors. Poland, the largest former transition country in Eastern Europe, is now an EU member. Poland is a typical competitor for Russia in European markets and an example of a successful transition. South Korea is a successful Asian Tiger that has an advanced economy; it can be considered a "former emerging economy." Spain, a developed European country, is a latecomer to the EU that has made major progress in catching up with Europe's leading economies. Germany is the largest and most advanced of the major EU economies.

b. Blank cells represent a negligible amount.

has a lower ratio of manufacturing exports to GDP (7 percent) than all the other countries, comparable only to the ratio for the relatively closed economies of Brazil and India and far behind the ratios for China (28 percent), South Korea (34 percent), and even Poland (25 percent). And it has by far the lowest share of manufacturing in overall merchandise exports (about 20 percent against more than 50 percent in any other comparator).

The low share of manufacturing in Russian exports is due to the low productivity and poor competitiveness of Russian manufactured goods (table 2-2). International comparisons of aggregate productivity usually rely on comparisons of output per worker, partly for reasons of data—those on fixed capital often are unavailable or unreliable—and partly because studies that compare TFP and labor productivity show the two to be closely correlated.[3]

Labor productivity in manufacturing in Russia is low even compared with that of most of the BRICS countries. Productivity is 50 percent higher in Brazil, two times higher in Poland, and three times higher in South Africa than in Russia. Value added per worker in Germany is ten times the figure for Russia. Manufacturing value added per worker is about the same in Russia as in China. Note that the relatively strong ruble in 2004 raises measured manufacturing output per worker using current exchange rates and that the adjustment for transfer pricing does the same. So in that respect, estimates of manufacturing productivity in Russia reported in table 2-2 are generous.

Benchmarking of TFP in BEEPS and Enterprise Surveys

A similar picture emerges when TFP is estimated directly using a very different data source, the Business Environment and Economic Performance Survey (BEEPS). Three waves of surveys were conducted, in 1999, 2002, and 2005, covering both manufacturing and nonmanufacturing firms. In 2004–05 the BEEPS was expanded to cover six developed OECD countries. For a number of years the World Bank also has been collecting data on manufacturing firms in various developing countries through the Productivity and Investment Climate Surveys (PICS), now called the Enterprise Surveys. The survey data can be used to estimate TFP levels in manufacturing firms in Russia and all the comparator countries considered here.

The results should be treated with some caution for a variety of reasons, however. Only data on gross sales, not on value added, are available for all the countries of interest. For the most part, the surveys cover small and medium enterprises, and they may not be representative of aggregate manufacturing.

Table 2-2. Productivity Indicators[a]

Indicator	Brazil 2004	Russia 2004		India 2000	China 2004	South Africa 2004	Poland 2004	South Korea 2004	Spain 2004	Germany 2004
		Unadjusted	Adjusted							
Manufacturing value added per employee (2004 US$)	11,094	6,723	7,226	1,908	6,894	21,116	15,532	40,473	50,180	68,640
Manufacturing value added per employee (Russia adjusted = 100)	153.5	93.0	100.0	26.4	95.4	292.2	214.9	560.1	694.4	949.9
TFP estimates for manufacturing firms (Russia = 100) based on BEEPS-PICS	209	100		139	102	350	208	493	369	452
Median employment	44	50		23	172	95	15	28	20	38
Number of firms	1,575	185		2,631	2,447	563	562	208	114	218
Annual manufacturing productivity growth (2000–04)										
Output	5.0	5.9		n.a.	10.6[b]	1.9	5.6	6.6	1.1	0.6
Employment	7.5	–4.3		n.a.	2.4[b]	3.5	–1.4	0.0	1.1	–1.2
Productivity	–2.3	10.6		n.a.	7.9[b]	–1.5	7.1	6.6	0.0	1.8
Monthly wages in manufacturing in (2002 US$)	$309	$142		$24	$111	$493	$469	$1,484	$2,834	$3,972
Memo items										
Industry value added per employee (2004 US$)	11,855	9,254	12,667	2,209	6,225	19,867	17,034	39,781	50,063	64,723
Industry value added per employee (Russia adjusted = 100)	93.6	73.1	100.0	17.4	49.1	156.8	134.5	314.1	395.2	511.0

Sources: Industry and manufacturing value added: UN national accounts data in local currency units converted at current exchange rates, with estimations for China, India, and Russia, where manufacturing is estimated from manufacturing, mining, electricity, gas, and water in 2004 and manufacturing share of manufacturing, mining, electricity, gas, and water is taken from a national source for an earlier year. India nominal value added data were converted from 2000 to 2004 rupees using the domestic inflation rate. Employment: ILO (2005). Monthly wages in US$: ILO (2005). Russian value added adjusted for transfer pricing effects (World Bank 2005d).

a. The table shows industry and manufacturing value added per employee in 2004 at current exchange rates. The exception is India, with productivity for 2000 in 2004 rupees and at the 2004 dollar-rupee exchange rate. The first column for Russia uses official Rosstat data, and the other adjusts Rosstat data for transfer pricing effects using the CEM methodology (World Bank 2005d). Transfer pricing moves profits from industry to trade. Most profits moved are for fuel and energy, only some for manufacturing. Industry is defined as manufacturing, electricity, gas, water, and construction.

b. Also includes electricity, gas, and water sectors.

And the sample sizes are small for most countries, including Russia. The results in table 2-2 are from a simple two-input (labor and fixed capital) Cobb-Douglas production function estimation using the TFP level of the firms in the Russia BEEPS of 2002 and 2005 as the benchmark. Despite all the caveats, the results are very similar to those from the comparisons of aggregate manufacturing value added: TFP in Brazilian and Polish small and medium enterprises is about twice that in Russia, and small and medium enterprises in the advanced market economies of South Korea, Spain, and Germany have TFP levels four to five times greater than those of Russian firms. Once again, Russia's productivity level is closest to that of China.[4]

Russia was an evident leader in productivity growth only in 2000–04, but that is not a cause for optimism. The period after the financial crisis of 1998 was one of abnormally high productivity growth due to increases in capacity use. A reported decline in the share of the shadow economy may have added to measured output growth. Those factors were mostly spent by 2004, and future productivity growth cannot be based on continuation of those trends. Also to be stressed is that Russia is the only country among those considered here where labor shedding has made such a large contribution to productivity growth. Manufacturing output growth in 2000–04 was not exceptional.

The low productivity in manufacturing would be less of a concern if it were matched with competitive (low) wages. Comparable cross-country data for wages in manufacturing are available only for 2002. They show that while Russia's manufacturing sector is about as productive as China's, it loses the competitive battle in labor costs: Chinese manufacturing wages are 30 percent lower than those in Russia. Per dollar of wages, one employee in manufacturing produced about $4.00 of value added in Russia, $5.20 in India, and $6.60 in China. But compared with wages in other countries, Russian wages in 2002 were still competitive: in Brazil, one dollar of wages added about $3.00 in value, in Poland about $3.50, and in other countries even less. But that competitive advantage no longer exists. Russia has been experiencing rapid wage inflation since 1999, with wages growing far faster than labor productivity.

The real wage in total industry in Russia (deflated by the producer price index) has increased by 72 percent since 1999. In 2004 the current dollar monthly wage in industry was over $250, an increase of 67 percent in just two years and a remarkable 266 percent increase over the $75 per month in 1999. Trying to compete internationally with cheap labor in other countries (not only China and India but also Brazil and South Africa) is not an option for the Russian manufacturing sector. In Russia, sales per worker are $6,800, well below sales for India ($8,600), China ($10,900), and Brazil ($12,300). But at $2,600 per worker, labor costs are fairly high compared with those in India ($1,300) and China ($1,400). While labor costs in Russia are still lower than those in Brazil ($4,900), real wages in Russian industry have been growing at a rate in excess of 15 percent a year, and that relative competitive advantage will probably disappear in a few years.

Dynamics of Employment and Productivity during the Transition (1992–2004)

It is well known that Russian manufacturing shrank significantly during the transition, both in relative and absolute terms: its share in total production fell from about 30 percent to 20 percent and it lost about 40 percent of jobs. Did job destruction and creation lead to higher productivity? Did the most efficient enterprises create new jobs? Although it would be interesting to see whether the strongest survived and the weakest left the market, we do not have data to analyze enterprises that ceased to exist during the period. The analysis is limited to firms still operating at the time of our survey and with information from the beginning of the transition. Comparability problems arise for some variables within that subset, so the focus is on a few comparable indicators for the whole period.

The subsample of firms that can be traced throughout the transition period includes 409 firms, about 40 percent of the total sample.[5] The very fact that the firms survived could be expected to bias the subsample toward better-performing enterprises, but the data do not support that assumption. In 2004 firms traced to the pre-reform period did not differ significantly from the rest of the sample in terms of productivity, so the results for the subsample are valid for at least 80 percent of the firms in the full sample (those created before 1992). The only caveat is that existing firms not represented in the sample or the subsample could be different. However, testing or controlling for censored data would require additional data collection outside the scope of this analysis.[6]

Total employment trended downward through the transformation period: the subsample had 40 percent fewer employees in 2004 than in 1991. Almost three-quarters of the firms (72 percent) lost jobs, and a little more than a quarter (28 percent) increased employment or maintained the same level. In a market economy, a firm's ability to keep or increase employment over a long period may be looked on as an indicator of competitiveness, and the factors underlying such competitiveness are worth investigating. Following the terminology in some of the literature (see Blanchflower and Burgess 1996), firms with lower employment are "job-destroyers" and those with higher employment are "job-creators."

Job-creators as a group generated additional employment even in the first half of the 1990s, when the economy was in recession, and generated it faster in the 2000–04 period of fast growth: net employment growth in job-creating firms increased from 105 percent in 1991–95 to 139 percent in 2000–04. Job destruction was more common in larger enterprises and job creation in smaller ones. In 1991, at the beginning of the transition, average employment was 1,417 per firm in the job-destroying firms and 441 in the job-creating group. By 2004, average employment was 722 and 658, respectively. Job destruction also speeded up over time: net employment growth in job-destroying firms was –70 percent in 1991–95 and –80 percent in 2000–04. Declines and increases in employment depended strongly on the sector and industry. In the food industry, 58 percent of firms were job-creators, while in textiles only 8 percent were. In the rest of industry the share of job-creators varied less, from 14 percent in machinery to 23 percent in the wood industry.

Initially, the smaller job-creating firms were nevertheless more "capitalized," with an average ratio of fixed assets to labor that was 1.4 times higher in 1991. That may be an indication not only of more fixed capital but also of newer and better capital. The difference became smaller during the transition, but it was still 1.2 in 2004. Since employment in the job-creator group grew significantly, the difference would indicate that job-creating firms also were more active in making new investments. The capital-labor ratio for job-creators in 2004 was slightly higher than that for new firms (those that reported having begun production after 1992).

The data on productivity for both groups suggest that Russian manufacturing went through "creative destruction," in the sense that net job creation occurred in more productive enterprises. It is worth noting that the productivity of job-creating firms increased during the transition. In 1992, labor productivity (measured by value added per employee) was 20 percent higher in job-creating firms than in job-destroying ones. By 2000 it was 56 percent higher, and in 2004 it was 57 percent higher. Redistribution of employment in favor of more productive enterprises resulted in significant growth of their share in total sales. In 1992, job-creators produced 17 percent of total output, and in 2004 their share more than doubled, to 37 percent, while their share in employment grew from 12 percent to 30 percent. The employment share of job-creating firms grew less rapidly than their share of value added produced but more than their share in total output.

The creative destruction story has another side, however. Did the destruction of jobs in job-destroyers lead them to become more productive? On the whole, no. Despite job cuts, they did not manage to increase their productivity up to the average rate. In 2004, labor productivity in job-destroying firms (value added per employee) was still 25 percent lower than the sample average and almost 60 percent lower than productivity in job-creating firms. That does not mean that cutting labor cannot help to increase productivity. The labor productivity of about 27 percent of job-destroying firms exceeded the sample average, and the productivity of more than 40 percent exceeded the industrial average. But for 60 percent of firms in the group, downsizing did not help much. There also was a group of evident outliers whose productivity was almost three times lower than average. That group was not small—16 percent of the sample, accounting for 11 percent of employment.

As seen, the likelihood that a firm will create jobs in the long run depends in large part on its sector and its endowment of capital inherited from the Soviet era. The trends for the capital-labor ratio indicate that job-creating firms are also more active in making investments, allowing them to keep their lead in capital-labor ratios, despite increases in employment. Overall, labor resources were redistributed in the right direction during the transition—from less to more productive enterprises, a reallocation that contributed to productivity growth in manufacturing. But downsizing, a passive adjustment strategy, did not lead to productivity improvements in 60 percent of firms. As a result, about 16 percent of the surveyed enterprises and 40 percent of firms traced to the pre-reform period were still falling behind, and the gap between that group and the rest of the industry was widening.

Industrial Heterogeneity

The 2005 Country Economic Memorandum (CEM) for Russia argues that the major source of future productivity improvements must come from reallocation of resources between incumbent firms and newer, more productive firms in leading sectors of the economy. Restructuring and the entry of competitive firms would drive such intrasectoral reallocation forward.[7] In order to characterize the nature and strength of the links between firm age and

Figure 2-3. Firm Creation in Russian Manufacturing, 1705–2005

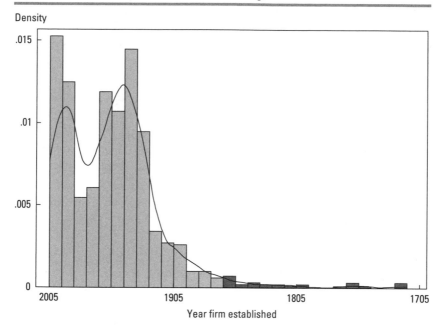

Source: LME Survey (2005).

productivity, the analysis in this chapter used the LME survey to investigate the heterogeneity of newer and older firms in productivity and in other characteristics.

The LME sample of medium and large manufacturing firms (see appendix 2) consists of two main groups of firms, new entrants during the transition and incumbent firms established in the Soviet era (figure 2-3). There also is a third, smaller group, of firms that date to before the twentieth century. A statistical description of that age profile would note bimodal distribution that peaks in the early 1990s and in the mid-twentieth century, with a fat tail. The origins of each of those waves of industrial entry reflect marked shifts in the economic system and industrial policy. Some caution is needed on the year of establishment, as managers may have reported a more recent (but still Soviet era) date for some factories constructed in the nineteenth century.

The productivity of enterprises in the sample (measured by value added per worker) has a much more regular profile, approximately log normal. That implies that while there is a great deal of heterogeneity in the productivity of

Russian manufacturing firms, there are no distinct industrial clusters with different average productivities. Indeed, many other firm characteristics also are distributed as log normal, including the size of the firm's workforce, the size of investments in fixed capital assets (or in machinery and equipment), the proportion of employees having attained a higher educational degree, and the amounts spent on R&D (see appendix 2).

Having found that labor productivity is approximately log normal, we checked whether younger firms entering during the transition were more productive than the incumbents from the Soviet and tsarist era. To test that hypothesis, we compared the labor productivity distributions for the firms established before and after 1990. They are not significantly different.[8] But one has to interpret that result with care because the sample does not include small manufacturing firms, arguably the new entrants into sectors with higher productivity. In addition, most or nearly all firms in the sample were privatized firms; very few were new private firms.

Because of the relationship between firm age, size, and productivity, it is not clear that newer firms were more productive than older firms. The reason is that labor productivity is closely connected to firm size—larger firms are more capital intensive and therefore would have higher labor productivity. And as older firms tend to be large, a new firm may have higher labor productivity than an older firm of the same size, but the average new firm is likely to have lower labor productivity than the average old firm.[9]

The analysis here does not support the hypothesis that the productivity profile is different for older and newer firms. In other words, the labor productivity distributions of the Russian manufacturing firms entering at different periods are statistically indistinguishable. Because of that, we believe that it is a reasonable approximation to frame the policy discussion in terms of measures that can support an "average" manufacturing firm as opposed to a target group with precise characteristics, though some selection problems and biases appear.[10]

Determinants of Productivity Growth

After fifteen years of transformation, the Russian productivity gap today cannot be explained simply by reference to transition shocks or to the inefficiencies inherited from the Soviet period. The relatively low productivity in Russia is even more puzzling in light of the country's rich natural resources and rich human capital, evident in an educated labor force and a history of major scientific and technological advances.

Absorption and R&D Expenditure

Much micro- and macroeconomic evidence now exists on the links between innovative activity, R&D expenditure, and productivity growth. Another link relevant to this study concerns the relationship between trade and absorption: openness to trade is especially important in facilitating the transfer of technology between developed, middle-income, and developing countries (chapter 3).

Not surprisingly, microeconomic data for Russia indicate a clear correlation between innovative activity by firms and their productivity level and growth. The Russia LME Survey of approximately 1,000 medium and large manufacturing firms collected information on a variety of measures of innovative activity: introduction of products and technology, acquisition of new technology, R&D expenditures, and so on. Simple log-linear estimations show that innovative activity, however measured, tends to be associated with firms that have high or growing levels of total factor productivity—indeed, with firms that are employing growing numbers of workers or that are investing and expanding their levels of fixed capital (see appendix 2 for details).

The puzzle in Russia is not the absence of a connection between technology adoption and growth at the micro level but in the low productivity of Russia's R&D sector. Simply put, although Russia has a large R&D sector, its output is unimpressive. Despite devoting significant resources at the aggregate level to R&D and innovative activity, Russia's current record of knowledge absorption is weak. And as shown above, it has not translated into higher levels of TFP.

The Soviet R&D legacy should have been a blessing. Russia began the transition with an R&D sector that was large by international standards and with a history of major technological achievements in its space program and military technology. UNESCO figures for the USSR in 1990 show the vast inputs devoted to R&D: spending of more than 5 percent of GDP and close to 6,000 researchers per million of population. Both measures of inputs are double the number found today in the advanced and technology-intensive economies of Germany and South Korea (figure 2-4).

Despite the significant decline of the R&D sector during the transition, the scale of inputs into R&D activity in Russia is still substantial. The number of researchers per million of population has halved, but that has taken Russia down only to the internationally high levels of Germany and South Korea. Spending on R&D has fallen substantially, to about 1 percent of GDP, but that amount is still above the levels observed in most of the other BRICS countries or in the EU 8. The definition of R&D inputs in these

Figure 2-4. Manufacturing Value Added per Worker and Researchers per Million Population

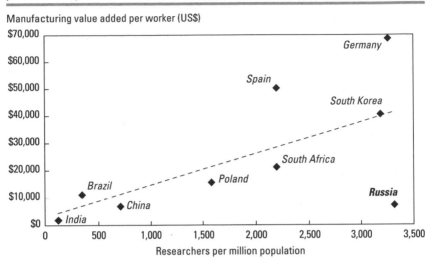

Source: World Bank (2002–2006); OECD (2004b).

international comparisons tends to understate the scale of R&D activity because it cannot fully capture the inputs devoted to imitating and adopting new technologies (see Keller 2004).

The coexistence of a large R&D sphere and low productivity in manufacturing indicates either low productivity in R&D institutions or weak links between R&D and the economy. Some evidence supports the first hypothesis (see table A2-2 in appendix 2). The number of scientific publications per thousand researchers in Russia is about the same as in China—around thirty—but significantly lower than in the other comparator countries. Researchers in Poland, India, Brazil, and South Korea are generating two to three times more scientific publications per person and German and Spanish researchers about six times more.

A very similar picture emerges with another indicator of the productivity of R&D spending—the number of U.S. patents per thousand researchers (see Jaffe and Trajtenberg 2002). Russia is at the same level as China and Poland, but Spanish researchers generate almost ten times more U.S. patents per person, Korean researchers sixty times more, and German researchers one hundred times more. The second hypothesis—poor links between R&D expenditure and industry—also is supported by the evidence, in this case by the high share of state-financed R&D expenditure and very low R&D activity at the firm level (see OECD 2005b).

Skills and Human Capital

A wide consensus now exists on the role and importance of human capital in the generation of economic and productivity growth, and considerable research since the late 1980s has explored the connection (see Krueger and Lindahl 2001 for a review). The connection is evident in the Russia LME Survey as well. Using the same methodology as used above for R&D activity, it shows that firms that have formal training programs—or those whose workforce includes a greater percentage of employees with higher education—have higher productivity. The differences are large and significant. Either a 20 percentage point difference in the share of employees with higher education or the existence of a formal training program is associated with 25 percent higher TFP (see appendix table A2-1 for further details).

As with R&D expenditure, the puzzle is not the connection among human capital, skills, and productivity at the microeconomic level—it is how Russia compares at the macroeconomic level. Enrollment rates in formal education in Russia are at least as high as in developed countries, not only for secondary school but also for institutions of higher learning. A very large portion of Russian students complete some form of university education—in the set of comparator countries considered here, only South Korea sends more students to university. The same picture emerges when workforce education and skills are considered: across the comparator countries, the micro-level BEEPS-Enterprise surveys show that Russian manufacturing firms have the most employees with higher education, the most managers with a university or higher degree, and skilled labor forces comparable to those in the leading countries used for benchmarking.

But the higher levels of skills and education in Russia are not being transformed into higher productivity. Russia is a clear outlier: other countries have either high productivity and a highly educated population or low productivity and a less educated population (figure 2-5). Russia (and to a lesser extent Poland, which is emerging from a similar economic system) combines high levels of skills and education with low levels of productivity.

The lack of a correlation between education and productivity in Russia is due to several factors. First, formal education indicators do not necessarily reflect employees' actual qualifications for their job or their skills. Second, many educated Russians are in some sense overqualified for the positions that they occupy—too many resources are going into producing grad-

Figure 2-5. Enrollment in Higher Education and Value Added per Employee in Manufacturing

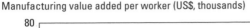

Manufacturing value added per worker (US$, thousands)

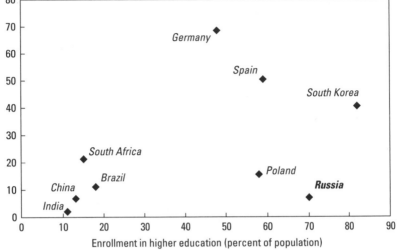

Enrollment in higher education (percent of population)

Source: UNESCO (various years) for enrollment figures; table 2-2 for value added per employee.

uates with skills and education that are not suitable for a low-productivity emerging economy. Third, the labor force training institutions are relatively ineffective—more suitable for generating workers for a centrally planned economy than for imparting skills for a dynamic market economy (chapter 4).

Investment Climate

If Russia is pursuing innovative activity on a large scale and has a highly educated workforce, why is productivity not higher? One answer is obvious: the R&D and human capital capacities are ineffective because they are deployed in an environment characterized by weak investment and ineffective economic institutions.

The investment climate has many aspects, and measuring its quality is challenging, especially across countries. The analysis here exploits the large-scale data collection conducted for the BEEPS-Enterprise surveys and uses a standard section in the questionnaires in which managers are asked about the constraints facing their businesses with regard to infrastructure, state regulations, macroeconomic stability, legal system, corruption, and so on. The results reported here refer to manufacturing firms only. A full set of comparisons is reported in appendix table A2-4 and includes regression analysis of the relative importance of different investment climate constraints in the selected countries.

A very useful feature of the data is that they include results for three separate surveys conducted in Russia, in 1999, 2002, and 2005. That allows for assessment of changes in the investment climate from the aftermath of the financial crisis of 1998 to the current period. Since 1999 the business environment in Russia has, in the perceptions of managers, improved significantly. The changes in some of the categories are a natural consequence of economic growth in the recovery period (access to finance, macroeconomic environment), and changes in others are due to economic reform (tax burden, licensing) and better state regulation. But most successes were achieved between 1999 and 2002. From 2002 to 2005 the situation changed little or even deteriorated. The danger here is that favorable improvements in the macroeconomic situation and in government finances may have led the government to reduce the priority given to improving the business climate further.

That is a serious problem. Comparisons with other countries show that Russia still has a long way to go: the Russian business environment in many aspects is significantly worse than in the most developed benchmark countries (South Korea, Spain, and Germany). The most serious gaps between Russia and those countries concern the effectiveness of the legal system, corruption, crime, and political stability (figure 2-6).

Compared with that of the poorer but rapidly growing BRICS countries, the Russian investment climate presents a mixed picture. Access to infrastructure—electricity, telecommunications, transport—is less of an obstacle in Russia than in India and China (see appendix table A2-3). That is expected, given that the two countries are still largely agricultural, whereas Russia has been largely industrial for many years. But Russian firms cite policy uncertainty and tax administration as bigger problems than their Indian and Chinese counterparts (chapter 5).

Conclusions

Russian productivity has been growing steadily since 1999—but from a very low level, especially in manufacturing. The sources of productivity and output growth lay in the sharp devaluation of the ruble in 1998, the decline of nonpayments and barter, the growth of capacity utilization, and

Figure 2-6. Ranking of Selected Investment Climate Constraints, Russia and Developed Economies[a]

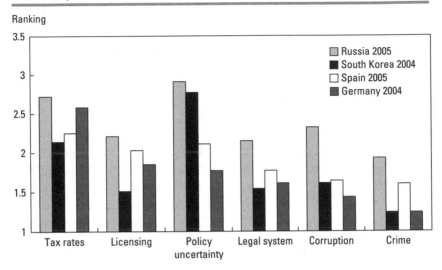

Ranking

Legend:
- Russia 2005
- South Korea 2004
- Spain 2005
- Germany 2004

Categories: Tax rates, Licensing, Policy uncertainty, Legal system, Corruption, Crime

Source: BEEPS (2006).
a. Ranking on a scale of 1 (*not an obstacle*) to 4 (*a major obstacle*).

the contraction of the informal shadow economy. Those factors were transient, so the growth that they supported may not be sustainable. Productivity in Russian manufacturing is lower than in most BRICS countries and uncompetitive because of rising real and dollar wages. The lack of competitiveness is clearly visible in the structure of Russian exports. While Russia is very much a part of the global economy, as evidenced by its high ratio of trade to GDP, the manufacturing sector produces mostly for the internal Russian market. Exports consist largely of fuel (oil and gas) and raw materials, and manufacturing exports as a share of GDP are very low by the standards of both other major emerging economies and developed market economies.

The paradox is that productivity in Russia is very low despite the significant resources devoted to R&D and to education and training of the workforce. The scale of inputs devoted to those activities is as high as in the leading industrial countries, but it results in productivity that is below that of most BRICS countries and far from that in the leaders. The investment climate, measured directly by surveys of managers, points to major improvements since the surveys started in 1999. Most of the improvements, however, were experienced in the immediate post-crisis period, and the rate of improvement between 2002 and the most recent survey in 2005 ranges from small to negligible or even negative. The overall quality of the investment climate is much worse than in the developed countries—and overall no better than in the poorer developing countries.

Notes

1. For a quantitative analysis, see the World Bank Country Economic Memorandum (CEM) for Russia (World Bank 2005d).

2. The structural changes between aggregate sectors of the Russian economy were to some extent distorted by the large-scale practice of transfer pricing, which diminished industrial output and exaggerated the share of trade. Nevertheless, the main trends in sectoral productivity stand even after correcting output for transfer pricing. More detailed analysis is in the CEM (World Bank 2005d).

3. That correlation reflects the fact that capital-output ratios vary much less across countries than do TFP levels.

4. The outlier country in the TFP results is India: firms in the Enterprise Survey have much higher levels of productivity than would be expected given the aggregate manufacturing output per worker. The likely explanation is that India has a large informal sector in manufacturing that has very low levels of productivity and is difficult to capture in a survey.

5. That does not mean that the rest of the sample consists of newly established firms. Actually, another 40 percent of firms in the sample started before 1992, but they cannot be traced back to the Soviet period because they changed their name or registration code or because they were not included in the available databases. This is a classic problem in constructing this type of panel data.

6. One way to collect the data would be to construct a sample representative of large and medium manufacturing firms in the base year, large enough to include a sizable proportion or all of the 409 firms in the LME Survey used in the present analysis. Then, by tracing the evolution of the firms forward, it would be possible to identify the characteristics of exiting firms and use that information to control for censored data. For a discussion of different approaches to collecting and constructing data sets for firm dynamics studies that compares the LME data set with other types of firm-level data, see Haltiwanger and Schweiger (2004). Another example of this kind of study is Scarpetta and others (2002).

7. The CEM (World Bank 2005d, p. 77) advances the following idea about the heterogeneity of productivity across Russian firms: "Given that the productivity improvements in Russia are likely to continue to be located within sectors, further restructuring within the largest sectors is crucial to unlocking growth. Russia's development, like that of other transition economies, will probably be dominated by competition between new, initially small and medium-size, but highly productive,

enterprises and old enterprises inherited from the previous system, with lower value added per worker and often in need of downsizing."

8. That finding is corroborated by the Kolmogorov-Smirnov statistic, which tests for the equality between two distribution functions.

9. Appendix table A3-7 shows that the dummy variable designating firms established after 1992 in which no share of common stock is owned by the government is not significantly correlated with the likelihood of engaging in R&D. Similarly, tables A3-2 and A3-3 indicate no significant correlation with the probability of introducing a new product or technology.

10. For example, the discussion of matching grants outlines general principles for program design that do not explicitly target specific groups of firms, but it also pays attention to selection problems that could lead to wastage and crowding out of R&D and how they could be resolved.

three
Fostering Knowledge Absorption

ITZHAK GOLDBERG, ENRIQUE BLANCO-ARMAS,

JOHN GABRIEL GODDARD, AND SMITA KURIAKOSE

The Russian Federation devotes considerable resources and manpower to research and development (R&D), yet the Russian economy lags behind other large OECD and middle-income economies in R&D-based outputs. Microeconomic evidence shows that firms facing stiffer competitive pressures also innovate more—and that firm-level R&D has a strong, positive, and significant association with technological and organizational innovation and knowledge absorption. The Russian government's initiatives to promote innovation do not appear to recognize the significant role of competition in fostering innovation and absorption.

Improving absorptive capacity—the ability to tap the knowledge in the world technology pool—can be a major driver of increased productivity growth. Yet that capacity is contingent on the effectiveness of trade flows, labor mobility, licensing agreements, and foreign direct investment. It also requires a good investment climate, education, and domestic R&D. This chapter argues that increasing the capacity and incentives of private firms to absorb knowledge and to innovate is critical. Using an empirical study of underlying firm characteristics, investments, and environmental conditions, it shows a positive and significant correlation between a firm's likelihood to absorb or innovate and the competitive pressures in its product market.

The distinction between knowledge absorption (introducing products and technologies new to the firm) and R&D/innovation (creating capital goods and final outputs new to the world) is important in a large economy like

Russia's. Although this chapter focuses on absorption, the complementarities between absorptive capacity and R&D/innovation are extensively supported by theoretical and empirical work, so R&D/innovation also is discussed at some length.

Specifically, the empirical work deals with a wide range of absorptive activities of firms, including the introduction of new and improved products and manufacturing technology, exports of technology-intensive goods, organizational change and outsourcing, and soft innovation through quality controls, certification, and automated systems.

This chapter first discusses the specific characteristics and relative strengths of domestic sources of knowledge absorption, including R&D and intellectual property, through international benchmarking. Cross-country comparisons are used to pinpoint potential obstacles to foreign sources of absorption and innovation operating through trade flows and foreign direct investment (FDI), and the determinants of R&D expenditures and absorption-related activities in Russian manufacturing firms are identified and also compared with international results. In conclusion, policies are presented that the government could undertake to support commercial efforts at knowledge absorption and innovation.

Domestic Sources of Knowledge Absorption and International Benchmarking

By international standards, Russia spends large amounts of money—and employs many workers—in research and development. Indeed, Russia now has as many researchers per capita as the R&D-intensive economies of South Korea and Germany. Domestic spending on R&D in Russia, even after plummeting in the early 1990s, was about 1.2 percent of the country's GDP in 2004—equivalent to China's but higher than that of other developing economies such as Brazil, India, and South Africa (0.9 percent, 0.8 percent, 0.7 percent respectively).[1]

Much of the expenditure is the legacy of Soviet socialism, under which industrial R&D grew large. The persisting effects, positive and negative, of that legacy have been discussed widely, and a recent World Bank report outlines some of the remaining inefficiencies: "Currently, many of the S&T (science and technology) resources are isolated both bureaucratically (in the sense that they are deployed in the rigid hierarchical system devised in the 1920s to mobilize resources for rapid state-planned industrial development and national defense), functionally (in the sense that there are few

Figure 3-1. Productivity of Russian Researchers

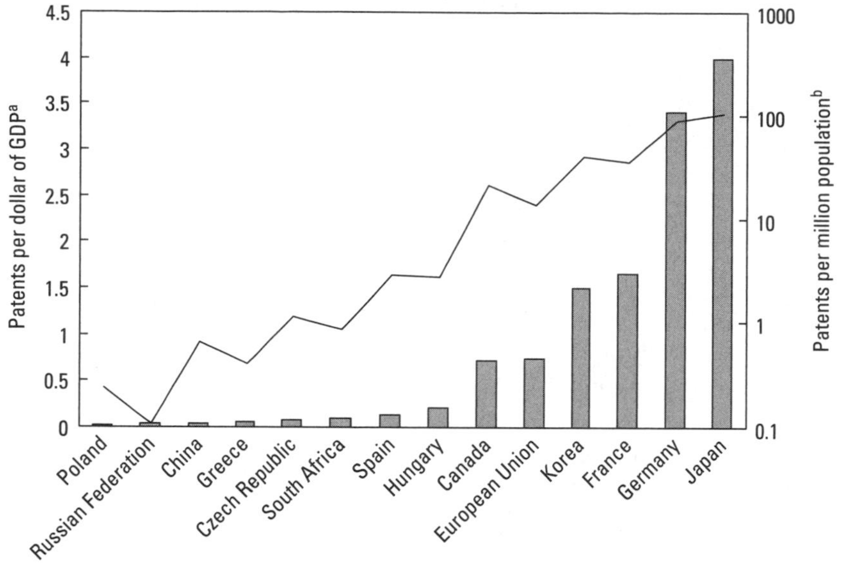

Source: World Bank (2006e) and OECD (2005b).
a. At purchasing power parity (2000).
b. Log scale.

links between the supply of S&T output by research institutes and the demand for S&T by Russian or foreign enterprises), and geographically (in the sense that many assets are located in formerly closed cities or isolated science/atomic cities). Overcoming the inefficiencies embedded in these sunk costs incurred during the socialist period and adjusting the S&T system to the demands of a market economy will require a major program of institutional and enterprise reform which, in turn, will make the task more daunting, although no less necessary."[2]

Despite the size of the R&D effort in both spending and personnel, Russia's manufacturing productivity has not benefited (figure 3-1). Based on the number of researchers, Russia's productivity should be among the highest—on par with that of Germany and South Korea. Instead, Russia's R&D activities fall well short of their potential.

The composition of R&D spending by economic sector changed in the 1990s, but it still remains financed largely by the government. In 2003 the Russian government was still financing 58 percent of R&D expenditures (the OECD average was 30 percent in 2002) and Russian industry financed

23 percent of total R&D outlays (the OECD average was 62 percent).[3] Private expenditures on R&D changed very little between 1999 and 2007.[4] Such imbalances have been underlined as a major problem in a recent study: "The Achilles' heel of the Russian innovation system is the weakness of corporate R&D, despite some encouraging developments over the last two to three years. The efforts to transfer near-market research from public organizations to business firms, to promote the creation of technology-based firms, to encourage private investment in R&D, and to attract R&D intensive foreign investment have not been entirely successful. The reasons are many but the fact is that business enterprises contributed no more than 20 percent of total R&D expenditure in 2002."[5]

Those expenditures did not seem to translate into R&D-related "outputs"— at least of the kind that can be measured and compared across countries, such as the number of international patents accumulated or the number of articles published in scientific journals.[6] The number of patent applications to the patent offices in the United States, the EU, and Japan per unit of GDP (0.1 patent per unit of GDP) was significantly lower than in OECD countries (4 patents per unit of GDP in Japan and 3.5 per unit of GDP in Germany).[7] Clearly, patents are only an imperfect proxy for cutting-edge innovation, given that much innovation takes place without patenting—improvements in the manufacturing process, for example, normally fall outside the domain of patents. Patents are an even worse proxy for knowledge absorption. Nevertheless, we believe that patents are a useful indicator of innovation and that registration in overseas markets is a more useful indicator of Russian innovation than patenting within Russia, for two reasons: first, Russian entrepreneurs tend to avoid registering patents locally due to weak enforcement of intellectual property rights (IPR) in Russia; second, they lack confidence that a Russian patent ensures international protection. The number of "triadic" patent applications by Russian entities to U.S., EU, and Japanese patent offices is significantly lower than the number by entities in OECD countries and in several non-OECD countries.[8]

Royalty and licensing fees paid by Russian entities in 2004 reached US$1 billion, an amount that was roughly 0.2 percent of GDP and equivalent to the amount paid in China and several other middle-income countries. Licensing and royalty fees received by Russian entities during the same time, however, were only US$220 million. That low figure, together with the modest patenting activity, suggests that the international commercial value so far realized by Russian R&D expenditures is limited.[9]

Figure 3-2. R&D Expenditure, by Economic Sector

Percent

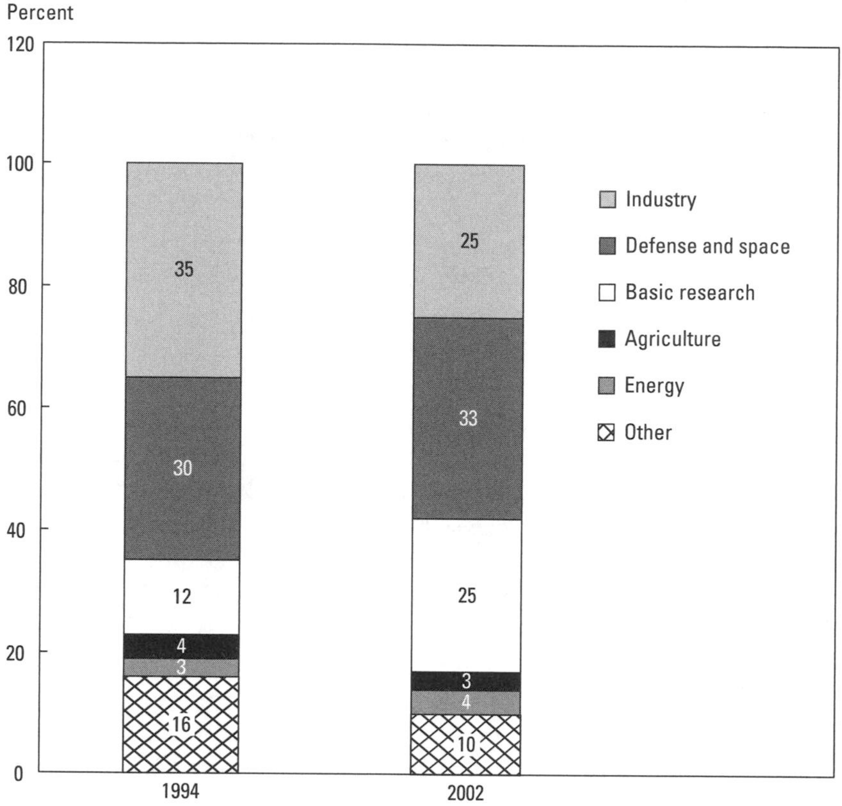

Source: HSE (2005).

The composition of R&D expenditure by economic sector, though, changed in the 1990s. A breakdown shows reduced emphasis on applied R&D for industrial purposes and, to a lesser degree, for agriculture (figure 3-2). R&D expenditure on defense and aerospace increased from 1994 to 2002, when expenditures on basic research more than doubled. But those expenditures did not seem to translate directly into standard indicators of research activity, such as the number of patents accumulated (per thousand researchers) or the number of articles by Russian researchers published in scientific journals.

The description of the Russian R&D sector in a 1994 OECD report captures fundamental characteristics that still affect the size and structure of the sector: "Once established, R&D organizations grew inexorably, following the pattern of extensive growth typical of the whole economy. There is no doubt that, in relation to the scale of the economy and its real level of development, Russia now has an excessively large S&T sector."[10] That observation is largely consistent with the data in chapter 2: the Russian R&D sector seems to be quite developed but surprisingly inefficient. The OECD report identified as a priority the need to downsize what it termed an "oversized, ill-adapted system in rapid deterioration."

Under the Soviet S&T system, the objective of servicing large state-owned enterprises (SOEs) and the defense complex undeniably molded the Russian innovation system.[11] Research was done mainly in specialized technology institutes that reported to their respective line ministries, subject to the central plan. Research institutes were not in universities, and they developed very narrow areas of specialization because lateral interaction between innovative agents was not encouraged by the central planning apparatus. Intellectual property generated anywhere was formally financed by the government and so belonged to the state. Dissemination of new knowledge, know-how, or technological advances from the most advanced establishments within the Soviet system—the isolated defense-oriented "Yaschik"—was prohibited.

Financing for research establishments was allocated largely on the basis of such input indicators as the number of scientists and not necessarily the research program. Historically the incentives for collaboration between most government-funded research establishments and enterprises were very weak. As a result, following the dismantling of the military complex and the privatization of the SOEs, the innovation system that remained could hardly meet the needs of the private sector.

In sum, the difficulties inherent in transitioning from a state-financed to a market-based innovation system still seem to constrain Russia's knowledge absorption capability. And private financing of R&D seems trapped at pre-transition levels.

Foreign Sources of Knowledge Absorption

Two potential channels of knowledge absorption and innovation are important for Russian industry:[12]

—*Trade.* Enterprises absorb knowledge through imported capital goods and technological inputs. Exporters benefit from their trade with suppliers and clients in more advanced markets through learning effects.

—*FDI*. Technology spillovers from foreign investors to suppliers and clients are beneficial for the destination country, and foreign entry by itself can increase knowledge absorption by competitors.

Trade

The diffusion of knowledge and technology through trade can be increased in two major ways: an increase in trade volume and an increase in the quality of trade (trading in goods with higher capital intensity).[13] Gains from international diffusion of technology amplify the overall productivity gain with greater openness. But it is not only the quantity of trade that matters—trading partners also make a difference.

The standard argument is that importing new vintages of capital goods can directly increase manufacturing productivity by increasing the capital-labor ratio and by raising the average quality of the capital stock. Consequently, a larger share of capital good imports from more advanced countries would be positively associated with industrial productivity and economic growth. In 2004 the Russian Federation imported $33.8 billion in capital goods, or 28 percent of total imports.[14] In 2005 the top five countries exporting capital goods to Russia were Germany ($9.3 billion, for 29.3 percent of the total), Finland ($3.3 billion, for 8 percent), the Netherlands ($2.6 billion, for 6.3 percent), Italy ($2.5 billion, for 7.2 percent), and China ($1.8 billion, for 4.4 percent). Overall, a large majority of Russia's imports of capital goods have come from partners that are economically and technologically more advanced than Russia.

In addition, simply trading with countries that have a more advanced knowledge and technology base—whether in capital goods or other commodities—can generate positive spillover in "learning" from buyers (for exports) or sellers (for imports).[15] As an approximate indicator of the potential supply and demand for learning, table 3-1 presents the volume of imports and exports for Russia's major trading partners and table 3-2 shows the top commodities in the trade. The tables point to the substantial share of Russia's exports to and imports from the EU and the United States; the concentration of exports in oil, gas, and natural resources; and the importance of capital goods.

Because of Russia's heavy reliance on exports of natural resources, the overall volume of trade is probably not a very good indicator of the potential for knowledge diffusion. It is more useful to look at the trade in parts and components with countries already well integrated into global production sharing networks, because trade in such intermediate goods can facilitate the

Table 3-1. Russian Exports and Imports, by Country of Origin and Destination, 2005

Exports	
Destination	Trade value (US$ billions)
Germany	19.9
USA	16.1
China	15.9
Turkey	12.9
Ukraine	12.8
Other reporters	138.2
Total exports	215.9
Imports	
Origin	Trade value (US$ billions)
Germany	21.0
China	13.2
Italy	7.5
Ukraine	7.5
Finland	7.1
Other reporters	63.7
Total imports	120.1

Source: UNCTAD (2006a).

Table 3-2. Russian Exports and Imports, by Type of Commodity, 2005

Top exports	
Description	Trade value (US$ billions)
Fuels and lubricants, primary	98.4
Industrial supplies, processed	54.5
Fuels and lubricants, processed	30.9
Industrial supplies, primary	11.3
Food and beverages, processed	3.7
Other commodities	17.2
Top imports	
Description	Trade value (US$ billions)
Industrial supplies, processed	25.3
Capital goods (except transport equipment)	24.2
Food and beverages, processed	12.9
Consumption goods, semi-durable	12.1
Parts and accessories of capital goods (except transport equipment)	9.6
Other commodities	36.0

Source: UNCTAD (2006a).

acquisition of new technology through vertical knowledge spillover between suppliers and customers operating in those networks.[16] It also is useful to focus attention on that type of trade because some of the literature has shown that "countries that promote exports of more sophisticated goods grow faster."[17]

Macroeconomic data show that most BRICS countries and some comparators, like Germany and Poland, are more integrated than Russia into global production networks. The growth of China's share of parts and components is exceptional, but all other BRICS as well as the other comparator countries also are exporting more parts and components, as a share of GDP, than Russia. The picture is similar for imports, where the evidence shows that Russia is only slightly ahead of India. Moreover, imports in parts and components are larger than exports, suggesting that Russian firms are not yet competitive enough in this area.

As mentioned, it is not only the amount of trade that helps a country to become better integrated in global production networks; trading partners also matter. Although the *total* flow of imports to and, more important, of exports from Russia is to a large extent directed from and to high-income OECD countries, trade in parts and components tells a very different story. While electrical parts and components are mostly imported from high-income OECD countries, Russia is exporting the vast majority of its own parts and components to countries in the Commonwealth of Independent States (CIS).[18] Using exports in parts and components as a litmus test for integration into global production networks, our evidence suggests that Russia's integration into those networks is less than complete. If it is true that exports can boost the spread of new manufacturing methods though learning from buyers, the data highlight the possible weakness of this channel.

Foreign Direct Investment

FDI can promote diffusion of international technology if the technological advantages of multinational firms do not remain restricted to one firm or its affiliates.[19] Technological spillover may take place in the recipient country through demonstration effects (imitation), labor turnover, or increased competition. The channels for spillover can be horizontal (originating in the entry of the multinational investor in the same sector) or vertical (originating in backward links when local suppliers supply multinational investors or in forward links when local customers buy from multinational investors).

Because a multinational has more incentive to promote local suppliers, backward links may be more widely observed than horizontal links, which inherently are associated with increased competition. Research by Javorcik (2004) finds a positive effect of FDI on Lithuanian local suppliers working through backward links. Another finding is that greater productivity gains are associated with projects partially owned by foreign entities (joint ventures), suggesting that domestic capital participation increases productivity spillover. That could serve as an interesting model for Russia: it might be able to attract FDI to complement domestic capital ownership and thereby increase productivity without yielding domestic firms' market share to direct foreign competition.

The evidence from Russia indicates that FDI inflows are lagging behind those of some BRICS comparators (see box 3-1),[20] suggesting that the benefits from international technology diffusion have flowed to only a few economic sectors, with FDI heavily concentrated in oil and natural resources.[21] At the same time, the large increases in FDI observed since 2002 suggest a growing balance within manufacturing and between the manufacturing and service sectors, indicating that the growing domestic demand for consumer goods is driving a consistent share of total FDI flows in Russia.[22]

Russian multinationals continue to dominate the outward FDI of the southeastern Europe and CIS region for FDI in joint ventures and mergers, accounting for 87 percent of the total in 2005.[23] Investment includes large deals to acquire and create joint ventures with enterprises in developed economies—notably Lukoil's purchase of Nelson Resources, a Canadian-based oil company, and the recently announced merger of the aluminum and alumina assets of RUSAL, the SUAL Group, and Glencore International. Such partnerships are likely to gain in importance, given evidence that foreign-invested enterprises (FIEs) have been important for increasing labor productivity and export competitiveness in such countries as China.[24]

One of the most powerful channels for technology diffusion is the information and communications technology (ICT) channel.[25] Usually, a good indicator of a country's capacity to leverage the ICT channel is the amount of FDI in communications, which in Russia remains extremely low (0.4 percent of total annual FDI in 2004–05).[26] Moreover, according to various private sources, such as WITSA (2006), the amount of ICT investment in Russia, as a percent of GDP, is substantially lower than that in Central and Eastern Europe (CEE) countries.

Note that neither trade in capital goods nor FDI inflows are sufficient for the successful diffusion of technology. A country must be ready to absorb

Box 3-1. Gains from Reducing Barriers to Trade and to FDI Flows in Russia

Russia stands only to gain by reducing its barriers to trade and FDI inflows and thus reaping the benefits of global integration, increased competitiveness, and improved access to business services.

Tariff barriers: The CIS has high average tariff and nontariff barriers, which would need to be reduced in the medium term in order to gain from international integration. For Russia in particular, Rutherford and Tarr (2006) shows that the average tariff increased between 2001 and 2003 from 11.5 percent to between 13 and 14.5 percent, placing its tariff rates (unweighted, or weighted averages) at a higher level than those of other middle-income countries, which average 10.6 percent. A reduction in the import tariff by 50 percent will produce gains to the economy on two counts: one, improved domestic resource allocation due to a shift in production to sectors where the value of production is higher, based on world market prices, and two, an increase in Russian productivity as a result of Russian businesses being able to import modern technologies. The second impact is more important for Russia.

Trade Restrictiveness Index: Kee, Nicita, and Olarreaga (2006) computes indicators of trade restrictiveness that include measures of tariff and nontariff barriers for ninety-one developing and industrial countries. Of the indicators for the manufacturing sector, one focuses on the trade distortions imposed by each country on imports and another focuses on market access for exports in the rest of the world. It is interesting to note that the trade restrictiveness index (TRI) for imports for Russia (.19) is lower than that for Brazil (.22) and India (.20) but higher than that for South Africa (.06), China (.12), and the European Union (.08). Russia's TRI is the highest in the Europe and Central Asia region, a reflection of the high tariff and nontariff barriers that it imposes on its imports. On the other hand, Russia faces less trade distortion on its exports from the rest of the world, China being the only country facing a lower level of restrictiveness.

Barriers to FDI: Russia fares worse than other countries in the region, attracting one of the lowest levels of FDI inflow. Among the key restrictions on foreign service providers in Russia are the monopoly of Rostelecom on fixed-line telephone services, the prohibition of affiliate branches of foreign banks, and the restricted quota on the share of multinationals in the insurance sector. The reduction of barriers to FDI in services alone would result in a

(continued)

**Box 3-1.   Gains from Reducing Barriers to Trade
and to FDI Flows in Russia (*Continued*)**

gain of the order of 3.7 percent of GDP, accounting for about three-quarters of
the total gains to Russia from WTO accession. The reduction in barriers to
FDI in the service sector would allow multinationals to obtain greater post-
tax benefits on their investments, encouraging them to increase FDI to supply
the Russian market. That in turn would lead to an increase in total service
providers in Russia, giving Russian users improved access to telecommuni-
cation, banking, insurance, and other business services; lowering the cost of
doing business and increasing the productivity of Russian firms using those
services; and providing a growth impetus to the economy.

Sources: Rutherford and Tarr (2006); World Bank (2005b); Kee, Nicita, and Olarreaga (2006).

---

foreign knowledge and manufacturing and sales methods. In Russia vertical
knowledge spillover could be hampered by the central planning legacy of
large industrial plants, which were more vertically integrated than Western
plants.[27] Moreover, local R&D, domestic research laboratories, and workers
with the right skills are key aspects of the process. Trade competition and
R&D expenditures are closely interrelated: unless a country is also well
endowed in R&D and invests in R&D, spillover is not likely.[28]

Knowledge Absorption Capacity:
Evidence from Firm-Level Surveys

The intensity and effectiveness of private investments in knowledge and technology absorption can be investigated through the survey data available for
Russia and for BRICS and EU comparator countries.[29] Russia has a very large
R&D sector (employing roughly the same number of researchers per capita as
Germany), but its output is comparable only to that of China, reflecting a
strong historical orientation toward military research; the obsolescence
afflicting R&D in certain fields now that the economy is more open to knowledge and technology exchanges; and the lack of effective links between public and private R&D. Here we use the LME Survey data and BEEPS data (see
the box in chapter 1 for a description of the surveys) to characterize the drivers of absorption in Russia, exploring both outputs and inputs of absorption
and comparing the results with those of comparator countries.

According to the LME Survey, knowledge absorption activities in Russia are associated with medium-low-technology and medium-high-technology manufacturing sectors.[30] The electrical equipment sector is a leader in introducing new or improved products, and the chemical industry introduces manufacturing technologies significantly more frequently than others. Firms in electrical equipment and chemicals and also in machinery are more likely to export technology-intensive manufactures. Those results suggest that capital-intensive sectors are adopting products and technologies more than labor-intensive industries. For example, only 29 percent of firms in the textile industry financed a new or improved product, while 47 percent of firms in other sectors did so. Results are similar for a new or improved production technology and technology-intensive exports. The food and wood sectors also exhibit weaker absorption.

Estimating the Knowledge Absorption Production Function: Methodology and Results

The econometric analysis presented here is meant to address three policy questions.

—First, what is the impact of investments by Russian firms in absorption and innovation inputs (for example, R&D expenditures and absorption-enabling investments in information technology) on key absorption outputs (for example, the introduction of new and improved products and manufacturing processes)?

—Second, how is the decision to allocate resources toward absorption and the capacity to adopt hard and soft technology related to a firm's characteristics and the wider economic environment? For example, it is generally argued that innovative activities increase with the size of the firm.

—Third, how does competitive pressure affect the frequency of investments in absorption, such as financing for the introduction of products, or the potential for exporting advanced technology products? Specifically, is competition increasing the propensity to innovate?

Our analysis begins to tackle those questions by characterizing the relationship between a firm's probability of introducing a new or significantly improved product or production technology and the firm's exports of high-technology goods, it characteristics, and environmental characteristics. In order to shed light on the underlying determinants of absorption outcomes, it also estimates a technology absorption production function,

$$Absorption = f(K, L, ICT, R\&D, COMPRESS, IC),$$

where K is access to finance; L represents workers' education, skills, and training; ICT captures various variables as proxies for technological capability, such as the availability of broadband Internet, a firm website, and an information technology department; $R\&D$ captures various measures of the expenditure on research and development and related metrics, such as purchase of machinery and equipment and purchase of patents and know-how; $COMPRESS$ refers to competitive pressures in the market; and IC stands for investment climate. See appendix 3 for a further description of the variables and econometric methods used in the regressions.

Technology absorption outcomes are the left-hand variable in the equation. They include the introduction of new or improved products and production technologies, which in general can be expected to be new to the firm or the country but not new to the world. Different types of investment—among which are two key outlays, for research and development and for purchases of new machinery and equipment—are complements in the outcomes of absorption. The absorption of products and knowledge often occurs along with the adoption of advanced production methods.

Our rationale for using these variables as indicators of absorptive and innovative capacity in Russian manufacturing firms is as follows. ICT variables are included because the most notable increase in productivity in manufacturing since the 1990s has been linked to the adoption of information and communication devices. The Internet allows businesses, their suppliers, and their clients to share and exchange vast amounts of information and knowledge. Indeed, like electricity and steam power, ICT is a "general purpose technology" that has the potential to spur growth as it spreads across different sectors of the economy, prompting a transformation in the organization of labor and production.[31]

ISO certification is a relevant and much-used management standard that attempts to raise quality to the international level directly. Because reaching ISO standards requires a minimum level of technological capability, ISO norms can be seen as a possible proxy for technology adoption. Moreover, because standardization reduces transaction costs, it enables economies of scale and eliminates duplication, both of which are good for productivity gains. ICT use and ISO certification therefore are not only indicators but also variables of interest themselves.

The relationship between firm-level R&D and innovative outcomes has been investigated thoroughly. The literature, particularly for OECD countries, generally finds a positive and significant association, yet the complexity and uncertainty surrounding knowledge-based activities means that

Table 3-3. Summary of One-by-One Regressions for Product and Process Innovation[a]

Independent variable	Firm introducing a new or improved product	Firm introducing a new or improved technology	Firm exporting technology-intensive products
Firm has a workforce that has tertiary education	(+)**		
Firm exports its products		(+)**	
Firm has a website	(+)***	(+)***	(+)***
Firm acquired technological innovations through purchase of patents, licenses, and general know-how from Russia or abroad	(+)***	(+)***	(+)***
Firm spends more than 1 million rubles on R&D expenditure	(+)***	(+)***	(+)***
Firm acquired technological innovations as a result of third-party R&D	(+)***	(+)***	
Firm has acquired ISO certification	(+)***	(+)***	(+)***
Firm faces financial constraints such as unavailable collateral	(−)*		(−)**
Firm is able to get loans from banks	(+)**		(+)**
Firm faces noticeable or considerable competitive pressure from domestic firms	(+)***		
Firm faces noticeable or considerable competitive pressure from imported products	(+)***	(+)*	(+)***

Source: LME Survey (2005).

a. Only significant results are shown. All regressions include a constant, explanatory variables (size, new private firm, firm holding, foreign owner), and sectoral dummies and use a random effects model. See appendix tables A3-2–A3-4 for detailed results. Significance is given by robust standard errors clustered by regions. *Significant at 10 percent; **significant at 5 percent; ***significant at 1 percent.

estimating a firm-level or aggregate relationship between absorption inputs and outputs is not a trivial task.[32] To investigate the relationship between private R&D and absorptive outcomes, we used a probit model for the sample of Russian firms (tables 3-3 and 3-4).[33] The results confirm a positive and significant relationship between investments in R&D and the three absorption outcomes: introducing new or improved products, introducing new or improved production technologies, and exporting technology-intensive goods.

The fact that Russian firms exhibit a positive association between R&D spending and absorption is definitely a positive sign of the capacity to modernize, especially for large and medium enterprises (LMEs) in manufacturing. But that does not imply that there are no more obstacles to making effective investments in R&D for Russian firms. Additional econometric estimations compare the probability of achieving an innovative outcome between firms in Russia and comparator countries (see table A3-6 in appendix 3, which describes the data and model used for the estimations). They show that the efficacy of absorption activities is higher in Russian firms than Chinese firms but lower in Russian firms than in firms in South Africa and Brazil. Therefore room exists for improving the innovation and absorption capabilities of firms and for correcting some of the external obstacles that reduce incentives to improve R&D expenditure outcomes.

As expected, there are some significant and positive correlations between absorption outcomes and absorption-enabling inputs, such as ISO certification and IT use. ISO certification is significant only for advanced technology exports in the full model (table 3-4). But when taken alone—with firm characteristics as controls—ISO certification turns out to be significant for all three absorption outcomes. IT use, in this case measured by the existence of a corporate website, is strongly associated with a higher likelihood of innovating. Finally, the purchase of intellectual property in Russia or abroad (patent rights, licenses for using inventions, production prototypes, and utility models) is strongly and positively associated with the probability of introducing product and process improvements at the firm level and positively associated with high-technology exports. That finding implies that technical knowledge codified in intellectual property rights contributes to a learning process that improves absorptive capability.

The coefficients related to other firm characteristics show mixed significance. Firm size is not related to introducing new or improved products or processes, but larger firms are significantly more likely to export high-technology products. That suggests that scale is a factor in export-oriented policies that would increase knowledge absorption. But there is a positive relationship between exporting and introducing new technologies (table 3-3), yet no evidence for a relationship with the other dimensions of absorption. Tertiary education level of employees has a positive impact on introducing new products (table 3-3), but that effect is lost in the full model (table 3-4), perhaps a reflection of the relatively weak impact of skills after adding other controls (chapter 4).

Table 3-4. Regression Results for the Full Model of Product and Process Innovation[a]

Independent variable	Firm introducing a new or improved product	Firm introducing a new or improved technology	Firm exporting technology-intensive products
Firms has less than 250 employees			(–)***
Private firm that was established after 1992			(+)**
Firm has a website	(+)***	(+)**	(+)**
Firm acquired technological innovations through purchase of patents, licenses, and general know-how from Russia or abroad	(+)***	(+)***	(+)*
Firm spending more than 1 million rubles on R&D expenditure	(+)***	(+)***	(+)***
Firm acquired technological innovations as a result of third-party R&D	(+)***	(+)***	
Firm has acquired ISO certification			(+)***
Firm is able to get loans from banks		(+)*	
Firm cites macroeconomic instability as an impediment for enterprise's activity and development	(–)*		
Firm faces noticeable or considerable competitive pressure from domestic firms	(+)**		
Firm faces noticeable or considerable competitive pressure from imported products			(+)**
Observations	729	729	729

Source: LME Survey (2005).

a. Only significant results are shown. See appendix table A3-5 for full regression results. All regressions include a constant, explanatory variables (size, new private firm, firm holding, foreign owner), and sectoral dummies and use a random effects model. Significance is given by robust standard errors clustered by regions. P values are given in brackets. *Significant at 10 percent; **significant at 5 percent; ***significant at 1 percent.

Lack of financing is often cited as a major constraint on the innovative activity of firms. We used two variables to gauge the effect of finance, one measuring firms' financial constraint and the other gauging access to financing and financial institutions. The estimation indicates a negative and significant relationship (table 3-3) between financing shortages and product or process improvements as well as export of technology-intensive products. Similarly, there is a positive and significant relationship between those two absorption outcomes and the access-to-financing variable, as expected (table 3-3). Because the finance variables and the size of the firm are highly correlated, if the model is estimated without the size variable, the finance variables become significant for all the absorption outcomes. With regard to investment climate variables, macroeconomic instability has a negative and significant effect on the probability that a firm will introduce a new product, suggesting that firms tend to absorb knowledge when the macroeconomic environment is stable (table 3-4).

Empirical Analysis of Soft Innovation and Organizational Change

The econometric analysis of the determinants of firm-level R&D expenditures (table A3-7 in appendix 3) reiterates many of the findings just reported. Again, firms that are larger and that have adopted information and communications technology and attained ISO certification are likely to spend more on R&D. The significance of ISO certification points to possible complementarities between the organizational capability of the firm and its capacity to conduct in-house R&D. In this case the educational level of the workforce also has a positive relation with R&D expenditure. Exporters have significantly greater R&D expenditures.

Even though public R&D spending in Russia is much larger than private R&D spending, only 23 percent of firms surveyed outsourced part of their R&D activities to third parties. The positive relation between third-party R&D and in-house R&D by firms underlines the fact that the two are probably complementary. Given the imbalances between public and private research, there is surely a great deal of room for additional collaboration.

To complete the analysis of innovativeness in Russian firms, we turned to the determinants of investment activities that aim to improve organizational capabilities. Such activities are referred to as "soft innovation" because they are tied to changes in processes and systems that seek to increase productivity of the existing capital stock and workforce. The econometric analysis examines five dimensions of soft innovation that reflect how firms absorb and implement production practices: restructuring the organization, hiring external management consultants, outsourcing functions and business processes to specialized third-party contractors, introducing input quality control for materials and production, and introducing an automated inventory management system.

The reason for enlarging the examination of knowledge absorption is that improving firms' organization can be critical for absorption and innovation, in a sense capturing how ready firms are to adopt and enhance new products and technologies. In the light of international differences in "innovative efficiency," readiness seems highly relevant for the ability of Russian firms to catch up (table A3-6 in appendix 3).

The results of the regressions show that organizational absorption is an investment activity that also is more likely in larger firms (table 3-5). Firm size apart, the significance of the other determinants really depends on the form of organizational change. The firms that are more likely to restructure are those that

—were established before 1992 (probably because they have an unfinished restructuring agenda)

—are less likely to face a financial constraint

—are more likely to face intense competitive pressure

—are more likely to be exporters of high-technology products

—are more likely to outsource R&D to third parties

—perceive themselves to be in environments where regulatory problems exist.

With regard to the direction of causality for some of the foregoing associations, one might expect that restructuring leads to an easing of the financial constraints and to greater R&D spending, but the data do not allow for testing of that question.

For firms to hire external management consultants, the significant determinants are having foreign equity participation, introducing a new or improved production technology (which points to the interrelatedness of hard and soft technology), outsourcing R&D, and being affected by macroeconomic instability. Business process outsourcing is more likely with firms that are part of a holding with foreign ownership. Input quality control is strongly associated with introducing a new product, an expected result. Last, the introduction of an automated inventory management system is positively associated with firms that have a more educated workforce, that have obtained ISO certification, and that have introduced new production technologies. The overall pattern suggests a very natural correspondence between the capabilities of the firms, particularly in their innovativeness, and decisions to implement costly management improvement measures to raise quality and optimize production systems.

Competition as an Incentive for Absorption

One of the most robust results drawn from the estimation of the absorption production function is that competitive pressures have a positive and

Table 3-5. Regression Results of the Full Model for Soft Innovation and Organizational Changes[a]

Independent variable	Firm reorganized organizational structure	Firm hired external consultants	Firm outsourced to third-party contractor	Firm introduced input quality control	Firm automated system of inventory management
Firms has less than 250 employees	(−)***	(−)**	(−)*		(−)**
Private firm that was established after 1992	(−)*				
Firm belongs to a group of small companies (holding)	(+)*		(+)***		
Firm with more than 51 percent of common stock owned by foreign individuals or company		(+)**	(+)***		
Firm has a workforce that has a tertiary education					(+)***
Firm exports its products					
Firm has acquired ISO certification					(+)**
Firm faces financial constraints such as unavailable collateral					
Firm is able to get loans from banks		(+)***	(+)*		
Firm faces noticeable or considerable competitive pressure from imported products	(+)**				
Firm introduced a new or improved product	(+)**	(+)*		(+)***	
Firm introduced a new or improved technology	(+)**				(+)*
Firm exports technology-intensive products					
Firm acquired technological innovations as a result of third-party R&D		(+)**			
Firm cites macroeconomic instability as an impediment for enterprise's activity and development		(+)**			
Firm cites regulatory constraints as an impediment for enterprise's activity and development	(+)**				
Observations	731	731	731	731	731

Source: LME Survey (2005).

a. Only significant results are shown. See appendix table A3-8 for detailed results. All regressions include a constant and sectoral dummies and use a random effects model. P values are given in brackets. *Significant at 10 percent; **significant at 5 percent; ***significant at 1 percent. Significance is given by robust standard errors clustered by regions.

Figure 3-3. Competitive Pressure and Absorption Activities

Percent likelihood that a firm will introduce a new product

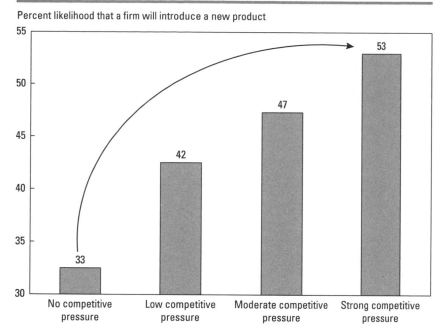

Source: Based on simulations using the LME survey; for details, see appendix 5.

significant effect on a variety of innovative and absorptive outcomes. To investigate that relation further in a Russia-specific context, we analyzed the evidence on competitive pressures from the firm-level data available.

We tested the hypothesis that competitive pressures have a positive impact on innovative activities of firms, using a variety of samples to test the robustness of the results (see appendix table A3-9 for the full range of specifications tested). In the LME sample, as expected, firms subject to competitive pressure were more likely to engage in innovative activities. In particular, competitive pressures coming from domestic firms were positively and significantly correlated with the introduction of new or improved products. Unexpectedly, competitive pressures from domestic firms were negatively correlated with exports of advanced technology goods.[34] Firms that faced significant competitive pressures were about 20 percent more likely to introduce new and improved products, controlling for sector, firm characteristics, and the like (figure 3-3). In contrast, firms that enjoyed monopolist positions or other forms of protection were less likely to change their products and production methods than firms facing greater competitive pressure. They also contributed to an unpredictable and uncertain regulatory environment. In sum, a monopolistic position can seriously hurt investments in technology absorption and innovation.

Competitive pressures arising from imports, by contrast, seems to bear most heavily on exports of advanced technology products, as captured by the econometric results in appendix table A3-9. Because high-tech exports often are considered a key element and a crucial contribution to sustained long-term growth, that finding seems especially important, particularly in light of the recent debate on diversifying the structure of the Russian economy.[35]

The robustness of the association between competition and knowledge absorption under different specifications is important given the methodological difficulties of the simultaneous determination of the two variables: industry structure shapes the incentives to adopt technology and innovate and innovative activities modify the competitive environment. The most recent theoretical and empirical thinking about that relationship points to an inverted U-shaped curve between competitive pressure and innovation.[36]

The upward sloping segment of the curve reflects the fact that product differentiation and cost advantages are more important when industries are more competitive—and that innovation and absorption are effective instruments for improving product quality and reducing manufacturing costs. In neck-and-neck industries, firms compete by lowering prices because their product lines and manufacturing processes are identical. Their absorptive and innovative activities therefore become a means of escaping price competition and allowing them to compete on quality and cost. The downward sloping segment indicates that very intense competition erodes firm profits and thereby reduces the resources available to invest in R&D.

The impact of competitive pressures on knowledge absorption, innovation, and productivity has been studied quite extensively. Carlin, Schaffer, and Seabright, using a data set from a BEEPS of nearly 4,000 firms in twenty-four transition countries, "find evidence of the importance of a minimum of rivalry in both absorption and growth: the presence of at least a few competitors is effective both directly and through improving the efficiency with which the rents from market power in product markets are utilized to undertake innovation." They conclude that "our findings strongly reinforce the message that unchallenged monopoly is a drain on dynamism."[37] Moreover, the *World Development Report 2005* on the investment climate focused on the importance of a vibrant, competitive business environment for firms' investments in skills, absorption, and innovation: "If firms are not subject to competitive pressures that stimulate technical progress and the demand for more skilled workers, then effective demand for education will be weak."[38]

The Role of Government in Supporting Absorption

The government of the Russian Federation has proposed strengthening existing programs and creating several new initiatives to promote absorption and innovation in smaller firms and larger industrial firms.[39] For smaller firms, the measures include more effective infrastructure (technology parks, incubators), and financial support for small firms and start-ups. Support for larger firms and the development of absorption networks and clusters include indirect measures to stimulate exports, quality certification assistance, cofinancing for ventures into global markets, support for patenting abroad, and support for the development of joint R&D projects. For the proposed measures to have the expected impact, it will be very important to translate them into specific interventions. The strategy does not appear to recognize the crucial role of competitive pressures in modernizing the Russian economy or the emerging trend toward increasing exposure to foreign R&D (primarily through FDI, imports, and licensing but also by encouraging mobility and exchanges abroad).

There have been many official efforts to support firms but information on the scope of those measures is scarce, limiting the possibilities of evaluating their impact. One of the most successful support instruments is the Fund for Assistance to Small Innovative Enterprises (Bortnik Fund), which has a budget of about $30 million a year. Although the fund has an important demonstration role, it has not had a major impact on the R&D sector in Russia, and it has yet to be replicated on a large scale (box 3-2).

Yakovlev (2006) addresses the extent of government support in Russia using information collected through an Enterprise Survey. Even though the perception exists that government support to enterprises has been limited, a quarter of firms surveyed received direct support for investment, absorption, or exports, although the amounts were low.[40] Among those types of support, support for exports appears least pervasive, with only 3 percent of firms

Box 3-2. Fund for Assistance to Small Innovative Enterprises

The Fund for Assistance to Small Innovative Enterprises (Bortnik Fund) was created in 1994 by the Russian government.[1] The budget, from the government, is 1.5 percent of total federal expenditures for civilian science. The fund supports small innovative companies through open competition. Proposals prepared by the competing companies are submitted to peer review by external reviewers from the science and business sectors (including representatives of banks and venture and investment funds). The financial share of the fund in the winning projects cannot exceed 50 percent, and the companies have the rights to the intellectual property created in the projects. The fund provides support only to projects included in a list of government-approved critical technologies.

In the late 1990s, the fund began to increase support to companies at the seed and start-up stages, obviously a riskier strategy. The change was prompted not only by the stabilization of the general economic situation but also by the fact that the financial resources of the fund were becoming larger. In addition, the return to the fund from earlier loans was stable and provided additional money.

In 2003 the fund initiated a program called START to support start-up companies. About half of the fund's budget—or $10 million when the fund was started in 2003 and approximately $15 million in 2006—has since been devoted to the START program. In its composition and instruments, the program resembles the U.S. Small Business Innovation Research (SBIR) program. The first results show that about 20 percent of supported firms managed to find investors and thus get support from the fund for the second year. That is an encouraging result showing that small firms create quite a few technology-intensive goods and services with commercial potential.

With a budget of about $30 million a year, the fund has not had a large impact on the R&D sector in Russia; it can only demonstrate the success of this or that instrument or approach. So far, it seems that the experience of the fund has not been replicated by other government agencies.

Saltykov and Kuznetsov did a cost-benefit analysis of a proposed bank loan for innovation infrastructure. The results for the Bortnik Fund show that the scale is small, that the number of participants is limited, and that the Bortnik Fund finances only firms with an impeccable credit history. It was concluded, therefore, that the fund does not allow for financing start-ups.

Source: Bortnik (2004); unpublished analysis by Boris Saltykov and Boris Kuznetsov.
1. Resolution no. 65 of February 3, 1994.

receiving it. At the same time, 28 percent of firms surveyed received indirect support through procurement contracts with the government. Almost half the companies surveyed (44 percent) received some sort of support, direct or indirect. Direct support was provided more often to companies that had had significant innovative activity or that exported a considerable proportion of their production.[41]

To enhance the role of government in supporting innovative firms in Russia, we recommend the following:

Proposal 1: *Reform the IPR regime to encourage researchers at public R&D institutes and universities to engage in private innovation while protecting the public IPRs—and support patenting activity of firms, especially patenting abroad and patenting by smaller firms with less capacity.* The legacy of the Soviet science and technology system is still having a negative effect on the orientation and overall level of appropriation and exploitation activities in the National Innovation System (NIS).[42] The incentive conflicts in the current arrangement have resulted in the de facto privatization of R&D activities, which can be observed in multiple scientific research teams based in the public system that provide R&D services on an informal but commercial basis to LMEs and SMEs. Some may see that as the encouraging beginning of an organic R&D industry. But there are negative consequences, including conflicts of interest between researchers and institutes, uncertainty about the ownership of technical results, and the government's loss of rents from the intellectual property generated through quasi-private research. Consider, on the other hand, India's Council of Scientific and Industrial Research: founded in 1942, it has evolved with the changing economic structure of the country to become an internationally competitive institute (box 3-3).

The government should consider additional policies to create incentives for spinning off research groups. The objective would be to lower the public financing burden for R&D institutes, foster commercial innovation and knowledge absorption by firms, and reallocate basic research funding in favor of universities. Although downsizing of R&D institutes has occurred, the most promising and active researchers have also been lost. The average age of those employed in R&D has risen along with the reduction in the number of personnel. University-based research would create a nurturing ground for young researchers, following the experience worldwide. In order to move to a more efficient and effective national innovation system, it will be important to hasten the dissolution of R&D institutes and

---

Box 3-3. From Autarkic Self-Reliance to Internationally Competitive Research and Development in India

India's Council of Scientific and Industrial Research (CSIR), founded in 1942, was modeled after the United Kingdom's Department of Scientific and Industrial Research. Predating most other specialized research and development institutes in India, it took on a wide range of functions, from promotion of scientific research to setting up research and development institutions and collecting and disseminating data on research and industry. In the first two decades after India's independence, it focused on building up an extensive research and development infrastructure, from metrology to research and development over a wide range of industries with a strong focus on supporting emerging industry, especially small and medium enterprises.

When India changed from an inward-oriented development strategy to a more external, market-driven strategy as a result of the 1991 crisis, the focus of the CSIR also changed, from technological self-reliance to "research and development" as a business. There was more emphasis on output and performance in a more competitive market and on doing research that was relevant for the productive sectors and that could earn income. Each laboratory was considered a subsidiary corporate entity. Incentives and rewards for meeting targets were introduced, and if laboratories did a good job of meeting their commitments on output and deliverables, they were given greater autonomy in operations. In addition, there have been continuous efforts to streamline the CSIR further to improve its effectiveness and efficiency.

Although the CSIR is going through further restructuring, the results have been impressive. Between 1997 and 2002 the CSIR reduced its laboratories from forty to thirty-eight and staffing from 24,000 to 20,000. At the same time, output increased noticeably. Technical and scientific publications in the internationally recognized journals increased from 1,576 in 1995 to 2,900 in 2005, and their average impact factor increased from 1.5 to 2.2. Patent filings in India increased from 264 in 1997–98 to 418 in 2004–05, and patent filings abroad increased from 94 in 1997–98 to 500 in 2004–05. Moreover, the CSIR accounted for around 50 to 60 percent of all U.S. patents granted to resident Indian inventors. The CSIR also increased its earnings from outside income from 1.8 billion rupees in 1995–96 to 3.1 billion rupees in 2005–06 (about $65 million). Today, it has 4,700 active scientists and technologists in thirty-seven research laboratories, supported by 8,500 scientific and technical personnel.

Source: Bhojwani (2006).

the teams within them that work on obsolete scientific and industrial problems.

Proposal 2: *To encourage productivity growth, provide incentives for firms to invest more in their knowledge absorption capacity. Specifically, more use should be made of instruments such as matching grants for supporting the absorption of new technologies and processes, access to ICT and ISO certification, and investments in soft technology.* Since the 1980s there has been increasing awareness in OECD countries of the benefits of matching grants in encouraging firms to share and manage risk.[43] We recommend matching grants because they encourage public-private risk sharing and orient the selection process toward the R&D programs most likely to generate outcomes with a high commercial impact.[44] The justification for supporting ICT technologies and international certification is that such investments have strong and positive effects on productivity and innovative behavior.

Clearly, there are major risks in allocating matching grants effectively— including program corruption, capture, and sectoral targeting. Therefore one prerequisite for success is an institutional design that would immunize the funding allocation from corruption and interference by political actors and other state or specific interests. A second prerequisite is neutrality: the program should not try to steer the grants in any predetermined direction ("picking winners").

To avoid government capture and failure, a matching grant program should be as neutral and transparent as possible. To ensure sufficient checks and balances, the decisionmaking process for funding allocations needs to include representatives from the private sector, academia, and civil society and foreign experts. An optimal design would include the following key elements:

—An independent institution with a clear mandate and control mechanism would be responsible for administration and funding decisions, keeping its mandate separate from other public policy goals.

—The funding decision would be made by an independent investment committee. To enhance transparency, the investment committee should be staffed with technical experts and foreign experts, who are less likely to be subject to political influence. A potential problem is the question of confidentiality and fear of industrial espionage.

—The investment policy and decisionmaking processes would be instituted and supervised by a board consisting of representatives of different government institutions and international advisers.

—Technical assessments of project proposals would be based on external peer reviews involving international experts when possible.

—All project proposals and decisions would be recorded, tracked, and made publicly available. E-government procurement technologies should be considered to aid the process.

A traditional approach to innovation, absorption, and R&D support for firms has been through tax incentives (tax credits or lower tax rates), widely used in Europe to encourage investors and companies to invest in R&D. But tax incentives have weaknesses that make them less applicable to postsocialist economies, and their weaknesses seem significant enough to preclude their use. First, tax benefits are meant to help existing enterprises that can use profits from related products to take advantage of the credits or offsets. But they do not help start-ups that have not yet accumulated sufficient profits and therefore cannot offset tax liabilities. Second, in countries with a weak tax enforcement system, tax incentives may promote distorting tax avoidance behavior rather than productive investment. Third, tax incentives cannot be used (as grants can) to promote networks and links between the private sector and universities and research institutes, which lie at the heart of the type of instrument that we recommend. The Institute of Economies in Transition (IET) study unsurprisingly finds that most respondents are keen about tax benefits.[45]

Proposal 3: *Private seed capital funds should be encouraged, but state-owned and state-managed venture capital (VC) funds proposed by the government should be avoided.* The government's program on "generating incentives for development of the manufacturing sector" envisages the establishment of an open joint stock company, a Russian venture company that would be a government-owned institution supporting innovation by participating in existing venture funds and by contributing to the creation of new funds. That would augment the existing provision of state financing for the creation and especially the expansion of new high-growth firms through venture funds, building on the experience and organization of the regional venture funds created in the 1990s with EBRD (Economic Bank for Reconstruction and Development) support. An open question is whether the funding is meant to be a transitory support leading to the creation of a private venture market. If so, the government would require an exit mechanism if and when a critical mass of venture projects was in place and incentives for private investment using venture funds were satisfied.

International best practices suggest that the government could seed the venture capital industry by investing in privately managed funds. In such public-private partnerships, government participation mitigates some of the risk in technology-oriented start-ups, and the seed capitalist provides commercial and managerial expertise. It still would be advisable for the seed capital program to be flexible in targeting small start-up high-technology companies by allowing public-private risk sharing with flexible contracting between investors and managers, free from excessive regulation, and the use of limited partnerships.

Internal financing by enterprises, government funding, and angel investors are all important in early-stage technological development (ESTD). But most important is the virtual absence of more mainstream intermediaries such as banks, private equity, and other institutional investors. Even in advanced and innovative economies, early-stage finance of innovative projects is undertaken directly by firms, if they have the resources, or by very specialized institutions, with a significant role for the government. Not surprisingly, internal funds account for the biggest share of ESTD financing in the United States because that is the most straightforward way of overcoming information asymmetries. Established enterprises know the track record of their own inventors and employees—and they typically have a better understanding of the market and the commercial potential of internally proposed innovations than outside agents do. Enterprises use the cash flows generated by established operations to finance innovation or to tap external funds on the basis of the strength of their balance sheet.

Angel investors are another important source of ESTD funding in the United States and to some extent in Europe. The term refers to successful entrepreneurs who look for new opportunities to invest private funds earned from their previous economic activities and are willing to invest in ESTD projects in technological fields that they understand well (having "been there and done that"). Studies of the behavior of angel investors frequently find that they are often heavily involved in commercial decisionmaking and that their "business support" function can be as important as the financing that they offer. Giving managerial advice and maintaining commercial control over the ESTD entrepreneur are typical functions of the angel investor and venture capital funding models—as well as internal funding models.

Given the short history of capital accumulation and profit-generating enterprises in Russia, internal financing by enterprises and angel investors is rare in the region and does not provide a viable basis for promoting innovation. The absence of angel investors is problematic not only from a funding perspective but also because they function as sources of managerial expertise, as information brokers, and as contacts to broader formal and informal networks of entrepreneurs and innovators. The role of government in Russia is therefore different from its role in OECD countries. The lack of angels and internal financing is acute, and the capacity of government agencies to take their place is extremely limited.

In that respect, some caution is warranted regarding the Russian government's initiative to establish venture capital companies with 100 percent state participation. International experience shows that publicly financed and managed venture capital funds may be ineffective in fostering the commercialization of new and improved goods and services and the expansion of innovative firms. The role of state-owned and state-managed venture capital funds in financing innovative projects in India, for example, was limited. Most of the funds set up in India during the recent relatively high-growth period (1995–2000) tended to be private funds, financed heavily from overseas by communities of nonresident Indians. It can be argued that the single most important factor for the VC and IT industries in India was the combination of returnees from the diaspora and a generous supply of engineering and IT talent. The successful businesses created from that pool of talent sparked spin-off and investment activities, which, in turn, influenced the government to improve business conditions further. The lesson is that directly intervening to manage the allocation of VC funds is unlikely to lead to the expected results.

When venture capital funds managed by government entities achieve commercial success, often it is because the funds are invested not in innovative ventures but in small, more mature companies with less risky product lines. Moreover, capture and rent seeking are prevalent and problematic because these types of funds are dominated by political interests.

One advantage of implementing proposals 2 and 3 simultaneously is that the synergies between the two can establish a more integrated framework for supporting entrepreneurial companies. A seed capital program aimed at promoting knowledge absorption is likely to work best when a grants program provides critical funding at the earlier stages of technological development, followed by private seed capital funds. The reason is that commercial venture capital funds typically avoid the risk connected with early-stage companies and target more established projects. Matching grants can fill the gap in the support framework for early-stage technology development.

In the more mature stages of technological development, seed capital provides funds to expand production and the customer base and supports the later (and most visible) stages of commercialization. To minimize the potential negative distortions of both proposals 2 and 3, the instrument design should ensure neutrality, whereby the government does not decide which sector or technology to support but responds to market demand.[46] When applied to matching grants or to the funding of seed capital funds, that translates into having the government establish universal criteria for submission and eligibility but allowing an independent entity to select projects for support through a transparent process.

Notes

1. These figures are from the OECD *Science, Technology, and Industry Scoreboard 2005* (OECD 2005). Not all figures were available for 2004, the most recent year, so figures for the most recent year available were used instead.

2. Watkins (2003).

3. OECD (2005). Not all figures were available for the most recent year (2004), so figures for the most recent year available were used instead. According to official Russian data for 2004, government expenditures on R&D were 59.6 percent of total expenditures (CSRS 2005, p. 75).

4. According to CSRS data (2005, p. 75) the share of funding from the "business enterprise sector" was 17.3 percent in 1998 and 21.4 percent in 2004. This indicator is quite difficult to decipher because it includes expenditures of state-owned enterprises and thus is not "private," but it gives an idea of the evolution over time.

5. OECD (2005b, p. 35).

6. The number of patents issued is highly influenced by export activity in a country. Given the fact that the application process implies costs to the owner of the knowledge, a patent may be pursued only when that knowledge has significant commercial value in the target market (such as the United States or European Union).

7. OECD (2005a).

8. The use of patenting in the United States as an indicator of knowledge was pioneered by Griliches (1994, 1998), followed by Jaffe and Trajtenberg (2002) and Lederman and Maloney (2003b).

9. Eurostat (2004).

10. OECD (1994). See also Rosstat (2004, p. 75) and OECD (2004b, p.192).

11. According to Boris Saltykov (Saltykov 2001), 75 percent of Soviet R&D was defense oriented. Basic science was usually emphasized because in certain areas the Soviet Union was the world leader.

12. Hoekmann and Javorcik (2006). A third channel is direct trade in knowledge through purchasing patents and licensing.

13. Coe, Helpman, and Hoffmaister (1995); Keller (2002).

14. Data from COMTRADE on "capital goods (except transport equipment) and parts and accessories thereof," classified as BEC-4. See UNCTAD (2006a).

15. Kraay (1999).

16. Global production sharing refers to the process whereby multinational corporations—through FDI—develop international production and distribution networks around the globe. This process facilitates production and distribution in different countries at different phases of the production process, enabling "true internationalization of the manufacturing process." Intra-industry trade, by contrast, refers to vertically integrated international networks that usually leverage a highly skilled labor force and specialized products.

17. Rodrik (2006a).

18. Most CIS countries have not yet made the transition from "buyer-driven" production networks (wherein countries can make use of cheap, unskilled labor to leverage labor-intensive activities, typically clothing and furniture manufacturing) to capital-intensive "producer-driven" networks. That transition is usually encouraged by rising wages, but economies rich in natural resources do not always face the same binding constraints (Broadman 2006).

19. Saggi (2006).

20. The FDI benchmarking analysis in the UNCTAD *World Investment Report 2006* (UNCTAD 2006b) also indicates that Russia has high FDI potential but low FDI performance.

21. World Bank (2006d).

22. Hare, Schaffer, and Shabunina (2004).

23. UNCTAD (2006b).

24. Whalley and Xin (2006) indicates that foreign-invested enterprises account for more than 50 percent of exports and 60 percent of imports and are a significant driver of economic growth (the authors calculate that around 40 percent of China's economic growth in 2003 and 2004 was due to FIEs). These enterprises have much greater average labor productivity than non-FIEs, and their export capabilities benefit from access to distribution systems and products tailored for export markets. Concerning absorption, the *World Investment Report* (UNCTAD 2006b, p. 188) argues that "the advantage of forming a joint venture from the perspective of technology diffusion within the host economy is that the local partners and the affiliate, which would be vested with a certain amount of technological and managerial expertise transferred from the parent firm, are likely to have close contacts and exchanges of personnel. Forming a joint venture is therefore the most obvious—and possibly the most effective—means by which local firms can acquire knowledge from TNCs."

25. Ark and Piatkovski (2004).

26. World Bank (2006d).

27. Hare, Schaffer, and Shabunina (2004).

28. Lederman and Maloney (2003a).

29. As in other studies using a production function approach and firm-level data, endogeneity is a possible problem in the estimations, owing to the two-way relationship between technology absorption and R&D spending, absorption outcomes and organizational change, and absorption decisions and competition. As a result, the description of the results is careful not to interpret the correlations in terms of causality but simply as an correlation between different investment activities and outcomes.

30. This follows the classification of industries in the OECD STAN Indicators, based on International Standard Industrial Classification (ISIC) Revision 3. The four technology categories are low, medium-low, medium-high, and high. Examples of low-technology industries include food, tobacco, wood, and paper products; beverages; and textiles. The high-technology manufactures are pharmaceuticals; office, accounting, and computing machinery; radio, television, and communications equipment; medical, precision, and optical instruments; and aircraft and spacecraft (OECD 2004c).

31. Helpman and Trajtenberg (1996).

32. For example, Acs and Audretsch (1988) confirms a positive relationship between R&D expenditures and the number of innovations in firms. The relationship is "sensitive to the total amount of innovative activity. That is, in industries in which there is little innovative activity . . . the correlation between all the measures of technical change becomes considerably weaker" (p. 682). The authors also refer to results in Griliches (1986) that show that the estimates depend on the definition and measurement of R&D.

33. Random effects and clustering are used to control for regional specific variables that may be driving innovative activities. This empirical model is meant to test for partial correlations and links between innovation outputs and inputs, but it is not an attempt to identify causal effects between those variables.

34. The evidence here is based on different indicators, mostly a firm's assessment of the level of competition in its main market. Even though we tested a number of different indicators and specifications, these findings should be interpreted more as confirmation of a quite developed part of empirical findings on the same topic.

35. Litwack (2005). As indicated by Rodrik, "China's experience indicates that it is not *how much* you export, but *what* you export that matters" (Rodrik 2006b).

36. Aghion and others (2002).

37. Carlin, Schaffer, and Seabright (2004, p. 20, 25). In this chapter we follow the example of Carlin, Schaffer, and Seabright in using measures of market power that correspond to the perceptions of individual firms regarding the competitive pressures that they face. They argue that "these are an important supplement to more conventional measures, such as shares of markets based on conventional industrial

classifications. These can help not just in illuminating the overall pressures faced by firms but also the way in which different constraints on managerial decision-making interact."

38. World Bank (2004, p. 157).

39. See the "Research and Development Strategy of the Russian Federation to 2015," approved in March 2006 (Ministry of Education and Science 2006).

40. Of firms receiving support, 5.6 percent received two or more types.

41. This is not the case for indirect support, so it cannot be affirmed that effectiveness is a consideration in the granting of procurement contracts. Exporting by itself is considered as a factor signaling effectiveness of firms.

42. OECD (2005b).

43. The following paragraphs are based on a World Bank report, "Public Financial Support for Commercial Innovation," which analyzes the various financial instruments to encourage innovation and recommends a series of reforms before those instruments can be put to good use (World Bank 2006c).

44. The importance of matching stems from the fact that it reduces the marginal cost of research to the firm. A firm facing a downward-sloping marginal research return schedule will always increase total expenditure when the marginal cost falls, precluding dollar-for-dollar crowding out.

45. CEFIR and IET (2006). Respondents in the IET survey expressed a preference for the introduction of incremental tax privileges for R&D costs and the purchase of foreign technologies.

46. World Bank (2006c).

four
Upgrading Skills

HONG TAN, VLADIMIR GIMPELSON, AND YEVGENIYA SAVCHENKO

Russia, even with its highly educated workforce, faces a growing shortage of skilled workers in industry. In the transition to a market economy, Russia's workforce underwent a wrenching reallocation of labor across industries and occupations, and many specialized and technical skills that workers acquired under central planning were no longer in demand.[1] Mismatches in the labor market became widespread, with sharp shortages of some types of skilled workers coexisting with excess supplies of others. The formal education system and the specialized vocational and technical training institutions in particular were poorly prepared to operate under the new market conditions and to supply the new skills that the market required. Employers who once hoarded labor are now reporting skill shortages as a major production constraint, and some are upgrading the skills of their existing workers through various training programs.

To raise labor productivity in industry, improve industry's international competitiveness, and participate more fully in the global knowledge economy, Russia must analyze the issue of skill requirements and develop policies to address it. Skill shortages can directly constrain production and prevent firms from meeting demand and using available inputs efficiently, with lower productivity as a consequence. And—indirectly—they can inhibit the absorption of new knowledge, a skill-intensive activity. With respect to the general economy, the mismatch between the skills that firms require and those that education and training institutions offer can waste scarce public and private resources. With respect to individuals, the mismatch leads to sunk investments in their human capital that yield low returns and unfavorable labor market outcomes.

Whether a corrective policy is appropriate depends on the cause of a skill mismatch. The likely causes include

—inadequate funding or governance of education and training institutions, which constrains them from responding to the needs of the market

—inappropriate labor regulations, which inhibit hiring and firing by firms to meet staffing shortfalls

—restrictive compensation policies, which prevent some employers from paying wages that are competitive enough to attract needed labor

—market failures in the training market, such as high turnover of trained workers, which inhibit the willingness of employers to invest in training to meet their own skill needs.

This chapter draws on the complete Russian Competitiveness and Investment Climate Assessment Survey—including the Large and Medium Enterprise Survey (LME Survey) and the Small Enterprise Survey (SE Survey)—and related research and information sources to gain insight into skill shortages and mismatches and in-service training. It examines recent trends in the level and quality of education, the effects of economic restructuring on the skill composition of the workforce, the returns to schooling, and the aggregate supply and demand for skills in the Russian labor market. Using data from firm surveys, it then characterizes the distribution and nature of staffing and skill shortages among different groups of manufacturing firms, thereby contributing to the understanding of reported skill shortages and staffing problems, including labor turnover, compensation policies, and the inhibiting effects of labor regulations. A discussion of worker training follows, presenting evidence on the distribution, intensity, and determinants of in-service training and the implications for productivity and wages. The chapter concludes with some policy implications.

Evolution of Human Capital in Russia

The transition from a centrally planned to a market economy has strongly affected the evolution of human capital in Russia. Before the transition, most of Russia's workforce was concentrated in industry and the service sector was underdeveloped. Educational attainment was high, but the educational system was oriented toward imparting narrowly defined technical skills at the expense of more general knowledge and skills. Wage inequality was artificially compressed, and rates of return to higher education were relatively low (in the 1 to 2 percent range).

That employment structure changed dramatically after 1991. In the first stage of the transition (1991–98), industrial restructuring was accompanied by decreases in employment and working hours and steep declines in real wages. The second stage (1999–2006)—against the backdrop of a dynamic recovery following the crisis of 1998 that positively affected all labor market indicators—led to rising returns to education and reports of skill shortages.

According to Barro and Lee (2001), in 2001 Russia had one of the most highly educated workforces in the world. For the population age twenty-five and over, Russia ranked seventh, with an average of 10.5 years of schooling. It was ahead of other BRIC and transition countries, as well as Germany, Japan, and the United Kingdom (appendix figure A4-1). Russia also had one of the highest shares of population age twenty-five and over that had a tertiary-level degree—more than half (57 percent), 13 percentage points more than in Canada and over 26 percentage points more than in other postsocialist countries[2] (see appendix figure A4-1).

Russia thus appears well situated to take advantage of knowledge-based economic activities requiring a well-educated workforce and a significant pool of researchers. In 2003 Russia had twice as many researchers per million population (3,371) as the Czech Republic, Hungary, or Poland (which averaged about 1,500) and five to ten times more researchers than Brazil (344 in 2000) or China (663). On that indicator, Russia was closer to France and Germany (which had about 3,200 researchers per million) but behind the United States and Japan (4,500 to 5,300). It benefited from downsizing in the science sector during the transition, so that now a significant proportion of the workforce that is not employed in the science sector has experience in research.

Despite its high formal educational attainment, Russia faces serious problems with the quality of education provided, including underfunding; low quality of instruction; the deterioration of secondary education, as measured by international standardized tests like PISA and TIMMS; and an orientation to teaching narrowly defined skills in professional education (see appendix 4).

High rates of educational attainment are not simply a legacy of the pre-transition period. While demand for higher education fell in the immediate post-reform period, enrollment rates rose again in the mid-1990s and today exceed the rates of the late 1980s. How much of that increase in educational attainment was the result of changes in the industrial and occupational composition of employment that accompanied restructuring? How much was the result of educational upgrading within industries and occupations? A decomposition of the effects of industrial and occupational changes suggests that while changes in the structure of industry and occupations contributed modestly to upgrading of the workforce in the early 1990s, most of the subsequent educational upgrading occurred independent of restructuring.[3] That the upgrading took place across the board, within all industries and occupations, suggests a strong, skill-biased process of change, reflected in technological change and in the transformation of organizational and institutional arrangements in the workplace. The demand for education is likely to increase in such an environment, given the comparative advantage of educated workers in implementing new technology or in responding to disequilibria.[4]

The rising returns to education in Russia help explain why the demand for education was so strong during the transition. Mincer-type wage equations suggest that private returns to an extra year of schooling prior to the transition were in the range of 2 to 3 percent, reflecting wage compression resulting from the administratively set "wage grid" system. The demise of centralized wage setting led to a rapid increase in the education premium. Returns to an extra year of education rose to about 7 to 8 percent in the first five years of transition and by an additional 2 to 3 percent in the later period, stabilizing at 8 to 10 percent by 2000–02 (see appendix 4).

When returns are differentiated by level of education, specialized training tends to yield lower payoffs than more general education. Vocational training increased the wages of secondary school graduates by about 5 percent. Tertiary professional and technical colleges, which provide training in specific skills, yielded wage increases of 13 percent for males and 20 percent for females. University-educated males earned 50 percent more than those who completed only secondary school, and the wage premium for university-educated females was about 70 percent. The high returns to university education explain why enrollment rates in higher education rose over the transition. And the fact that schooling returns stayed high despite the increasing supply of educated workers indicates that the demand for higher education was very strong, exceeding supply.

Skill Constraints and Labor Shortages

Given the concerns raised by the deteriorating quality and relevance of education and training in Russia, evidence from firm surveys, including the Russia LME Survey, provides insights into how employers perceive labor and skill shortages, whether their perceptions are valid, and which firms are most affected. Several factors may constrain enterprises from responding to perceived skill shortages—particularly labor turnover, compensation policies, and labor legislation.

Respondents to the Russia LME Survey ranked "lack of skilled and qualified workforce" as the number-two investment climate constraint to enterprise growth and development (the number-one constraint was taxation). Small enterprises with fewer than 100 employees also ranked the skill constraint as major or severe, though not as highly as regulation or access to and cost of finance (see appendix 4).[5] The skill constraint is not new, but it has been growing with the transition from a planned to a market economy and with the rapid economic growth since the late 1990s.

Time-series data from the quarterly Russia Economic Barometer surveys provide insights into how overstaffing or understaffing in enterprises has changed over the last two decades.[6] Before the 1998 financial crisis, the proportion of firms reporting that they were overstaffed relative to expected output in the coming year was high—in 1997, 38 percent of firms noted that they had redundant personnel. The strong recovery in industrial output after 1998 brought the proportion of overstaffed firms down to less than 15 percent.

The proportion of firms reporting that staffing was not sufficient to meet expected demand started to grow after 1998, and by 2004 almost one in four firms reported understaffing against expected output. The shift from overstaffing to labor shortage is consistent with labor use rates, which grew from around 70 percent in the mid-1990s to 90 percent, almost full use of the workforce, in 2005. The shortages also grew with output, which increased 1.5 times over 1999–2005 as employment in the corporate sector fell slightly.

In the 2005 Russia LME Survey, about 60 percent of surveyed managers rated their current staffing as "optimal" relative to current output while 27 percent rated their firm as "understaffed" and 13 percent as "overstaffed." On average, understaffed firms were short of personnel by 17 percent, while overstaffed firms had 15 percent more workers than they needed (see appendix 4). That means that a sizable fraction of Russian enterprises had difficulties adjusting the size of their workforce to levels dictated by their output.

The probability and levels of understaffing were highest for firms operating in the textile industry, where more than 50 percent of surveyed firms reported less than optimal staffing, with the staffing gap averaging 22.6 per-

Table 4-1. Staffing and Workforce Skills, by Skill Category

Classification of enterprises	Managers	Professionals	Other white collar	Skilled workers	Unskilled workers
Skills and qualifications of workforce a major or severe constraint					
Yes	51.1	51.8	68.4	53.8	60.3
No	40.1	38.0	40.1	25.5	38.0
Overall staffing in the firm					
Optimal	3.0	11.8	0.7	37.0	4.9
Understaffed	8.1	37.0	4.4	95.6	29.3
Overstaffed	3.9	14.8	2.3	42.2	6.3
Total	4.5	19.1	1.9	53.6	11.7

Source: LME Survey (2005).

cent relative to the desired level. New firms established in or after 1992, small enterprises with fewer than 250 employees, firms involved in metallurgy and machine building, and government-controlled firms (those having more than 25 percent public ownership) also were more likely to report understaffing. Overstaffing was more prevalent among large firms (those having more than 1,000 employees) and firms involved with chemicals.

Enterprises were concerned not only about overall staffing but also about the desired mix of skills. That finding was borne out by firms reporting understaffing in several occupational groups—managers, professionals, other white-collar employees, skilled workers, and unskilled workers. Firms that ranked "skills and qualifications of the workforce" as a major or severe constraint were more likely to report understaffing in the different skill groups than were those that did not rank skill constraints highly (table 4-1). As might be expected, firms that had less than optimal staffing were also more likely than other firms to report understaffing in all skill categories, especially skilled workers (95 percent) and professionals (37 percent). Interestingly, firms with optimal or more than optimal staffing also reported shortages in the same two skill categories. Specific shortages, especially of professional and skilled workers, can coexist with overall optimal staffing or overstaffing. That fact hints that firms face difficulties in adjusting and reallocating their workforce.

The extent to which skill shortages are a problem varies across units within firms. Most firms identified two major problems—lack of technological capacity and lack of skilled and qualified workers, both concentrated in operating units, that is, on production lines. A much smaller fraction of firms reported those as major problems in their economic, human resource, and research and development units (see appendix 4).

Firms experiencing skill shortages cited several reasons for understaffing. The four most commonly cited were lack of workers with needed skills in the local labor market (72 percent), lower wages than at other firms (41 percent), high labor turnover (30 percent), and high competition for workers in the local labor market (23 percent). Those reasons are consistent with an inadequate supply of workers with relevant job skills in the local labor market, high labor turnover rates, and noncompetitive wages and salaries.

Labor Turnover

During the transition to a market economy, labor turnover in Russian firms has been higher than in firms in other former USSR countries. In 2004 the average rate of new hires was about 29 percent, while the job separation rate was 31 percent, giving the Russian economy a gross labor turnover rate of about 60 percent. Those turnover indicators are even higher if only industry is considered, with hiring, separation, and gross turnover rates of 30, 35, and 65 percent, respectively.[7]

The high turnover rates were not neutral with respect to skills. Managers surveyed in the Russia Economic Barometer were asked to compare the skill mix of those who were newly hired or separated to the skill mix of those who remained. Throughout 1996–2005, more than a third of all managers reported deterioration in the quality of their workforce, about half reported no change in quality, and a tenth reported some improvement in quality due to labor turnover. The low quality of newly hired workers, not the high quality of separations, may have been responsible for the reported deterioration in quality. Almost half of the firms hired workers who had lower-quality skills, while only 10 percent hired workers who were more skilled. The proportion of firms that experienced an improvement in workforce quality through job separations was roughly equal to the proportion that experienced a decline. The net outcome, at least for one segment of the firms surveyed, was that the overall quality of the workforce fell.

Compensation Policies

Respondents to the Russia LME Survey listed noncompetitive wages as one reason for understaffing. If that is true, noncompetitive wages may account for the inability of firms experiencing labor or skill shortages either to retain their skilled workers or to hire equally or more skilled workers from the open labor market, as the Russia Economic Barometer data indicate. Firms may not offer competitive wages if they have below-average performance and profitability—that is, if they are unable to pay wages that are high enough to retain their most skilled workers or to fill vacant positions with the skilled labor that they need.

Gimpelson (2004) used data from a survey of 300 large and medium firms in Russia to investigate whether skill shortages were driven by supply or by demand constraints and to find out what enterprises were doing to respond to reported skill shortfalls.[8] The analysis suggested that understaffed firms had lower labor productivity, profitability, and average wages than both optimally staffed and overstaffed firms. And if low-efficiency firms (those with low labor productivity, profitability, or wages) declared that they had labor or skill shortages, they were more likely to use workers with mass (generic) skills supplied by the traditional vocational education system. In contrast, efficient firms were more likely to search for workers with specific or unique skills, who were in limited supply.

A similar pattern of reported staffing and firm performance emerges in the 2005 Russia LME Survey, which includes a much larger sample of industrial enterprises. Understaffed firms fared the worst on all performance indicators. Though understaffed, they lost employment and showed negative net employment change over the previous year. Overstaffed firms, by contrast, were in slightly better economic shape and showed significant (and needed) downsizing over the preceding year. The best performance in labor productivity and profitability was by firms with optimal staffing. They paid wages that were comparable to those paid by overstaffed firms and significantly above those paid by understaffed and low-productivity firms.

Labor Legislation

Russian enterprises may also be constrained from meeting reported skill shortages by employment protection legislation (EPL). An emerging literature suggests that overly strict employment protection legislation can impair hiring and firing, stifle job creation, and lead to higher unemployment. Labor legislation—regarding minimum wages, social benefits and guarantees, employment contracts, and layoff regulations—can change the labor costs that employers face and, if strictly enforced, lower their incentives to hire new workers or discharge redundant ones, even when warranted by labor demand.

On the World Bank's "Doing Business" scale, Russia got a score of 30 on rigidity of employment, comparable with that of China but significantly lower than that of either Brazil or India, which had scores of 56 and 62 respectively.[9] Russia's index of employment rigidity was closer to the average for OECD countries and lower than that of most other transition countries except for the Czech Republic. According to the index, firing costs—measured in weeks of wages given as compensation for discharge—also were significantly lower in Russia than in other BRIC countries.

The index may understate the extent to which employment protection regulations in Russia constrain the staffing decisions of employers[10] because they are poorly and selectively enforced; their impact on staffing flexibility, therefore, may differ from one firm to another.[11] The actual "rule of law" is selective and varies by region, sector, age of firm, and segment of the legislation.[12] In large and mostly unionized firms (which account for roughly two-thirds of total employment in Russia), EPL is more strictly enforced, while the same provisions are barely binding on small firms. Instead of reducing uncertainty, Russia's EPL regime increases it (through non-enforcement) and differentiates firms by their mandatory labor costs. Firms that enjoy discretion in applying the rules may avoid paying social benefits to their workers. Firms that abide by the rules—typically large and medium firms—avoid creating new jobs and maintain a low-wage policy; many rely on small firms as flexible suppliers of labor.

Not surprisingly, managers in the Russia LME Survey did not rank EPL as significant a production constraint as the shortage of skilled labor.[13] Even so, about 17 percent of respondents did rank it as a notable constraint. In a separate question on labor regulations, only 40 percent of respondents believed that labor regulations did not create major problems for their enterprise. One-fifth reported that rules on hiring foreign labor created serious difficulties, 19 percent pointed to hiring and firing rules, and 15 percent stressed regulations regarding working hours. Overstaffed firms tended to select hiring and firing rules, working hours regulations, and rules on timing of wage payments as the most constraining labor regulations. Understaffed firms tended to stress rules governing the minimum wage and the hiring of foreign workers. Although the use of short-term contracts is restricted by labor law, 38 percent of surveyed firms reported using them to hire about 10 percent of their workforce.

Labor adjustment costs induced by the EPL are likely to make it more difficult for firms to search for and hire skilled workers. The regression estimates in appendix table A4-6 suggest that the EPL index is positively associated with the difficulties that firms experience in searching for and hiring professionals and skilled workers. The higher the sum of EPL rankings as a constraint, the more severe the search and hiring difficulties reported by firms for both groups. Firms able to circumvent employment protection legislation were less likely to rank searching for and hiring skilled labor as a problem. The results also confirm that firms paying low, noncompetitive wages were more likely to report difficulties in searching for and hiring skilled labor.

In-Service Training

One possible solution to skill shortages in the local labor market is for employers to train or upgrade the skills of their existing workforce. The hiring-versus-retraining debate is discussed in Lazareva, Denisova, and Tsukhlo (2006). In the authors' survey of 1,000 industrial enterprises in 2004, 56 percent of firms considered retraining existing workers to be the most efficient way to meet skill shortages, 35 percent preferred hiring from the external market, and 25 percent preferred agreements with education and training institutions.

The BEEPS and LME Survey data show that selected comparator countries in East Asia and Latin America had a higher incidence of training than transition economies in Eastern Europe and OECD countries, with South Asia especially far behind (see appendix 4).[14] How did training incidence in Russia compare with that in its BRIC competitors—Brazil, India, and China? At 58 percent, Russia trailed behind China (92 percent) and Brazil (59 percent), but it was way ahead of India (17 percent).[15]

The Russia LME Survey elicited data about the skill groups that received in-service training and the number trained. It suggests that managers, professionals, and skilled workers are the three skill groups most likely to benefit from in-service training, consistent with the kinds of skill shortages that firms reported. On average, 10 to 11 percent of managers and professionals and about 8 percent of skilled workers received formal training.

Those figures, which are extremely low by international standards, suggest that in-service training is not firmly entrenched in Russian firms. World Bank (1997) estimated that in Malaysia—a fast-growing East Asia country that also ranked skill shortages highly—24 percent of managers, 32 percent of professionals and technicians, and 13 to 16 percent of production workers received formal in-service training.[16] So while many more Russian firms train their employees, they provide training to a smaller number of them than do their fast-growing counterparts in East Asia.

Russia stands out among the BRIC group with respect to the very small share of its workforce trained within the firm (7.7 percent of skilled and

Figure 4-1. Percent of Workforce Trained and Percent of Firms Providing In-Service Training in Russia and Selected Countries

Percent of workers   Percent of firms

☐ Skilled workers trained   ■ Unskilled workers trained
— Firms that provide employees with training

Source: LME Survey (2005).

1.4 percent of unskilled workers) compared with that of Brazil (53 percent and 45 percent) and China (44 and 28 percent) (figure 4-1 and appendix table A4-7).[17] The share of workers trained through in-service programs also was lower in Russia than in several other transition countries (12 percent and 45 percent for skilled and 6 percent and 13 percent for unskilled workers respectively) and selected developing countries (47 percent and 70 percent for skilled and 34 percent and 53 percent for unskilled workers respectively), and it was significantly below the share in OECD countries as a group (typically above 50 percent). It is possible, though unlikely, that the low estimates for Russia are a statistical artifact.[18] The recent survey of enterprise training practices in Lazareva, Denisova, and Tsukhlo (2006) reports a somewhat higher figure for Russia—about 20 percent of workers—though it is still below figures for OECD countries.

Which firms trained, and where did workers get their training? The incidence of in-service training was higher among larger, export-oriented firms and firms that invested in research and development. Long-established firms were more likely to provide in-service training than newer firms. Domestically owned firms tended to train more than foreign-owned firms, and government ownership made no difference in the likelihood of training.

Localities rated moderate in investment risk tended to have a higher incidence of training than minimal-risk or high-risk regions.

The probit-regression analysis in appendix table A4-8 reinforces the correlations reported. First, it shows that the likelihood of in-service training is higher in larger firms (those with more than 250 employees) and in localities with moderate investment risk than in either low- or high-risk regions. Second, firms that employ a larger proportion of workers with higher education also are more likely to train. The empirical evidence from many countries indicates that both types of skills—educational attainment of the workforce and post-school training—are highly correlated.[19] Educated workers are not only more productive in performing given tasks but are thought to be more adept at evaluating new information and learning from it.

The probit regression analysis shows that firms that engage in R&D and, to a lesser extent, export-oriented firms also are more likely to train. The technology literature suggests that much of the productivity gain from introducing a new or improved product or technology is realized through intensive learning by doing.[20] To use new technology, firms have to adjust management, reorganize production lines, and upgrade worker skills. Export orientation also can have a salutary effect on training. Employers that export have greater incentives to train their workers to produce high-quality products meeting the exacting standards of foreign buyers and to increase labor productivity to meet competitive pressures.[21]

The analysis shows also that training by external sources tends to be more common among long-established firms in which the government has a controlling interest and in export-oriented firms with a high share of highly educated workers. Their reliance on external training appears to be a carryover from the pre-transition period, when many state-owned enterprises had arrangements to hire graduates trained in specific areas by related vocational and technical training institutions. In contrast, in-house training is shaped less by the share of highly educated workers and more by the firm's export orientation, location in moderate investment risk regions, and R&D spending. Employers appear to rely more on in-house training when industry or work-relevant skills are not available locally or when innovative activities require intensive on-the-job learning and training specific to the new technologies being developed or used.

Are firms that reported understaffing more likely to train to meet skill shortfalls? Surprisingly, no. Reported understaffing was not correlated with in-service training, nor were employer assessments of occupation-specific understaffing. In fact, overstaffed firms were more likely than those with optimal staffing or lack of staff to provide in-service training. One explanation, consistent with table 4-1, is that shortages of specific skills can coexist with overall optimal staffing or overstaffing, so even overstaffed firms train. Another explanation is that there are various sources of demand for training—training is required not just to make up numerical labor shortfalls, but also to meet the need for specific skills related to exporting and adopting new technologies.

So why do Russian firms not train in house to meet skill shortfalls? Although information on why employers might not train or might train very little was not elicited in the Russia LME Survey, it is available in the World Business Environment Survey (WBES). The WBES asked firms to rank statements about what factors influenced their decisions on how much to invest in training workers.[22] Firms that did not train gave the following key reasons for not training:

—use of "mature" technologies that did not require training or skills upgrading

—inability to afford training, which might suggest a weakness in financial markets

—high labor turnover of trained staff, an externality that prevents firms from recouping the cost of training.

—adequate informal on-the-job training or the ready availability of skilled workers in the labor market.

Productivity and Wage Outcomes of Training

In-service training makes sense only if an employer's investment in training employees and upgrading their skills yields positive returns in higher productivity and profits. If formal training is associated with higher firm-level productivity, as suggested by the preponderance of evidence from both industrial and developing countries, which source of training (in-house company programs or training by external providers) has the largest impact on productivity?[23] If training increases productivity, employers also need to determine whether to share productivity gains from training with workers through higher wages and if so, how much. That decision depends on how easily skills gained from training can be transferred to other potential employers.[24]

A production function approach was used to estimate the productivity impact of training (see appendix 4).[25] It is worthwhile to note some parameters estimated by the models before turning to the training results. First, consistent with results reported by other studies of the Russian economy, the estimated production function parameters of capital and labor coefficients are positive and statistically significant. Second, consistent with the belief that education raises productivity, the production function results indicate that increased educational attainment of one year in a firm's workforce is associated with higher firm-level productivity of about 4 to 5 percent. Third, the productivity of regions with moderate or high investment risk is 27 to 33 percent lower, respectively, than productivity in regions with low investment risk. It appears that firms in moderate- to high-risk regions have greater incentives to train in house to compensate for skill shortfalls in the local markets and for their lower overall productivity.

The production function results support the hypothesis that training is associated with higher productivity. The measure for any formal in-service training is positive and statistically significant at the 1 percent level, suggesting that training is associated with a 22 percent increase in firm productivity. When training is disaggregated by source, only external training is significant. But when firms are distinguished by whether they rely only on in-house training, only on external training, or on both in-house and external training, the results suggest that using both sources of training is most productive, leading to a 28 percent increase, while using only external training sources is associated with a 17 percent increase in productivity.

Similar positive effects of training are found on average monthly wages in firms (see appendix 4). In general, Russian employers pay higher wages when enterprises are large (having more than 250 employees) and export oriented, when they engage in R&D activities, and when they employ a more highly educated workforce. Consistent with the earlier training-productivity finding, enterprises that train also pay monthly wages that are 16 percent higher than nontraining firms, a difference that is statistically significant at the 1 percent level.

The wage effects of training differ by training source, depending on whether firm-level or occupation-level wages are studied. The firm-level results suggest that external training is associated with the largest wage gains (18 percent), while the wage effects of in-house training programs are not statistically significant. Occupation-level wages are most strongly affected by in-house training (16 percent), a result that is statistically significant, but they are not affected by training from external sources. When wages are averaged across occupations, firm-level mean wages may conceal considerable within-firm variation in wages by skill or occupation. That dispersion of skill-wage differentials within and across firms is better explained by in-house training

Table 4-2. Innovation and Training Variables

	Sample size		Percent of firms that provided training	
Independent variable	Yes	No	Yes	No
Firm spent more than 1 million rubles on R&D	211	779	0.79	0.67
Firm introduced new process or technology	293	697	0.80	0.65
Firm purchased patents, licenses, or know-how	161	829	0.74	0.69
Composite innovation indicator	463	527	0.77	0.63

Source: LME Survey (2005); authors' calculations.

than by external training, possibly reflecting skill-wage premiums associated with innovating firms that rely on in-house training.

Training and Knowledge Absorption Capacity

Training and knowledge absorption are complementary, in the sense that a firm's capacity to innovate or to absorb new knowledge—and benefit from absorption—depends on the skills and training of its workforce. The previous analyses already have shown in-service training and R&D spending (a crude measure of knowledge absorption) to be highly correlated. Training is also highly correlated with other indicators of innovativeness—such as third-party R&D or licensing of patents and know-how, introduction of new production technologies, and export of high-tech products. The more pertinent issue is not just whether training and absorption are correlated but whether absorption is possible without a highly skilled and trained workforce.

A composite indicator variable was used as the measure of absorption.[26] Table 4-2 shows the distribution of firms for each of the variables that make up the composite absorption indicator: 463 firms are defined as being "absorptive" according to their R&D spending, and those so defined are more likely to train (77 percent) than those that are not (63 percent). Each of the absorption variables that goes into the composite indicator is similarly correlated with training. Bivariate probit analysis confirms that training and absorption decisions are made jointly (appendix table A4-11).

Moreover, the regression analysis shows that when a firm both trains its workers and innovates, the impact on productivity is greater than it is for no training or innovating, only training, or only innovating (and it is the only significant effect in the endogenous model). The wage regression using predicted values suggests that all three states—just training, just innovating, and both activities together—are associated with wage gains. Curiously, innovating but not training has the largest coefficient. The alternative "exogenous" wage model also yields different results: "just training" and "investing in both" show wage gains but "just innovating" does not.

Policy Implications

Together, the analyses of the Russia LME Survey data and comparisons of their findings with those from other developed and developing countries suggest that employer perceptions of shortages of skilled and qualified workers are accurate. They tell a broadly consistent story about the nature of skill shortages:

—Demand for educated and skilled workers is high and rising.

—The educational and training system is underfunded beneath the tertiary level and faces numerous challenges, including deteriorating quality and lack of response to industry's need for skilled workers.

—The industrial sector faces high labor turnover (which inhibits training) and constraints on its ability to adjust its workforce and workers' mix of skills.

—Some noncompetitive enterprises are unable to pay wages that are competitive enough to attract and retain workers who have the skills that they need.

The analyses suggest that most enterprises have not responded to skill shortages by training their employees in house or by training more of them, despite the productivity and wage gains that might come from such investments.

These results have implications for training policy in Russia. It is clear that Russian industrial enterprises underinvest in training their employees. While the incidence of training is high, the proportion of employees provided in-house training in different skill categories is one of the lowest among the countries with data available, both high-income and developing countries. If in-service training is critical to the effective use of new technologies and to productivity growth, as the literature and the estimates reported in this chapter suggest, then Russia's underinvestment in workforce skills places it at a relative disadvantage to its OECD, BRIC, and East Asia competitors. Improving the investment climate in Russia should have a salutary effect on business operations and growth and should create incentives for the private sector to invest in both physical and human capital. Policies to foster greater technological change also should induce more in-service training, given the evidence of a strong training-knowledge absorption nexus.

Market failures diminish employer incentives to train, and whether a policy response is appropriate depends on the nature of the market failure. While not Russia-specific, available WBES data suggest that three market failures—the high cost of training, training externalities from the turnover of skilled workers, and information problems—are key constraints for training.

When costs are high, financial sector reforms to improve access to funding for all kinds of investments, including training, are likely to be most important for smaller enterprises. When employer incentives to train are low because of turnover or "poaching" of skilled workers by other employers, mandates or collective action to get all firms to train can help internalize some of the externalities. The Human Resource Development Fund of Malaysia has, since its introduction in the mid-1990s, increased training among firms.[27] When poor information is the constraint, the appropriate policy response is to disseminate widely the evidence on the productivity benefits of training, best practices in training, and information about the services offered by different public and private sector training providers and the cost of services.

The Russian government should consider putting in place employer-targeted training policies to remedy the underinvestment in in-service training. It can draw on the experiences of many other countries, both industrialized and developing, that have used payroll-levy training funds, tax incentives for employer-sponsored training, and matching grants. Designing a training policy appropriate for Russia is beyond the scope of this chapter, but the global experience with training levies[28] suggests several lessons:

—Employers should be closely involved in the governance of levy funds, as in Argentina, Brazil, and Chile, which have vested supervision of levies in industrial bodies.

—Policies should be designed to increase competition in training provision from all providers, both public and private, including employers.

—Levy funds should be earmarked strictly for training and not diverted to other government uses, as happened with training levies in several Latin American and African countries.

Although international evidence shows that levy schemes can increase training by enterprises, such schemes also have problems. Levies have been inequitable in the sense that they tend to benefit large employers more than small or medium employers. Employer reactions to the schemes also have been mixed, with many firms, especially smaller businesses, feeling that a levy is simply another tax that offers them very little benefit. That may also be the response of many Russian firms that already face relatively high payroll taxes, unless they are reassured that funds earmarked for training will not be diverted elsewhere and that training funds will be used effectively and transparently.

Training levies do not work especially well for small and medium enterprises (SMEs), the group of enterprises in Russia that exhibited the lowest incidence and intensity of in-service training. The experiences of China, Malaysia, Brazil, and Chile suggest that SMEs are not likely to adopt training policies and that targeted training programs are required to reach such firms. Encouraging training in small and medium enterprises may require more active approaches to address systemic weaknesses both in training and technological capabilities and in access to finance. Mexico's experience with training programs for SMEs offers some lessons.

An alternative is to use matching grants, which can help to develop a culture of training, although by themselves grants will not expand the training market. The most successful schemes are demand driven, implemented by the private sector and intended to sustain training markets. Chile and Mauritius report good results from using private agents to administer their schemes. Higher investments in training have been matched by fewer enterprise failures. A side benefit has been a new network of industry management training consultants available to enterprises that want to invest in enterprise-based training.

Singapore has a program to build up its stock of industry trainers, and Japan's Industrial and Vocational Training Association has trained more than 30,000 industry trainers in the past thirty years. It is important to generate training capacity in enterprises and increase the propensity of workers to undertake training. Grants should not be restricted to state-run training institutions. Funds should strengthen and diversify the supply of training and stimulate demand. Strong training cultures have been established in much of Europe, in Japan, Korea, and Singapore, and (judging by the levels of in-company training) in Brazil and Chile.

Whatever training policy is eventually adopted in Russia, it is imperative that enterprises and employer associations have meaningful input into the design of the training system so that it is responsive to their needs and to those of other key stakeholders. Where warranted, industry could take joint responsibility with government for the management and delivery of training, as in Brazil.

At the institutional level, involving Russian employers in the management of individual vocational and technical institutes should help ensure a steady flow of information about the skills needed by local industry—as well as opportunities for instructors to upgrade their knowledge and for students to be placed with employers. The Indian government is taking a similar approach in its efforts to reform the country's moribund public sector industrial training institutes. It introduced Institutional Management Committees (IMCs) in 1998 to involve employers in overseeing the operations of the industrial training institutes. There are now 350 IMCs in eighteen states, with more in the pipeline. IMCs are supported by the Confederation of Indian Industries and the Federation of Indian Chambers of Commerce and Industry, with each IMC chaired by a local industry representative. As currently structured, however, IMCs have limited decisionmaking powers because most states in India do not allow industrial training institutes to exercise significant financial authority, nor do states give IMCs incentives to revamp the training that they offer. Moreover, IMCs may not retain student fees and other nontraditional sources of revenues from, for example, delivering tailored training courses to employers.

Employers also could form public-private partnerships to deliver demand-driven, low-cost training that is largely self-financing. Malaysia's Penang Skills Development Centre suggests how the private sector in different Russian regions can partner with state governments in the reform and management of tertiary-level professional and technical institutes.

Notes

1. According to Sabirianova Peter (2001), more than 40 percent of all employed workers in Russia changed occupation during 1991–98, two-thirds of them during 1991–95. The author termed this mass occupational change the "Great Human Capital Reallocation."

2. This result was due in part to the very high proportion of the population that attended professional and technical colleges (or SSUZ, in Russian). Considering only attendance at university-level institutions (or VUZ, in Russian), Russia, at a rate of 21 percent, still ranked in the top ten countries, sharing ninth and tenth place with Japan.

3. A shift-share approach is used to decompose changes over time in educational attainment attributable to different components: one that measures the results of shifts in the industry and occupational composition of employment, holding education constant; another that measures the contribution of rising education, holding industry and occupation mix constant; and a third interaction term. The

1992–97 decomposition uses six education groups, fifty occupation groups, and fifteen industry groups, while the 1997–2002 decomposition relies on seven education, thirty-two occupation, and nineteen industry groups.

4. See appendix 4; Schultz (1975); Bartel and Lichtenberg (1987); and Tan (2005).

5. In addition to ranking each constraint on a scale of 1 to 5, with 5 being a severe constraint, enterprises in the LME and SE surveys also were asked to identify the most severe constraint from the previous list. This alternative ranking yielded broadly similar findings, with lack of a qualified workforce being ranked third by medium and large enterprises and second by small enterprises.

6. IMEMO, various years.

7. Rosstat (2006).

8. The survey in Gimpelson, conducted jointly by the Higher School of Economics (HSE) and the Russian Public Opinion Research Center (ARPORC), surveyed 304 industrial enterprises located in thirty regions of Russia in 2003. The respondents were personnel managers.

9. World Bank (2006a).

10. Until 2002, employment in Russia was regulated by the Code of Laws on Labor (KZOT); reforms to the code in 2001 eliminated many contradictory and obsolete requirements but left the employment protection section of the code almost unchanged. The major positive change was to abolish trade unions' veto power over mass layoffs. The new code required employers to hire employees on standard open-ended contracts with a full-time work week and restricted the use of fixed-term employment contracts to specific cases (prompting employers to use more temporary contracts on the pretense that they met the code's conditions). In spring 2004, Russia's supreme court ruled against the more liberal interpretation of that section of the legislation and directed that fixed-term contracts signed illegitimately had to be treated as open ended.

11. In a recent World Bank study, Rutkowski and Scarpetta (2005), the authors argue that despite strict employment protection regulations, flexible enforcement gives CIS countries considerable labor market flexibility.

12. Regulations pertaining to layoffs are enforced better than regulations on overtime work.

13. There are simple and quasi-legal ways to deal with EPL constraints and turn labor-management relations into something close to employment at will. First, employers can pressure workers to quit voluntarily. Second, there is an informal practice of pressuring workers to submit an application to quit voluntarily at the same time that the worker applies for a job. That allows managers to date the application and initiate a "voluntary" quit at any moment and at no cost. These and other informal practices can result in high labor turnover driven by quits with almost no layoffs.

14. The seventeen countries clustered by region include Germany, Greece, Ireland, Portugal, South Korea and Spain (OECD); China, Malaysia, and Thailand (East Asia);

India and Sri Lanka (South Asia); Brazil and Chile (Latin America); and Bulgaria, Lithuania, Serbia, and Russia (Eastern Europe).

15. We adopted a common weighting scheme based (arbitrarily) on the size distribution of firms in the India Enterprise Survey. In India the size distribution of micro (15 or fewer workers), small (16–100 workers), medium (101–250 workers), and large enterprises (more than 250 workers) was 40, 44, 7, and 8 percent respectively; the corresponding size distribution for the pooled LME and SE surveys in Russia was 12, 16, 29, and 43 percent respectively.

16. In the Malaysian ICA survey, employers ranked the skills and education of the workforce as the number one "severe" or "very severe" investment climate constraint (World Bank 2005c).

17. The sample is restricted to countries included in BEEPS (2006) or in Enterprise Surveys (World Bank 2002–2006) that asked about in-service training and the shares of skilled and unskilled workers that received formal training. Skilled workers are defined to include managers, professionals, and skilled production workers, while unskilled workers include unskilled production workers and other nonproduction or other white-collar employees.

18. In the LME Survey, firms reported shares of workers trained in several ranges, including an open-ended "35 percent or more." In calculating shares trained, the mean for the last interval was generously assumed to be 45 percent, possibly biasing training estimates for Russia upward. Tabulations of the small sample of Russian firms in the BEEPS also revealed low shares of workers trained relative to shares in other countries in the BEEPS sample.

19. See Tan and Batra (1995) for estimates on the education-training relationship in five developing countries in East Asia and Latin America and Tan (2000) and World Bank (1997, 2005c) for related training analyses for Malaysia.

20. Enos (1962); Bell and Pavitt (1992).

21. Tan and Batra (1995); Batra, Kaufman, and Stone (2003).

22. The World Business Environment Survey (WBES) was an Enterprise Survey sent to more than 10,000 firms in eighty countries between late 1998 and mid-2000. The analyses reported in Batra, Kaufman, and Stone (2003) are based on a special survey module that focused on competition, trade, firms' technological capabilities, and worker training in twenty-eight of the WBES countries.

23. Cross-sectional studies have found a strong positive association between in-service training and firms' productivity and wage levels (Tan and Batra 1995; Batra, Kaufman, and Stone 2003).

24. Becker (2002); Tan (1980); and Acemoglu and Pischke (1998).

25. Production functions are economic models used to measure the average relationships between output and inputs, such as capital equipment, labor, intermediate inputs, raw materials, and energy. Production functions are estimated in logarithmic form so that the estimated parameters can be interpreted as elasticities.

Some studies use a gross output measure; others (including this one) rely on a value-added specification.

26. The composite indicator equals 1 if a firm has substantial R&D spending (more than a million rubles); has purchased technology licenses, patents, and know-how; or has introduced new production processes. If not, the indicator is 0.

27. Taiwan and Singapore are two other East Asia economies that have used direct reimbursement of approved training expenses, funded through payroll levies, to encourage firms to train their employees. A training grant scheme in Taiwan led to dramatic increases in training, which continued after the program ended in the 1970s. Singapore used a levy on the wages of unskilled workers to finance training grants to employers to upgrade worker skills. The Skills Development Fund's aggressive efforts to raise awareness of and increase direct training among firms led to a steady rise in training, especially among smaller firms. See Tan (2000) for an extended discussion of the Malaysian experience and an impact evaluation of the Human Resource Development Fund (HRDF) policy.

28. Middleton, Ziderman, and van Adams (1993); Gill, Fluitman, and Dar (2000).

five

Improving the Investment Climate

RAJ M. DESAI

In addition to the skill base of the workforce and the capacity of firms to absorb technology, the investment climate—government policies and actions that shape the opportunities and incentives for firms to invest productively, create jobs, and expand—also affects the productivity and growth of Russia's economy. Following the financial crisis of 1998–99, a combination of favorable macroeconomic conditions and major regulatory reforms to the business environment in 2000–02 propelled Russia's economic expansion.

However, the Russian investment climate, although much improved in recent years, is still characterized by significant administrative costs, policy-induced risks, and formal and informal barriers to competition—all limiting the innovative and productive potential of the private sector. It also is characterized by unevenness in the treatment of different kinds of firms. Some firms benefit from relatively minor investment climate obstacles, while for others the obstacles are far more severe. Preferential treatment of some influential firms—long recognized as a problem in the Commonwealth of Independent States and Eastern Europe—continues to affect the Russian economy and can deter investment, innovation, and growth.[1] Since 2003 the investment climate has also suffered from growing uncertainty about regulatory and policy changes and about the character of government-business relations.

Investment climate policies provide numerous opportunities to redistribute resources toward favored firms. Therefore, policies that would benefit the economy as a whole may not be implemented because they cannot be used to reward loyalty or to strengthen personal ties between public officials and particular privileged firms. Governments may suppress competition—for example, by conferring monopolies, devising market restrictions, or tolerating cartels. Tax systems may become riddled with special exemptions, or they may be enforced selectively. And because the investment climate encompasses a wide range of policies—from tax rules to labor regulations to finance—reforms to the investment climate in any country often require profound changes in the process of government, in the way the public sector does business, in the relationships between public officials and firms, and in the mechanisms of accountability, transparency, and restraint:

—Competitive legislatures would permit disenfranchised groups to challenge the authority of incumbents, making it more difficult for executive branch policymakers to make implicit transfers to firms without legislative approval.

—The tendency of governments to grant preferential treatment to some firms could be checked by increasing the transparency of decisionmaking by public officials and by creating vehicles through which broad constituencies can express their collective demands.

—A free and independent media could make the public aware of the costs of corrupt practices.

—Embodying formal rules and processes in national constitutions that establish effective veto points in the decisionmaking process—such as checks and balances on different branches or levels of government—could constrain arbitrariness and business clientelism.

But countries do not have to implement proposed reforms all at once. They can reap benefits by addressing important investment climate constraints in a way that gives firms the confidence to invest.[2] Recent reviews of case studies around the world suggest that investment climate reforms can be initiated by seizing opportunities to place reform on the policy agenda—in much the same way that administrative reforms were implemented in the early part of this decade by a new Russian government.[3] To that end, the proposals offered in this chapter are modest. They are intended to ensure that the proposals in previous chapters will be supported by complementary reforms of the investment climate—and that the incentives of key actors to support reforms will be strengthened. In particular, the chapter argues for a clear government commitment to establishing stable conditions for private business, including a competition policy that allows tangible and intangible assets to be acquired and exchanged by small and medium firms. Along with that commitment, the government must give a greater voice to those who demand more market openness, it must encourage greater investment in the nonresource sector, and it must promote further economic diversification.[4]

Around the world, the most innovative economies are characterized by high levels of competition. Russia is no exception. In large part, competitive pressures develop not from centralized, top-down efforts to create them from scratch or solely from the efforts of public agencies to police the common market against monopolistic behavior. They develop from a policy environment that encourages businesses to start up and that enables fledgling companies to find customers for products without significant policy-induced costs, risks, or barriers to competition—formal or informal. As shown in chapter 3, firms facing the weakest pressures from domestic and foreign competitors innovate the least. This chapter explores in further detail the obstacles that Russian firms face in doing business, the consequences, and how the obstacles might be ameliorated.

Cross-National Comparisons

In comparing the severity of investment climate constraints across countries, it is important to evaluate the choices facing an investor planning to finance an enterprise in different countries.[5] Figure 5-1 compares the severity of constraints in Russia with those in China and India, controlling for sector, size, year, whether firms were exporters, and whether they were foreign-owned.[6] To control for the overall propensity to complain, responses of firms are included for a question on macroeconomic instability—a catch-all to capture systemic attitudes toward the investment climate.

Figure 5-1 identifies three major problems for Russian firms relative to problems for firms in China and India: policy uncertainty (relative to India), tax administration (relative to India and China), and access to finance (also relative to India and China). Russian firms are generally more likely than firms in either of the other countries to consider those constraints binding on their activities. The opposite is true for all other constraints, indicating that Russian enterprises are less likely to complain about them than are other firms.

But in the past two years, reforms have slowed on some fronts, regressed on others. Surveys confirm the worsening of corruption, informal practices,

Figure 5-1. The "Russia" Effect on Investment Climate Constraints[a]

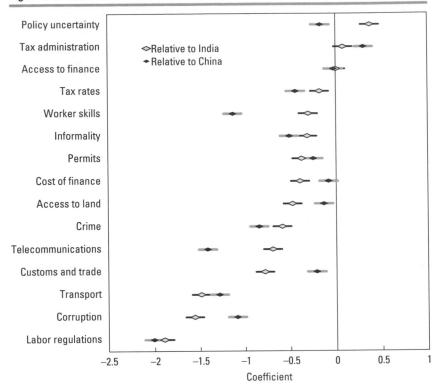

Source: LME Survey (2005).

a. Figure shows coefficients of the "Russia" country dummy variable generated from two separate ordered-logit estimations of each of the individual constraints, with +/– 95 percent confidence intervals. In addition to the Russia dummy variable, additional control variables include size, sector, exporter, and foreign-owned dummy variables, as well as a binary variable coded 1 if the firm considered macroeconomic problems to be an obstacle (moderate, major, or severe) or 0 otherwise.

and the quality of the legal system, among other areas. As figure 5-2 shows, while fewer firms considered infrastructure, finance (cost and access), land, and taxes to be major obstacles in 2005 than they did in 2002, several areas show deterioration. The percentage of firms that viewed labor (skills and regulations) as a major obstacle increased by 7 percentage points. Higher increases were registered for crime and the quality of the legal system (10 percent), policy unpredictability (10 percent), and corruption (24 percent).

Many costs to firms are a normal function of commercial activity, but government policies and behavior can impose additional costs. For example,

Figure 5-2. Change in Russian Firms' Perceptions of Investment Climate
Constraints, 2002–05

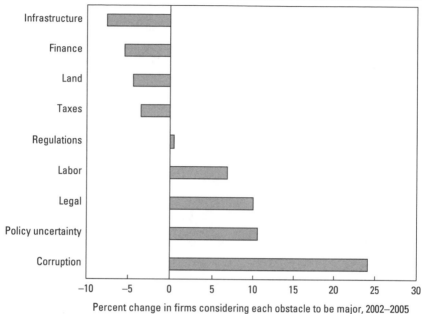

Percent change in firms considering each obstacle to be major, 2002–2005

Source: BEEPS (2006).

it takes less time and money (as a share of per capita income) and requires
a smaller number of procedures to start a business in Russia than in Brazil,
China, or India (table 5-1). Even so, as figure 5-3 indicates, the losses that
Russian firms suffer because of delivery delays, infrastructure problems
(mainly utility service disruptions), crime, and bribes are approximately

Table 5-1. Business Start-up Costs, Selected Countries

Country	Year	Procedures to start a business (number)	Time to start a business (days)	Cost of starting a business (percent of per capita income)
Brazil	2005	17	152	10.1
China	2005	13	48	13.6
India	2005	11	71	61.7
	2003	12	29	8.4
Russian Federation	2004	9	36	6.7
	2005	8	33	5

Source: World Bank (2006a).

Figure 5-3. Administrative and Transaction Costs as a Percent of Sales in Selected Countries

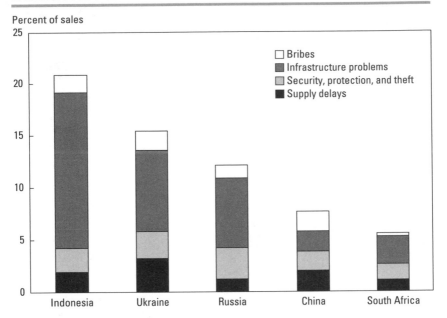

Percent of sales

Legend:
- Bribes
- Infrastructure problems
- Security, protection, and theft
- Supply delays

Countries: Indonesia, Ukraine, Russia, China, South Africa

Source: World Bank (2002–2006).

12 percent of total sales—about 50 percent larger than those suffered by Chinese firms and twice as large as those for South African firms.

Corruption imposes its own costs. While there has been some improvement over the past few years, the average bribe paid by firms in acquiring a business license and in their dealings with inspectors, tax collectors, and the courts increased between 2002 and 2005, in sharp contrast to the declining trend for those kinds of bribes in the former Soviet states, Central Europe, and the Baltic region. According to the BEEPS, the percentage of firms stating that bribery is frequent in fire, building, environmental, and health and safety inspections was higher in 2005 than in 2002, while the CIS region overall exhibited a decrease.

Differences among Small, Medium, and Large Enterprises

Many of the foregoing findings on the investment climate were confirmed in separate surveys of large, medium, and small enterprises undertaken for this book. Firms of all sizes put taxes, uncertainty (both macroeconomic

Figure 5-4. Firms' Most Severe Investment Climate Constraints, by Firm Size

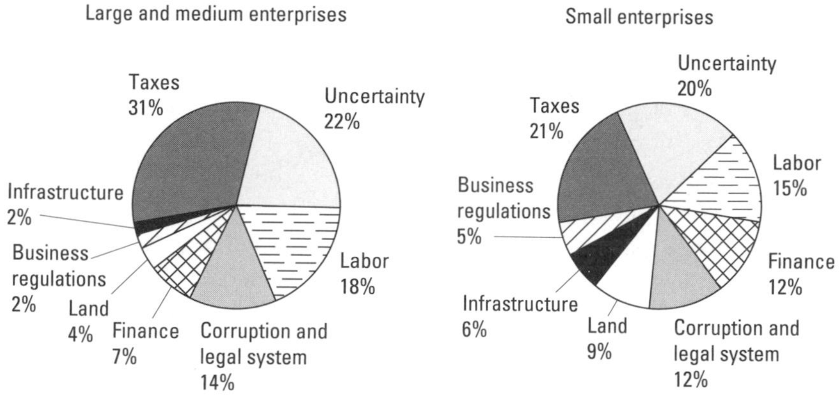

Large and medium enterprises

Small enterprises

Taxes
31%

Uncertainty
22%

Infrastructure
2%

Business
regulations
2%

Labor
18%

Land
4%

Finance
7%

Corruption and
legal system
14%

Uncertainty
20%

Taxes
21%

Labor
15%

Business
regulations
5%

Finance
12%

Infrastructure
6%

Land
9%

Corruption and
legal system
12%

Source: LME Survey (2005); SE Survey (2005).

and policy induced), and labor problems at the top of their list of complaints. Figure 5-4 shows the percentages of large, medium, and small firms that ranked different categories of investment climate constraints as "the most important impediment" to their activities and development. Taxes, uncertainty, and labor top the list of major obstacles for Russian enterprises of all types. Smaller firms, however, tend to rank financial issues and land issues as their most severe obstacles.

Regulatory and Policy Uncertainty

Investment is deterred by uncertainty. Firms' confidence in the future—which is based, to a great extent, on expectations of the stability and predictability of government policies—is critical. A major concern of firms of all sizes is the unpredictability of economic and regulatory policy changes and inconsistency in public officials' interpretation and enforcement of regulations. Note that bribes and policy uncertainty are separate concerns. They can be related, in that excessive bribe taking can create costs, exemptions, and inconsistencies in regulatory enforcement for the firms from which bribes are extracted. But bribes are more properly thought of as a "cost" of doing business, while regulatory uncertainty is more appropriately considered a "policy-induced risk." Unlike market-based risks, risks created by policy and regulatory instability are fully under government control and—except for the risk of expropriation—are generally more difficult to insure against. So the latter risks can unnecessarily thwart investment, knowledge absorption, and competitiveness because entrepreneurs cannot predict their potential losses due to shifts in government policy.

In enterprise surveys the predictability of state regulations improved little between 2002 and 2005, with about 60 percent of firms indicating that regulatory unpredictability constituted a moderate or major concern to business. Russian firms still face a very uncertain policy environment characterized by unpredictable changes in regulations and by inconsistent application of existing rules. While informal practices and crime are less of a concern than uncertainty, they also have worsened for Russian firms. According to the World Economic Forum, Russia ranks 75 among 117 countries in terms of regulatory unpredictability (China ranks 48, India 50, and Brazil 65).

The BEEPS confirm that policy uncertainty can generate uncertainty in other areas. Russian firms that perceive a high level of policy-induced uncertainty also have less confidence that their contractual and property rights will be enforced. The BEEPS also suggest that the views of surveyed firms on the predictability of state regulations improved little between 2002 and 2005, indicating the need for continuing the effort to reform the regulatory regime. In both of the surveys (BEEPS and LME), around 60 percent of firms in the manufacturing sector—and firms overall—suggested that regulatory unpredictability constituted a moderate or major business concern.

Administrative, Regulatory, and Tax Issues

After 2001 Russian federal authorities undertook reforms to streamline the regulatory regime and reduce administrative constraints. New laws were introduced for inspections (in 2001), licensing (2002), registration (2002), simplified taxation (2003), and regulations (2003). Reforms of tax and customs administration took place in the same period, with the enactment of a new land code (in 2001) and customs code (2003). These reforms reduced the administrative barriers facing the private sector and improved the business community's perception of the regulatory regime, although some evidence of recent reversals was detected in joint monitoring of the regulatory regime by the Center for Economic and Financial Research (CEFIR) in 2001–05 in collaboration with the World Bank and the U.S. Agency for International Development.[7]

Tax Administration

The 2003 Law on the Simplified System of Taxation for Small Enterprises offered a reduced number of taxes and levies to small firms that adopt the simplified system. According to the CEFIR monitoring study, firms that adopted the simplified tax system paid almost six different taxes and levies in 2005, compared with more than nine types of taxes in 2002. Those firms also gave much more optimistic subjective assessments of taxation.[8]

However, the recent reforms appear to have had a small effect on business perceptions of tax rates and tax administration. More than 50 percent of firms still considered them a problem, and tax administration was more problematic in Russia than in the CIS as a whole or in Europe and Central Asia.[9]

Medium and large enterprises in particular devoted considerable employee time to interactions with officials of the Tax Inspectorate (forty-five person-days a year for a median firm), much more than with those of other control bodies such as the police or the sanitary-epidemiological agency. A median small enterprise also spent two times more person-days dealing with the Tax Inspectorate than with the other control bodies (five person-days and two person-days, respectively), although the numbers were much lower than those for medium and large enterprises.

Of the eleven different ministries and federal services, the Federal Tax Service was assessed by medium and large enterprises as having much more of a negative impact on their business activities than any other ministry or federal service. Forty-six percent of respondents stated that the activity of the Federal Tax Service affected their business negatively, while no other ministry or service was given such an assessment by more than a quarter of surveyed firms.

Uncertainty in Asset Ownership

The landmark mass privatization of 1992–94 passed to private owners all physical assets (buildings, equipment, inventories, transport, and utilities) in 17,000 medium to large enterprises and in hundreds of thousands of small businesses.[10] It did not, however, fully transfer control rights over two key assets: land and intellectual property. Both remain largely in the public domain.

Although buying or leasing land and premises is less problematic for larger firms, smaller firms continue to face obstacles. Surveys suggest that while some firms manage to go through the procedure relatively quickly (two to three months), for others it can easily take well over a year. As reported in the fourth round of CEFIR monitoring, in 2003 about 90 percent of the firms trying to purchase land failed to finish the procedure in half a year. In the fifth round, the length of the procedures came down only slightly.

CEFIR's monitoring surveys indicate that one of the chief sources of the problem is the lack of competition in real estate markets. Businesses continually complain that there has been very little privatization of land and that the limited privatization that has occurred has been characterized by severe inconsistencies, nontransparency, and favoritism. Other surveys reinforce these findings with complaints about the "need to rely on connections," excessive discretion, and a higher degree of corruption associated with real estate transactions than with most other administrative procedures; these surveys also find that potential foreign investors, in particular, were concerned about access to land.[11]

Municipal Landlords

The new Land Code of the Russian Federation explicitly calls for the land beneath privatized buildings to be privatized as well, thus allowing land and buildings to be consolidated in a single property registry. But most usable land remains in the hands of municipal governments. Although new federal legislation constrains municipalities' legal discretion in setting rents and lease terms, officials still abuse their dominant position through selective use of administrative barriers—more often to favor some firms over others or to exercise undue influence over local business development.

Many regions and municipalities have instituted mechanisms to privatize real estate, but few are transparent or fair, and the authorities have little incentive to improve their procedures and thereby advance land reform. There is some evidence that regions that adopted legislation on land privatization ahead of the federal law (the Land Code) were also the ones that continued to take the lead in land reform after the law's enactment. While the Land Code did clarify the overall principles governing land transactions, it did not necessarily persuade unwilling regions to initiate land reform and land privatization.[12]

As a result, few firms have managed to gain access to land. Among small and medium enterprises (SMEs) surveyed by CEFIR, only 6 percent owned land. From surveys conducted in fifteen regions of firms that carried out land or real estate transactions in 2004 (mostly medium firms), the proportion of respondents reporting ownership rights to land was about 18 percent.[13]

Administrative barriers in land acquisition procedures deter many firms from applying for land ownership. For example, even the relatively straightforward procedure of applying for ownership rights to land under a building already owned by a business takes an average of eleven procedures involving eight agencies, seventeen documents, about 220 days, and 70,000 rubles. Land transactions also are magnets for corruption. On average, according to "business intermediaries" who carry out such transactions on a regular basis, more than half of privatization transactions involved "unofficial payments." Firms that carried out such procedures on their own behalf reported a somewhat lower level of bribes (about 36 percent), but about 25 percent of them were required to pay "sponsorships" to various foundations suggested by government officials and more than 20 percent had to pay for other burdens, such as paving a nearby road.

Delineating and Protecting Property Rights

Key policymakers—including representatives of the Duma, the Ministry of Economic Development and Trade, the Federal Antimonopoly Service, regional authorities, the Russian Urban Institute, and the private sector—have agreed on the need to create a competitive environment and a functioning land market, the lack of which has already begun to constrain economic growth. Three major issues hinder market relations in the land and real estate sectors:

—*Legal deficiencies.* There continue to be major deficiencies in the conceptual approaches of the law and inconsistency among various statutes governing land and construction (use of land and forest, town planning) and specific procedural rules on registration of the associated rights.

—*Lack of interest on the part of municipalities and officials in developing competition in the land and real estate market.* The real estate market has been monopolized, inflating prices, blunting equal access to the facilities for sale, and nurturing corruption.

—*Lack of an appropriate informational and legal basis for land market development.* Most land plots have not been registered in the cadastre, and rights to real estate objects (in reality unified objects, such as adjacent land, buildings, and infrastructure) are fragmented and governed by separate and sometimes conflicting laws and regulations.

Intellectual Property Rights

Firms also face uncertainties about the ownership of intangible assets, particularly intellectual property rights (IPRs), which complicate the collaboration of research institutes with private firms, inhibit technology transfer, impair the development of spin-off companies into independent and growing businesses, create conflicts of interest for the institutes, and may even give rise to conflicts between the goals of individual researchers and their organizations. Russia's IPR regime has two main weaknesses:

—First, the assignment of IPRs remains unclear. In the 1990s Russia introduced patent and other IPR laws in which inventions registered through "author's certificates" (the prevalent form of registration in the Soviet economy) and new technology developed with state funding remained de jure state property. However, there is ongoing debate about who owns the IPRs: the inventor, the inventor's employer (research institute or enterprise, either state-owned or private), or the Russian government.

—Second, registered IPRs are weakly protected due to the inability or unwillingness of public authorities to police producers and importers of pirated goods and to prosecute violators—a particular concern for foreign investors and exporters facing copyright piracy or patent infringement by domestic producers or importers.

Different countries have different rules for allocating IPRs developed in private settings with public funds. In the United States the Bayh-Dole Act (1980) gave universities the right to patent all discoveries resulting from federally funded research in order to make their technology-transfer activities more effective and to facilitate commercialization through patent assignments (sales), licenses, and spin-offs. The act reduced IPR disputes (previous U.S. law did not provide a clear answer to the question of who held the right to patent federally funded research).

The rise in university patenting in the United States during the ensuing period and the reports of university discoveries generating significant licensing revenues are persuading European policymakers to consider similar legislation. Although funding of private research by the European Commission does not come with conditions on the ownership of resulting IPRs, national rules governing the ownership of results from publicly supported research differ. Some countries give exclusive ownership to academic inventors (Finland, Iceland, Italy, and Sweden). Others give universities the right to own patents on their research (Austria, Belgium, Denmark, France, Germany, Ireland, Netherlands, Norway, Poland, Spain, and the United Kingdom).

Allocating intellectual property rights is one of the most discussed problems in Russian science and technology policy, especially for intellectual property created with budget expenditures, because of contradictions between the laws on patents and on public procurement. A draft new law that would resolve the contradictions by transferring intellectual property ownership to research institutions has been approved by the Council of Ministers but not officially enacted. The use and disposal of tangible assets theoretically owned by the state is poorly regulated in practice, since it is difficult to exercise control over the more than 10,000 state-owned enterprises (the "unitary enterprises") that currently exist.

Scarcity of corporate R&D is the Achilles' heel of the Russian innovation system. Business enterprises contribute less than 20 percent of national R&D expenditures, while the state finances more than 60 percent. Most government-funded research and development is carried out by research institutes, design bureaus, and business enterprises. As a result, 90 percent of all IPRs registered in Russia are created with state support. Russian inventors often file patent applications merely to register a "patent pending" for their inventions. Lacking funds, many Russian firms fail to commercialize their inventions, something that differentiates Russian firms from firms in the developed market economies, who view patenting as simply a first step to commercialization. Since it is costly to keep patents in effect for the seventeen years allowed by law, Russian patent holders tend to stop maintaining their patents after four to five years. As a result, only 35 percent of registered patents in Russia are active, and the rest cannot be enforced if competitors copy the patented invention. Patenting abroad is prohibitively expensive for most Russian technology-intensive firms. Hence it is difficult to put the intellectual property of Russian innovators to sufficient productive use; moreover, the ability of intellectual property to strengthen innovators' position in the markets for technology-intensive goods and services is inadequate, perpetuating Russia's specialization in raw material industries.

Despite the controversies and the incompleteness of Russia's IPR laws, most observers agree that the content and quality of the laws correspond to international standards. The institutions and procedures to enforce the laws, however, remain weak. They need to be strengthened to comply with the WTO's Agreement on Trade-Related Aspects of Intellectual Property Rights (TRIPs), one of the stumbling blocks in Russia's accession to the WTO. The market share of pirated goods is high, rising to 97 percent of computer software, 85 percent of optical disks, 75 percent of audio records, and 45 percent of printed works.

Russian arbitrage (commercial) courts hear up to 200 cases a year related to violations of IPRs, half of which are initiated by foreign plaintiffs. Often cases are resolved before a verdict is reached. In only a few cases are defendants found guilty.

Barriers to Competition

Around the world, the most innovative economies are characterized by high levels of competition. In Russia, too, firms facing the strongest pressures from domestic and foreign competitors innovate the most. Table A5-1 suggests that the investment climate in Russia can be improved significantly by enhancing competition and strengthening consultations between the public and the private sector.

Competition Policy

The Russian antitrust regime, with the Ministry of Antimonopoly Policy and Entrepreneurship Support (MAPES) at its center, was put in place early in Russia's transition and has gradually increased the severity of punishment for violations of antitrust laws. The Law on Competition and the Restriction of Monopolistic Activity in Goods Markets, passed in 1991, consisted mainly of cease-and-desist orders for violators. Subsequent amendments and supplementary legislation expanded the responsibilities of regulators and sanctions on offenders. In 1999, as part of a response to anticompetitive actions by financial institutions, the antimonopoly regime underwent further reform, establishing MAPES as a cabinet-level ministry.

In 2004 the Russian Federation was the first non-OECD economy to participate in the OECD's Regulatory Reform Programme, which reviewed Russia's efforts to foster competition, innovation, and economic growth. The review identified several flaws in the Russian regulatory framework—structural and legal problems, excessive caseloads and limited capacity, and an enforcement mechanism characterized by weak sanctions for some transgressions and limited investigative powers. In March 2004, MAPES was replaced by presidential decree with the Federal Antimonopoly Service; some of the functions of MAPES, including consumer protection, commodity exchange supervision, small and medium business support, and telecommunications tariff regulation, were passed to other ministries.

Despite limitations, authorities in Russia have helped create more competitive conditions, reducing barriers to the movement of goods and services and establishing consumer protection legislation.

Addressing competition law and policy in Russia requires amendments to multiple laws and decrees and to the organization and operations of the new Federal Antimonopoly Service and the local, regional, and federal governments. More important, expectations for centralized, top-down approaches to competition policy often are based on a presumption that the reforms will yield results and change the incentives of the main actors in a somewhat predictable fashion. Experience suggests that this is far from the case in a country as large and regionally diverse as Russia—and in a government as multilayered.

That does not imply that reforms of the kind recommended by the OECD review are not important. There is, however, an imperative to strengthen the demand for competition from the bottom up—to empower and support the natural constituencies for competition and market openness.

Competitive Pressures

Monopolistic firms tend to obtain more favorable treatment than other firms from government authorities. They tend to suffer less from any given investment constraint, to pay less in bribes to secure government contracts, to suffer less from nonpayment by customers, and to spend less on protection payments. Their differential treatment is most likely due to loopholes, exemptions, or special exceptions in existing legislation, as well as the discretionary interpretation and application of regulations by public authorities (table 5-2).

Previous analyses of enterprise performance in Russia revealed that firms that received preferential treatment from federal and regional governmental authorities tended to receive tax breaks, investment credits, direct subsidies, guaranteed loans, access to state property, and the creation of special economic zones on the sites of specific enterprises.[14] The World Bank's Country Economic Memorandum for the Russian Federation noted that firms controlled by regional private owners as well as foreign investors were most likely to receive preferential treatment. It also found that selective, preferential treatment toward the most politically influential firms had adverse effects on the performance of less influential regional firms.[15]

In a similar vein, the business surveys conducted for this book suggest that certain categories of firms face a more favorable investment climate. Firms facing weak competitive pressures from domestic and foreign manufacturers (the least innovative firms) tend to encounter lesser constraints in conducting business, while firms facing greater competitive pressures also face a more severe investment climate. Because firms facing the greatest competitive pressures are also the most innovative, investment climate constraints

Table 5-2. Costs of Business and Competitive Pressure for Russian Large and Medium Enterprises[a]

Constraint	Firms facing the least competitive pressure	Firms facing the most competitive pressure
Percent likelihood of paying bribes to get things done	29.5	49.2
Percent of contract value paid in bribes for government procurement	0.9	2.6
Overemployment (percent of workforce)	5.1	12.2
Percent likelihood of nonpayment by customers	29.2	71.7
Protection payments as a percent of sales	0.2	0.7

Source: LME Survey (2005).

a. Estimates are based on stochastic simulations of regressions in table A5-3 in appendix 5. All estimates control for size, age, former SOE status, and location of firms.

do the most harm to precisely the companies that could serve as engines of diversification of the Russian economy. (Tables A5-2 and A5-3 in appendix 5 show the relationship between the competitive pressures that firms face and the severity of various investment climate constraints.)

Figure 5-5 represents these findings. After controlling for firms' systemic favorable biases toward the investment climate in general as well as size, age, sector, and regional location, the analysis shows that firms facing competitive pressures are more likely to face harsher governance constraints (such as a poorly functioning legal system, policy uncertainty, crime, and unfair competition), less access to and higher costs of finance, higher taxes and a weak tax administration, more problems with labor (skill shortages and regulations), and steeper administrative barriers (customs and licensing barriers).[16]

What accounts for the apparent punishment of the most innovative firms? State capture. Powerful private interests come to control legislative and regulatory systems, guaranteeing themselves a stream of uninterrupted benefits, protections, and rents. State capture does not, however, benefit private firms alone. Local and national public officials also benefit in numerous ways—whether through direct payments from captor firms or through political financing (campaign contributions) by firms. Meanwhile, firms that are not captors do not benefit, and they may be targeted by public officials—inspectors, tax authorities, and politicians—who extract benefits from them.[17] Firms facing the greatest competitive pressures also pay more in bribes to obtain contracts with the government, tend to have bloated payrolls (presumably because they are restricted from laying off workers),

Figure 5-5. Investment Climate Gap between Competitive and Noncompetitive Firms[a]

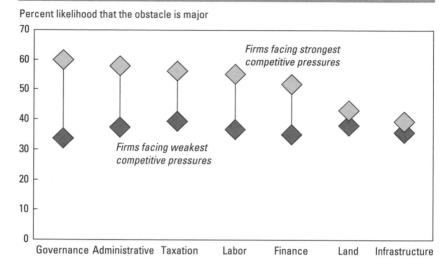

Percent likelihood that the obstacle is major

Firms facing strongest competitive pressures

Firms facing weakest competitive pressures

Governance   Administrative   Taxation   Labor   Finance   Land   Infrastructure

Source: LME Survey (2005).

a. Estimates are generated from stochastic simulations of regressions in table A5-2 in appendix 5, which control for firm size, membership in financial-industrial conglomerates, sector, region, and systemic bias toward the investment climate.

and tend to encounter more nonpayment by customers (table 5-2). How can the most vulnerable firms protect themselves from such adverse effects of state capture?

Business Associations

Business associations can serve as a "leveler" among firms. Although firms that belonged to business associations reported more severe investment climate constraints (in both objective and subjective terms) than those that did not, association members also were more likely to introduce new products and new technologies (appendix table A5-4). Moreover, firms that did not belong to business associations and that faced strong competitive pressures were more likely to have excess labor and to pay more in bribes for government contracts; they also were less likely to believe that regulations were predictable. Among firms belonging to business associations, the gap in perceptions between firms facing strong and weak competitive pressures disappears. The combination of competitive pressure and business association membership has the most favorable effect on investment climate costs and uncertainties (appendix table A5-5). The problems of excess employment, regulatory burdens, regulatory unpredictability, and severity of bribe payments for government contracts are less constraining for competitive firms belonging to business associations than for either members of business associations or for firms facing competitive pressures alone.

There are two possible explanations for this "beneficial" effect. First, Russian firms belonging to business associations report that one of the most valuable services that associations provide is access to information on regulations, pending legislation, the economic policymaking process, standards, accrediting, and markets—information that may better equip business association members to anticipate regulatory and policy shifts, to prepare for changes in laws, and to identify "loopholes" or ways around often complex regulatory regimes. Second, it is possible that firms—especially smaller and medium firms—that band together are better protected from rent-seeking or predatory public officials. Consequently, they may pay less in bribes for commonplace tasks and procedures than firms outside business associations.

Russia's SME associations have achieved considerable success in forging strong working relationships with their government counterparts, and Russian business associations as a whole have been characterized more by positive market-supporting behavior than by the negative rent-seeking behavior typically assumed of them.

Ineffective representation at the national level had been a concern for small business leaders for some time, so they approached the government to gauge its receptivity to working with a unified association of entrepreneurs. The response was very positive. The administration's support prompted the smaller associations to unite, leading to the creation of the Association of Organizations of Small and Medium Enterprises (OPORA) in 2001. OPORA's mission is "to create positive conditions for the development of entrepreneurship in Russia, to represent and defend the interests of entrepreneurs in dialogue with all levels of government, and to participate in the creation of a national 'middle class' on the basis of the best traditions of national entrepreneurship and Russian business culture."[18]

One of OPORA's first major projects, participating in the government's program to reduce administrative barriers, focused on improving conditions for Russian entrepreneurs by reducing the role of government rather than by lobbying the government for concessions. To foster innovation, OPORA focuses on changing the environment for Russian small businesses. As large consumer goods companies enter the market and consumers become more discerning, the small consumer goods trading operations that helped so many entrepreneurs get started have much less potential.

Business associations can, however, quickly become instruments of cronyism. Consultative mechanisms, therefore, should be inclusive, welcoming input from their core membership. Broadening policy dialogues to include representatives of a wider range of interests—including consumers, taxpayers, and owners and employees of smaller businesses—can enfranchise previously excluded groups.

Recommendations

The enterprise surveys conducted for this report—and comparisons of their findings with those from other developed and developing countries—suggest that employer warnings of policy constraints are real and should be heeded. They tell a broadly consistent story about the investment climate hurdles encountered by potentially innovative, dynamic firms. What should be done to improve the competitiveness of Russian firms and unlock their full innovative potential? Four things stand out:

—Privatize municipally held land.

—Improve the allocation of intellectual property rights.

—Strengthen the consultative basis for regulatory decisions.

—Adopt one of several review mechanisms to deal with existing regulations.

Privatize municipally held land. Improving the process for privatizing land requires greater use of auctions and tenders for vacant land and greater transparency with respect to procedures. It also requires lower prices, especially for land beneath already privatized buildings. Many bureaucrats involved in land and real estate privatization and registration appear to create or threaten delays to encourage payments for "speedy processing." One way to deter such behavior would be for the Ministry of Economic Development and Trade to draft new legislation to impose time limits on the processing of applications; a nonresponse from an agency would be taken as approval of an application, and officials would be required to submit official written explanations for any refusals, citing objective reasons. The Ministry of Economic Development and Trade should also require annual statistical reporting by regions and municipalities regarding land and real estate ownership, lease rights, privatization transactions, modes of privatization, and prices. The Federal Antimonopoly Service might use official statistical data and survey data to identify possible abuses of market power by public sector bodies (such as municipal administrations) and to prosecute such cases as anticompetitive practices.

Improve the allocation of intellectual property rights. A current draft of the Civil Code allows research organizations to become owners of intellectual property rights for technologies developed using government funds "provided that the procurement contracts do not specify otherwise." Research and business communities are rightly concerned that this open-ended provision would allow public authorities to continue to exercise ownership for subsequent IPRs and prevent closer cooperation between innovators and firms.

At the end of 2005 an important step was taken toward improving the legal regulation of intellectual property created with public funding. According to Decree 685, "on the procedure for disposing of the rights to the results of activity in the sphere of science and technology," the rights to the results of public-funded activity may be transferred to the inventor or researcher (with some notable limitations). This decree has not yet granted the direct authors of inventions the right to dispose of their intellectual property fully and at their own discretion. And several aspects of the decree need to be further specified, including the conditions for transferring the rights to the inventor or researcher, the obligations of the state in the early stages of technological development, and the procedures for determining the amount of the compensation.

Strengthen the consultative basis for regulatory decisions. Difficulties in informing market participants about new and forthcoming legal and regulatory changes stem in part from Russia's unfinished transition. A degree of regulatory instability is thus inevitable and generally well understood by market participants. But the government should intensify its efforts to develop adequate mechanisms to consult the business community and inform market participants in advance of new measures. Regulatory transparency and predictability are especially important for small domestic investors and for foreign investors, particularly potential investors, because they are less familiar than incumbent firms with the national legal and regulatory environment. Small and medium firms, moreover, are a natural constituency to demand openness and competition in markets.

Government consultations with business groups can produce higher-quality regulations that achieve legitimate aims at the least possible cost. They also permit basing regulatory decisions on objective analysis and transparency. But they should be inclusive, obtaining input from the groups' core membership. Broadening policy dialogues to include representatives of a wider range of interests, including consumers, taxpayers, business owners, and employees, also can enfranchise groups previously excluded from policymaking. Russia now has a fairly well-developed network of business associations representing large and small firms alike; in practice, however, the associations rely heavily on personal ties with regional and federal government authorities for access and information, and lack of connections often is considered a strong barrier to access.[19]

Public disclosure of regulatory agreements as part of a broader framework for better information sharing by the government can promote consumer rights, encourage rule-based enforcement of obligations, and reduce incentives for corruption. Several countries have standards for public disclosure—say, by posting the full content of infrastructure contracts and regulatory and administrative procedures on government websites.

Adopt one of several review mechanisms to deal with existing regulations. Although licensing and regulatory reforms in 2001–03 streamlined administrative barriers, business regulation in Russia often is complicated by older rules that are still on the books. The Russian Federation should consider implementing one of the approaches used in Mexico, Hungary, and other countries to eliminate obsolete regulations. Requiring governing authorities to document and justify all business regulations to the national governing body by a given deadline, for example, has yielded positive results in several countries.

Notes

1. Yakovlev and Zhuravskaya (2005).
2. World Bank (2004e, p. 57).
3. Kikeri, Kenyon, and Palmade (2006).
4. World Bank (2005a).
5. It is difficult, however, to do so by looking at mean responses of firms to questions on Enterprise Surveys regarding their perceptions of the investment climate, for three reasons. First, the totals do not control for different distributions of firm types across countries and thus do not accurately show the "country" effect of firms' locations. Second, the scoring differs between Russian firms (four categories of severity) and firms from Brazil, China, and India (five categories). Third, the totals do not account for the propensities of firms to "complain" about investment climate constraints in general.
6. The benefit of the ordered-logit is that it enables analysis of the effects of various explanators on changes in categories of severity, rather than on the actual likelihood that a firm selects a particular category—and thus avoids difficulties in

comparison that may arise due to the fact that the number of allowable categories differs across countries.

7. CEFIR (2005).

8. CEFIR (2005).

9. BEEPS (2006).

10. Ownership was transferred primarily through a system of vouchers distributed to Russian citizens, with certain reservations of ownership made for enterprise insiders.

11. FIAS (2004a, chapters 1 and 4).

12. A notable exception to this is Tomsk Oblast, which made use of the opportunity to promote reform.

13. FIAS (2004a).

14. Slinko, Yakovlev, and Zhuravskaya (2003).

15. World Bank (2005d).

16. Investment climate constraints were generated using principal component weightings of individual impediments, generating normally distributed, continuous variables with mean 0. The results also control for firm size, whether or not the firm is a member of a holding company or financial-industrial group, and a firm-specific, systemic "optimism" or favorable bias toward the investment climate. Sectoral dummies also are included.

17. Frye (2002).

18. Yermakov and Kaganov (2000).

19. OECD (2006); Aidis and Adachi (2007).

Appendix 1

The Large and Medium Enterprise (LME) Survey sampled approximately 1,000 medium- and large-scale manufacturing enterprises. The survey stratified the sample according to the following characteristics: sectoral affiliation, size (based on the number of permanent employees), and location.

Sectoral Classification

Table A1-1 lists sectoral activity and approximate number of firms in the population based on the 2003 Russian census of enterprises. The selected sectors of medium and large enterprises included around 75 percent of all enterprises in manufacturing, which were responsible for 87 percent of total output.[1]

Size

In addition, the sample was stratified according to enterprise size, in order to ensure adequate representation of both medium and larger enterprises. A small number of very large enterprises (more than 10,000 employees), however, were excluded from the survey (heads of very large enterprises being harder to interview, the time and effort required to gather all necessary information from the largest firms being more difficult, and so forth).

Location

It is likely that regional factors could affect enterprise competitiveness (due to regional differences in the investment climate as well as regional wealth). Thus, the sample was further stratified by region. The LME Survey, for logistical reasons, did not sample all eighty-nine oblasts and autonomous regions of the Russian Federation. Rather, firms from forty-nine regions were sampled from both urban and rural locations. One hundred forty-two enterprises were in Moscow and the Moscow Oblast, and seventy-four were in Saint Petersburg and its oblast. The two capitals included more than 20 percent of the surveyed enterprises, which corresponds to the share of those regions in the "universe" of enterprises. About half of the enterprises in the sample were located in regional capitals, about 40 percent in noncapital cities, and about 10 percent in the countryside (villages and settlements).

Table A1-1. Sectoral Structure of Russian Manufacturing Firms

Code	Activity	Number of medium and large enterprises	Percent of the total	Output (fourth quarter 2004)[a]	Percent of total output
D	Processing industries	18,969	100.0	5,018.6	100.0
DA15	Food products	5,129	27.0	969.8	19.3
DB	Textile and sewing industry	1,733	9.1	76.5	1.5
DD	Timber and woodworking industry	780	4.1	82.6	1.6
DG	Chemical production	628	3.3	394.0	7.9
DJ	Metallurgy and metalworking	1,299	6.8	1,480.3	29.5
DK	Machinery and equipment	2,412	12.7	337.9	6.7
DL	Electrical, electronic and optical equipment	1,602	8.4	319.1	6.4
DM	Transport vehicles and equipment	834	4.4	697.2	13.9
	Total number of enterprises	14,417	76.0	4,357.4	86.8

Source: Rosstat (2006).
a. Output in billions of rubles.

Table A1-2 compares the final sample to the universe of firms in the enterprise census. The table shows some oversampling of firms in sectors with a rather small number of enterprises (chemical and timber sectors). In general, however, the sampling structure was close enough to the universe of firms. Similarly, the distribution of employees shows some oversampling in the timber and chemical sectors.

Table A1-3 shows the distribution of enterprises by legal form of organization. The majority of surveyed enterprises were joint-stock companies (opened or closed). About 9 percent of the enterprises in the sample were state-owned enterprises.

About 80 percent of firms were established during the Soviet period or earlier, while 20 percent began operations after 1991. Forty-five percent of the enterprises exported their products directly or through intermediaries (but the share of revenue attributable to exports was more than 10 percent for only about 20 percent of them). About one-third of surveyed enterprises were a part of larger structures (holding companies).

An extensive analysis of the conditions facing small enterprises (less than 100 employees) was beyond the scope of this book. Nevertheless, a second survey of limited scope (from four regions and fourteen industrial sectors) of 304 small enterprises (SE Survey) also was completed.

Table A1-2. Estimation of Sample Parameters, by Sector in the Selected Regions

Parameter	Food production (DA 15)	Textiles and garments (DB 17–18)	Timber and woodworking (DD 20)	Chemicals (DG 24)	Metallurgy and metal working (DJ 27–28)	Machinery and equipment (DK 29)	Electrical, electronic, and optical equipment (DL 30–33)	Transport vehicles and equipment (DM 34–35)	Total
Number of enterprises in the database of the State Statistics Committee (>100 and <10,000 employees across fifty regions)	1,886	655	346	390	766	1,096	1,031	556	6,776
Ideal proportional number in the sample based on the enterprise census	281	98	51	58	112	162	154	83	1,000
Adjusted number in the sample (minimum ninety; the rest are represented proportionally)	253	90	90	90	101	146	139	90	1,000
Actual number of enterprises in the sample	248	92	84	88	103	155	142	90	1,002
Distribution (all firms)	28.00	9.87	5.14	5.79	11.37	16.27	15.31	8.25	100.00
Distribution (sample firms)	24.75	9.18	8.38	8.78	10.28	15.47	14.17	8.98	100.00
Employees (all firms)	651,023	268,227	157,240	422,081	621,225	640,307	688,839	655,099	4,104,041
Employees (sample firms)	92,514	38,854	43,212	84,830	79,795	91,555	90,138	100,514	621,412
Distribution of employment (all firms)	15.86	6.54	3.83	10.28	15.14	15.60	16.78	15.96	100.00
Distribution of employment (sample firms)	14.89	6.25	6.95	13.65	12.84	14.73	14.51	16.18	100.00

Source: LME Survey (2005).

Table A1-3. Classification of Enterprises in the Final Sample, by Organizational and Legal Status

Enterprise status	Number of observations	Percent of the sample
Limited liability company	229	22.85
Public corporation (joint-stock company)	480	47.9
Closed corporation (joint-stock company)	229	22.85
State-owned enterprises and other forms of enterprises	56	5.59

Source: LME Survey (2005).

Note

1. As part of its effort to harmonize with international norms, in 2004 the Russian statistical authority changed its sectoral classification nomenclature from the Soviet-era classification based on "industries" (known by its Russian acronym *OKONH*) to one based on "economic activities" (OKVED). The newer system largely conforms to the EU's Classification of Economic Activities (NACE) and the International Standard Industrial Classification (ISIC).

Appendix 2

The estimation methodology uses simple log-linear equations to test for the correlation between measures of innovative activity and measures of productivity and growth. The correlations reported include several key characteristics of firms known to be related to productivity and growth from other studies. They include size, ownership (new firm established after 1991—the dataset includes virtually no state-owned enterprises), export activity, and regional characteristics. The regression results are shown in table A2-1.

The findings can be summarized as follows. First, absorptive activity, however measured, is basically uncorrelated with total factor productivity (TFP) (as shown in column 1, when TFP is estimated using the log of value added, and column 3, when TFP is estimated using the log of sales), where TFP is productivity after accounting for capital and labor inputs. The exception is R&D spending, which is positively though not robustly correlated with higher TFP. This result is supported by work done on other countries. Wiesner (2005) shows that R&D activities are an important factor in explaining productivity growth for OECD countries. He further suggests that the elasticities of total factor productivity to R&D are lower in Europe and Japan than in the United States, suggesting more efficient use of R&D capital in the United States, the existence of greater enabling institutions, or both. The failure to find a correlation between innovative activity and TFP is essentially a multicollinearity problem.

Innovative activity is strongly and positively correlated with both the capital-labor ratio (column 5) and labor productivity (columns 2 and 4). In essence, firms that are absorbing and creating products and technology are firms that also have lots of fixed capital, and after the endowment of fixed capital is accounted for, there is little for absorption to explain. That may be either a measurement problem (measuring the flow of capital services is notoriously difficult, measuring R&D activity even harder) or a kind of double-counting problem (many of the R&D activity measures in the LME Survey imply fixed investment, which is also captured in the fixed-capital measure).

The findings for training measures are similar but stronger; the difference is that the multicollinearity problem is lower or absent. Training measures are positively correlated with both TFP and labor productivity—and positively correlated with the capital-labor ratio. The explanation may lie in how labor and capital inputs are measured. Labor is measured in

Table A2-1. Innovation, Skills, and Firm Characteristics versus Productivity and Growth Measures in Russia[a]

Item	(1) TFP (VA)	(2) Log L VA/L	(3) TFP (sales)	(4) Log sales/L	(5) Log K/L	(6) TFP growth	(7) Log sales growth	(8) Log L growth	(9) Log K growth
Innovation									
Financed introduction of new product	0.101	0.196**	0.040	0.264**	0.263**	0.064*	0.094**	0.038*	0.044
Financed introduction of new technology	0.046	0.185*	0.025	0.224**	0.138	0.038	0.068*	0.040*	0.098*
Exported advanced technology finished products	0.074	0.249**	0.010	0.187**	0.339**	0.011	0.011	0.021	-0.022
Acquired tech innovation									
Through own R&D	0.148*	0.275**	0.068	0.175**	0.282**	0.045	0.045	0.034	-0.024
Through third-party R&D	0.029	0.108	0.030	0.141*	-0.002	0.072*	0.079**	0.022	0.056
Through purchase of machinery or equipment	0.087	0.179*	0.034	0.133	0.098	0.039	0.050	0.033	0.062
Through purchase of patent, licenses, or know-how	0.034	0.150*	-0.012	0.246**	0.219*	0.047	0.087**	0.053**	0.088*
R&D/sales	0.165	0.291**	0.058	0.269**	0.283*	0.037	0.058	0.025	0.117
R&D expenditures > 0	-0.005	0.004	-0.002	-0.004	0.004	-0.001	0.003	0.005*	0.008
R&D expenditures > 1 million rubles	0.198*	0.388**	0.076	0.329**	0.504**	0.075*	0.071	0.030	0.030
Skills									
Percent of workforce with higher education	0.011**	0.016**	0.003*	0.017**	0.009*	0.002	0.001	0.001	-0.004*
Percent of workforce with any formal training	0.215**	0.370**	0.077	0.346**	0.362**	0.043	0.061	0.058**	0.040
Other characteristics									
SME	-0.144	-0.291**	0.057	-0.277**	-0.374**	-0.070*	-0.117**	-0.070**	-0.139**
New private firm	0.286**	0.111	0.090	0.156	-0.425**	0.020	0.097*	0.052	0.098
Exporter	0.133	0.296**	0.050	0.258**	0.405**	0.021	0.045	0.035*	0.043
To CIS countries	0.011	0.378**	0.042	0.332**	0.436**	0.010	0.034	0.035	0.022
To developed countries	-0.037	0.118	0.038	0.113	0.453**	0.007	0.018	0.019	0.107
To developing countries	-0.064	0.246**	0.062	0.209**	0.433**	0.067*	0.089**	0.043	0.097
National/regional capital	0.262**	0.302**	0.121**	0.302**	0.224*	-0.016	-0.026	-0.017	-0.092*
Population > 500k	0.301**	0.353**	0.165**	0.380**	0.320*	0.033	0.025	-0.019	-0.022
Regional IC risk	-0.163**	-0.178**	-0.082*	-0.177**	-0.149*	-0.011	-0.01	0.003	-0.041
Observations	657–784	708–847	675–815	776–989	896–917	696–890	765–975	765–988	712–911

a. TFP (VA): Log (value added in 2004). Value added in 2004 = (sales in 2004 – purchase of materials in 2004) / (number of employees in 2004). TFP (sales) = Log (sales in 2004). TFP growth: Log (value added in 2004) – Log (value added in 2003). *Significant at 10 percent; **significant at 5 percent; ***significant at 1 percent.

numbers of people, so there is no correction for "labor quality." Fixed capital, by contrast, is measured by value, so high-quality capital gets a larger value than low-quality capital. Since quality is not captured by our labor input measure, there is an observed relationship between labor quality (skills) and TFP.

The picture is similar for growth of TFP, inputs, and output (columns 6–9). Most knowledge absorption measures are uncorrelated with TFP growth. Only a few are positively correlated, and even then the statistical significance is not great. But absorption is positively correlated with the growth of both inputs and output: employment growth, growth of fixed capital (investment), and growth of sales. That can again be interpreted as a kind of multicollinearity problem, because absorption activities are correlated with measures of growth of inputs and output but not with the residual (TFP). The results for training measures are complementary: they are correlated with growth in sales and especially employment.

The findings for size (SME dummy) and new private ownership complement this picture. Smaller firms have lower labor productivity levels, but that is driven by their lower capital intensity. Thus, when a TFP equation includes a measure of fixed capital, the TFP levels of SMEs are not significantly lower than those for larger firms. New private firms also are less capital-intensive than privatized firms, but they do not have lower labor productivity, and their TFP, after accounting for labor inputs are accounted for, is higher.

SMEs are shrinking rapidly in both inputs and output, so their TFP growth is only modestly lower than that of larger firms. New private firms are growing somewhat faster than privatized firms in terms of outputs but not inputs, but the difference is not great, so their TFP growth is no faster. Export activity is not associated with higher TFP; exporting firms are capital intensive, and that explains their higher labor productivity. Interestingly, firms growing in both TFP and sales are the ones exporting to developing countries rather than to the developed West or the Commonwealth of Independent States.

Finally, there is a very strong relationship between city type (national or oblast capital) or city size and productivity: firms in the large cities have much higher levels of productivity. That is true of TFP, labor productivity, and capital intensity. When we move to growth, however, the city type–population relationships disappear. Roughly speaking, the duality gap between big-advanced and small-backward cities is not changing: low-productivity firms in the smaller cities and rural areas are not falling farther behind firms in the major cities and capitals, but they are not catching up either.

The regional investment climate (IC) risk measure, from an external source, captures a single classification (low, medium, high).[1] The IC risk measure is strongly negatively correlated with productivity (a move up one category is associated with 20 percent lower productivity). The IC risk measure is not (as may have been supposed) correlated with other characteristics of firms, such as industry and size, that also influence productivity. The industrial structure of the sample, as well as the average size of firms, is very similar in groups of regions with different risks.

Table A2-2 presents detailed data on innovation activity in Russia and the selected comparator countries. The first panel shows the level of R&D inputs, as measured by R&D spending as a percentage of GDP and by the number of researchers per million population. Where possible, figures are shown for the most recent year available, plus a snapshot from one to two decades earlier. It is worth noting, in addition to the patterns and developments in Russia discussed in the main text, how the countries that have made the most gains in catching up—China, South Korea, and Spain—have also significantly increased the scale of their R&D activity during the same period. The contrast between East and West Germany in 1989 also is noteworthy—East Germany, like Russia and the rest of the USSR, also had a large but economically relatively ineffective R&D sector.

Note the discrepancy between the figures for R&D spending in 1990 in Russia (2.0 percent) and the USSR (5.7 percent). Both figures come from the UNESCO yearbooks, various years. No explanation is offered in these sources, but it is possible that treatment of military R&D spending could account for some of the difference.

The second panel presents R&D outputs, as measured by the number of scientific and technical journal articles[2] and utility patents ("patents for invention") granted by the U.S. Patent and Trademark Office. The data in the third panel on R&D productivity (output per thousand researchers) were calculated using the data in the first two panels.

Notes

1. Expert Rating Agency (2006).
2. World Bank (2006e).

Table A2-2. Basic Indicators of R&D Input and R&D Productivity for Selected Countries

Measure	Brazil	Russia	India	China	South Africa	Poland	South Korea	Spain	Germany
R&D inputs									
R&D as percent of GDP (year)	0.93 (2004)	1.17 (2004) 2.03 (1990) **USSR** 5.66 (1990)	0.85 (2000) 0.56 (1982)	1.44 (2004) 0.60 (1996)	0.76 (2001) 0.82 (1983)	0.58 (2004) 1.00 (1985)	2.63 (2003) 0.57 (1980)	1.11 (2003) 0.44 (1981)	2.49 (2004) (1989) **West** **East** 2.79 3.37
Researchers per million population	344 (2000) 175 (1981)	3,319 (2004) 6,697 (1990) **USSR** 5,856 (1990)	119 (1998) 131 (1982)	708 (2004) 410 (1991)	307 (2001) 270 (1983)	1,581 (2004) 1,533 (1985)	3,187 (2003) 484 (1980)	2,195 (2003) 510 (1981)	3,261 (2004) (1989) **West** **East** 2,236 7,819
R&D output									
Scientific papers per million population	42 (2001)	109 (2001)	11 (2001)	16 (2001)	52 (2001)	149 (2001)	233 (2001)	382 (2001)	530 (2001)
U.S. PTO patents granted per million population	12 (1981)	132 (1993)	13 (1986)	1 (1981)	65 (1985)	107 (1985)	4 (1981)	63 (1981)	412 (1991)
	0.6 (2004) 0.2 (1981)	1.2 (2004) 0.3 (1994) **USSR** 1.7 (1980)	0.3 (2004) 0.0 (1980)	0.3 (2004) 0.0 (1981)	2.7 (2001) 2.0 (1983)	0.4 (2004) 0.3 (1985)	92.1 (2004) 0.2 (1980)	6.2 (2004) 1.5 (1981)	130.6 (2004) 96.0 (1991)
R&D productivity									
Scientific papers per thousand researchers	104 (2000)	31 (2001)	86 (1998)	28 (2001)	164 (2001)	100 (2001)	81 (2001)	194 (2001)	165 (2001)
U.S. PTO patents per thousand researchers	1.6 (2000)	0.4 (2004)	0.7 (1998)	0.4 (2004)	8.5 (2001)	0.3 (2004)	26.1 (2003)	3.3 (2003)	42.6 (2003)

Source: R&D inputs: UNESCO (various years) and OECD (2004b). R&D outputs: World Bank (2006e) and USPTO (various years). R&D productivity: derived from data for R&D inputs and R&D outputs.

Table A2-3. Formal Education Indicators, Skills, and Productivity, Selected Countries

Indicator	Brazil	Russia	India	China	South Africa	Poland	South Korea	Spain	Germany
Gross enrollment ratios by International Standard Classification of Education (ISCED) level (2002)									
Secondary (ISCED level 2 and 3)	110	93	50	67	89	103	91	115	100
Higher education (ISCED level 5 and 6)	18	70	11	13	15	58	82	59	48
Manager/employee education level									
Skilled production workers (percent of workers)	40.5	78.9	63.5	13.0	44.7	89.9	85.3	76.5	85.8
Employees with university-plus education (percent of employees)	8.5	34.5	19.0	n.a.	11.5	13.6	36.8	15.8	9.8
Top manager with university-plus education (percent of firms)	50.7	87.9	88.2	80.1	71.0	57.7	n.a.	n.a.	n.a.

Source: UNESCO (2006) for secondary education figures; Eurostat (various years) for higher education figures; World Bank (2002–2006) for workforce education.

Table A2-4. Investment Climate Constraints[a]

Constraint	Brazil 2003	Russia 1999	Russia 2002	**Russia 2005**	India 2002	China 2002	South Africa 2003	Poland 2005	South Korea 2004	Spain 2005	Germany 2004
Telecoms	1.60 >>	n.a.	1.46	**1.36**	1.63 >>	1.92 >>	1.49 >	1.50 >	1.37	1.73 >>	1.17 <<
Electricity	2.17 >>	n.a.	1.43	**1.55**	2.56 >>	2.31 >>	1.72 >	1.54	1.46	1.66	1.18 <<
Transport	2.32 >>	n.a.	1.61	**1.63**	2.11 >>	2.16 >>	1.88 >	1.62	1.65	1.91 >	1.55
Land access	1.96 >>	n.a.	1.67	**1.67**	1.75	1.90 >	1.26 <<	1.55	1.44 <	1.74	1.63
Land title	n.a.	n.a.	1.84	**1.63**	n.a.	n.a.	n.a.	1.65	1.41 <	1.73	1.48
Tax rates	3.80 >>	3.62 >>	2.60	**2.72**	2.58	2.68	2.31 <<	3.43 >>	2.14 <<	2.25 <<	2.58
Tax administration	3.45 >>	3.27 >>	2.72	**2.80**	2.50 <<	2.41 <<	1.86 <<	3.00 >	1.82 <<	2.01 <<	2.42 <<
Customs	3.15 >>	2.25	2.39	**2.24**	2.48 >	2.45 >	2.38	2.61 >>	1.92 <<	2.05 <<	2.25
Licensing	2.60 >>	2.37	2.12	**2.21**	2.14	2.01 <	1.46 <<	1.96 >>	1.51 <<	2.03	1.85 <<
Anticompetitive practices	3.29 >>	2.62 >	2.30	**2.35**	2.22	2.22	1.98 <<	2.49	1.97 <<	2.13	2.05 <<
Labor regulations	3.46 >>	1.90	1.70 <<	**1.96**	2.42 >>	2.50 >>	2.86 >>	2.68 >>	1.68 <<	2.26 >>	2.26 >>
Labor skills	3.09 >>	n.a.	2.19 <<	**2.48**	2.13 <<	2.68 >	2.77 >>	2.40	1.73 <<	2.37 >>	1.95 <<
Financial access	3.18 >>	n.a.	2.31 <	**2.06**	2.13	2.32 >>	1.76 <<	2.80 >>	1.85 <<	2.15	2.04
Financial cost	3.70 >>	3.49 >>	2.37	**2.53**	2.33 <	2.32 <	2.11 <<	3.21 >>	1.94 <<	2.15 <<	2.22 <<

(continued)

Table A2-4. Investment Climate Constraints[a] (*Continued*)

Constraint	Brazil 2003	Russia 1999	Russia 2002	Russia 2005	India 2002	China 2002	South Africa 2003	Poland 2005	South Korea 2004	Spain 2005	Germany 2004
Policy uncertainty	3.76	3.54	2.88	**2.91**	2.42	2.62	2.21	3.22	2.77	2.11	1.77
	>>	>>			<<	<<	<<	>>		<<	<<
Macro environment	3.80	3.62	2.82	**2.80**	2.37	2.58	2.71	3.25	2.93	2.34	2.10
	>>	>>			<<	<		>>		<<	<<
Legal system	2.80	2.22	1.97	**2.15**	n.a.	n.a.	1.87	2.55	1.54	1.77	1.61
	>>						<<	>>	<<	<<	<<
Corruption	3.43	2.59	2.20	**2.32**	2.82	2.42	2.08	2.31	1.61	1.64	1.43
	>>	>			>>		<		<<	<<	<<
Crime	3.05	2.63	1.94	**1.93**	2.12	2.15	2.59	2.13	1.24	1.60	1.24
	>>	>>			>	>	>>	>	<<	<<	<<
Organized crime	n.a.	2.57	1.75	**1.73**	n.a.	n.a.	n.a.	1.91	1.15	1.49	1.26
		>>						>	<<	<<	<<

a. Investment climate evaluated by firms responding to World Bank Enterprise Surveys. Rows correspond to answers to the question "*How much of an obstacle is X to the operation of your business?*" (1 = *not a problem*, 4 = *very big problem*). Results use manufacturing firms only. Entries are country means, controlling for firm size; statistical significance is vis-à-vis Russia in 2005. Significance and sign at the 5 percent and 1 percent levels are indicated by >>, >, <, and <<.

Appendix 3

Table A3-1. Descriptive Statistics[a]

Independent variable	Observations	Mean	Standard deviation	Minimum	Maximum
Size (< 250)	1002	0.4241517	0.4944604	0	1
New private firm	1002	0.1996008	0.3998999	0	1
Workforce tertiary education	979	19.25506	13.48214	0	100
Website	996	0.7439759	0.4366545	0	1
Firm holding company	1001	0.3226773	0.4677341	0	1
Exporter	1002	0.4530938	0.4980435	0	1
Foreign owner	808	0.0371287	0.1891943	0	1
New/improved product	1002	0.4560878	0.4983167	0	1
New/improved technology	1002	0.2954092	0.4564543	0	1
Export technology-intensive products	1002	0.2315369	0.4220253	0	1
R&D expenditure (> 1 million rubles)	961	0.2237253	0.4169571	0	1
Third-party R&D	1002	0.2215569	0.4155018	0	1
Machinery and equipment	1002	0.4491018	0.497651	0	1
Intellectual property	1002	0.1007984	0.3012119	0	1
ISO certification	981	0.3792049	0.4854367	0	1
Financial constraints	1002	0.1896208	0.3921967	0	1
Macroeconomic instability	1002	0.5698603	0.4953427	0	1
Access to finance	1002	0.8313373	0.3746407	0	1
Domestic competitive pressure	1002	0.6706587	0.4702088	0	1
Imports competitive pressure	1002	0.4510978	0.4978513	0	1
Foreign producer competitive pressure	1002	0.2844311	0.4513684	0	1
Reorganized organizational structure	1002	0.5000000	0.5002497	0	1
Hired external consultants	1002	0.1506986	0.3579335	0	1
Outsourced to third party	1002	0.0868263	0.281721	0	1
Automated inventory management system	1002	0.3103792	0.4628799	0	1
Introduced input quality control	1002	0.6007984	0.4899789	0	1

Source: LME Survey (2005).

a. All independent variables are defined in table A3-10.

Table A3-2. Results of One-by-One Regressions for Introduction of New or Improved Product[a]

Independent variable	(1)	(2)	(3)	(4)	(5)	(6)
Size (< 250)	−0.41***	−0.38***	−0.35***	−0.40***	−0.28***	−0.39***
	[0.00]	[0.00]	[0.00]	[0.00]	[0.00]	[0.00]
New private firm	0.13	0.17	0.19	0.16	0.16	0.17
	[0.28]	[0.18]	[0.14]	[0.20]	[0.21]	[0.16]
Food	−0.02	0	0.03	−0.05	0.04	0
	[0.87]	[0.97]	[0.84]	[0.72]	[0.80]	[0.98]
Textile	−0.58***	−0.62***	−0.62***	−0.63***	−0.54***	−0.54***
	[0.00]	[0.00]	[0.00]	[0.00]	[0.01]	[0.01]
Wood	−0.57***	−0.64***	−0.60***	−0.63***	−0.57***	−0.54***
	[0.01]	[0.00]	[0.00]	[0.00]	[0.01]	[0.01]
Chemicals	−0.09	−0.11	−0.11	−0.14	−0.19	−0.1
	[0.64]	[0.56]	[0.57]	[0.46]	[0.34]	[0.60]
Metallurgy	−0.35*	−0.32*	−0.29	−0.30*	−0.33*	−0.28
	[0.06]	[0.07]	[0.11]	[0.09]	[0.07]	[0.13]
Electric	−0.05	−0.01	−0.03	−0.02	−0.06	−0.01
	[0.75]	[0.97]	[0.86]	[0.90]	[0.72]	[0.94]
Transport	−0.30*	−0.34*	−0.34*	−0.33*	−0.40**	−0.33*
	[0.10]	[0.06]	[0.07]	[0.07]	[0.04]	[0.07]
Firm holding company	−0.08	−0.07	−0.05	−0.06	−0.11	−0.09
	[0.45]	[0.46]	[0.60]	[0.51]	[0.30]	[0.36]
Foreign owner	−0.24	−0.22	−0.17	−0.29	−0.18	−0.15
	[0.34]	[0.37]	[0.50]	[0.25]	[0.49]	[0.56]
Workforce tertiary education	0.01** [0.05]					
Exporter		0.14 [0.18]				
Website			0.58*** [0.00]			
Intellectual property				0.65*** [0.00]		
R&D expenditure (> 1 million rubles)					0.66*** [0.00]	
Third-party R&D						0.66*** [0.00]
ISO certification						
Financial constraints						
Access to finance						
Macroeconomic instability						
Regulatory constraints						
Infrastructure constraints						
Domestic competitive pressure						
Imports competitive pressure						
Foreign producer competitive pressure						
Constant	0.11	0.18	−0.24	0.2	0.07	0.08
	[0.46]	[0.21]	[0.14]	[0.10]	[0.62]	[0.53]
Observations	787	808	802	808	770	808
Number of region code	49	49	48	49	48	49

Source: LME Survey (2005).

a. All regressions include a constant and sectoral dummies and use a random effects model. Significance is given by robust standard errors clustered by regions. P values are in brackets. *Significant at 10 percent; **significant at 5 percent; ***significant at 1 percent.

(7)	(8)	(9)	(10)	(11)	(12)	(13)	(14)	(15)
−0.35***	−0.38***	−0.39***	−0.42***	−0.42***	−0.43***	−0.42***	−0.40***	−0.42***
[0.00]	[0.00]	[0.00]	[0.00]	[0.00]	[0.00]	[0.00]	[0.00]	[0.00]
0.17	0.17	0.19	0.17	0.17	0.17	0.18	0.18	0.17
[0.16]	[0.15]	[0.12]	[0.16]	[0.17]	[0.17]	[0.14]	[0.13]	[0.15]
−0.04	−0.07	−0.09	−0.07	−0.06	−0.06	−0.12	−0.02	−0.07
[0.79]	[0.64]	[0.56]	[0.62]	[0.67]	[0.66]	[0.43]	[0.89]	[0.63]
−0.64***	−0.65***	−0.66***	−0.64***	−0.65***	−0.65***	−0.66***	−0.70***	−0.66***
[0.00]	[0.00]	[0.00]	[0.00]	[0.00]	[0.00]	[0.00]	[0.00]	[0.00]
−0.57***	−0.66***	−0.68***	−0.65***	−0.64***	−0.64***	−0.66***	−0.63***	−0.66***
[0.01]	[0.00]	[0.00]	[0.00]	[0.00]	[0.00]	[0.00]	[0.00]	[0.00]
−0.12	−0.11	−0.11	−0.1	−0.11	−0.1	−0.13	−0.13	−0.11
[0.52]	[0.57]	[0.56]	[0.59]	[0.56]	[0.60]	[0.50]	[0.49]	[0.56]
−0.31*	−0.30*	−0.35*	−0.31*	−0.34*	−0.33*	−0.33*	−0.29	−0.31*
[0.09]	[0.09]	[0.05]	[0.09]	[0.06]	[0.07]	[0.07]	[0.11]	[0.08]
−0.06	−0.02	0.01	−0.03	−0.01	−0.02	−0.01	−0.01	−0.02
[0.70]	[0.90]	[0.97]	[0.87]	[0.95]	[0.90]	[0.94]	[0.93]	[0.89]
−0.38**	−0.34*	−0.35*	−0.34*	−0.33*	−0.34*	−0.33*	−0.31*	−0.33*
[0.04]	[0.06]	[0.06]	[0.06]	[0.07]	[0.06]	[0.07]	[0.10]	[0.07]
−0.07	−0.07	−0.05	−0.07	−0.07	−0.07	−0.08	−0.07	−0.07
[0.50]	[0.47]	[0.62]	[0.48]	[0.45]	[0.46]	[0.44]	[0.48]	[0.45]
−0.23	−0.2	−0.18	−0.19	−0.22	−0.2	−0.15	−0.21	−0.18
[0.37]	[0.41]	[0.48]	[0.45]	[0.39]	[0.44]	[0.54]	[0.40]	[0.46]

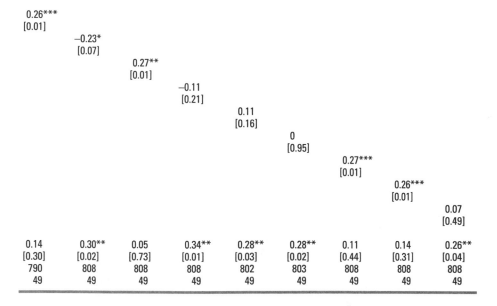

(7)	(8)	(9)	(10)	(11)	(12)	(13)	(14)	(15)
0.26***								
[0.01]								
	−0.23*							
	[0.07]							
		0.27**						
		[0.01]						
			−0.11					
			[0.21]					
				0.11				
				[0.16]				
					0			
					[0.95]			
						0.27***		
						[0.01]		
							0.26***	
							[0.01]	
								0.07
								[0.49]
0.14	0.30**	0.05	0.34**	0.28**	0.28**	0.11	0.14	0.26**
[0.30]	[0.02]	[0.73]	[0.01]	[0.03]	[0.02]	[0.44]	[0.31]	[0.04]
790	808	808	808	802	803	808	808	808
49	49	49	49	49	49	49	49	49

Table A3-3. Results of One-by-One Regressions for Introduction of New or Improved Technology[a]

Independent variable	(1)	(2)	(3)	(4)	(5)	(6)
Size (< 250)	−0.32***	−0.24**	−0.25**	−0.29***	−0.19*	−0.29***
	[0.00]	[0.02]	[0.01]	[0.00]	[0.06]	[0.00]
New private firm	−0.18	−0.15	−0.13	−0.15	−0.14	−0.13
	[0.19]	[0.26]	[0.32]	[0.26]	[0.30]	[0.31]
Food	−0.28*	−0.19	−0.25	−0.29*	−0.16	−0.24
	[0.07]	[0.24]	[0.11]	[0.06]	[0.33]	[0.13]
Textile	−0.42**	−0.37*	−0.42**	−0.40*	−0.28	−0.33
	[0.05]	[0.08]	[0.05]	[0.06]	[0.18]	[0.12]
Wood	0.07	0.08	0.09	0.1	0.13	0.17
	[0.74]	[0.70]	[0.67]	[0.63]	[0.55]	[0.43]
Chemicals	0.16	0.12	0.12	0.11	0.04	0.15
	[0.42]	[0.52]	[0.54]	[0.57]	[0.83]	[0.43]
Metallurgy	−0.17	−0.17	−0.14	−0.14	−0.12	−0.12
	[0.38]	[0.37]	[0.44]	[0.45]	[0.52]	[0.51]
Electric	−0.12	−0.11	−0.16	−0.14	−0.2	−0.13
	[0.50]	[0.51]	[0.36]	[0.42]	[0.26]	[0.45]
Transport	−0.3	−0.33*	−0.34*	−0.31	−0.33	−0.32
	[0.13]	[0.10]	[0.08]	[0.11]	[0.11]	[0.11]
Firm holding company	0.11	0.11	0.12	0.12	0.11	0.09
	[0.28]	[0.29]	[0.24]	[0.26]	[0.30]	[0.41]
Foreign owner	−0.22	−0.31	−0.24	−0.35	−0.28	−0.24
	[0.42]	[0.27]	[0.38]	[0.21]	[0.33]	[0.39]
Workforce tertiary education	0					
	[0.55]					
Exporter		0.24**				
		[0.03]				
Website			0.39***			
			[0.00]			
Intellectual property				0.60***		
				[0.00]		
R&D expenditure					0.67***	
					[0.00]	
Third-party R&D						0.47***
						[0.00]
ISO certification						
Financial constraints						
Access to finance						
Macroeconomic instability						
Regulatory constraints						
Infrastructure constraints						
Domestic competitive pressure						
Imports competitive pressure						
Foreign producer competitive pressure						
Constant	−0.26*	−0.47***	−0.63***	−0.38***	−0.53***	−0.45***
	[0.10]	[0.00]	[0.00]	[0.00]	[0.00]	[0.00]
Observations	787	808	802	808	770	808
Number of region code	49	49	48	49	48	49

Source: LME Survey (2005).

a. All regressions include a constant and sectoral dummies and use a random effects model. Significance is given by robust standard errors clustered by regions. P values are in brackets. *Significant at 10 percent; **significant at 5 percent; ***significant at 1 percent.

(7)	(8)	(9)	(10)	(11)	(12)	(13)	(14)	(15)
−0.23**	−0.28***	−0.28***	−0.31***	−0.29***	−0.30***	−0.31***	−0.30***	−0.31***
[0.03]	[0.01]	[0.01]	[0.00]	[0.00]	[0.00]	[0.00]	[0.00]	[0.00]
−0.13	−0.13	−0.11	−0.13	−0.13	−0.13	−0.13	−0.13	−0.13
[0.35]	[0.33]	[0.41]	[0.32]	[0.32]	[0.32]	[0.32]	[0.32]	[0.31]
−0.24	−0.30*	−0.31**	−0.27*	−0.26*	−0.26*	−0.30*	−0.26*	−0.29*
[0.12]	[0.05]	[0.04]	[0.08]	[0.10]	[0.09]	[0.05]	[0.09]	[0.06]
−0.42**	−0.42**	−0.43**	−0.43**	−0.39*	−0.39*	−0.41**	−0.46**	−0.42**
[0.05]	[0.05]	[0.04]	[0.04]	[0.06]	[0.06]	[0.05]	[0.03]	[0.05]
0.16	0.06	0.04	0.08	0.11	0.11	0.07	0.08	0.07
[0.46]	[0.78]	[0.84]	[0.72]	[0.61]	[0.61]	[0.74]	[0.70]	[0.75]
0.14	0.14	0.14	0.16	0.17	0.18	0.14	0.12	0.15
[0.46]	[0.47]	[0.47]	[0.41]	[0.37]	[0.36]	[0.47]	[0.53]	[0.45]
−0.18	−0.15	−0.18	−0.16	−0.15	−0.15	−0.16	−0.14	−0.16
[0.34]	[0.44]	[0.33]	[0.39]	[0.43]	[0.44]	[0.40]	[0.46]	[0.41]
−0.2	−0.13	−0.11	−0.12	−0.1	−0.1	−0.13	−0.13	−0.13
[0.25]	[0.43]	[0.53]	[0.48]	[0.56]	[0.55]	[0.46]	[0.44]	[0.45]
−0.39*	−0.33*	−0.33*	−0.32	−0.29	−0.3	−0.32	−0.3	−0.32
[0.05]	[0.09]	[0.09]	[0.11]	[0.14]	[0.14]	[0.11]	[0.13]	[0.11]
0.11	0.11	0.13	0.1	0.09	0.09	0.1	0.11	0.1
[0.30]	[0.30]	[0.20]	[0.34]	[0.38]	[0.38]	[0.31]	[0.30]	[0.32]
−0.3	−0.26	−0.24	−0.26	−0.26	−0.26	−0.24	−0.26	−0.25
[0.27]	[0.34]	[0.38]	[0.35]	[0.34]	[0.35]	[0.37]	[0.34]	[0.36]
0.30***								
[0.00]								
	−0.21							
	[0.12]							
		0.31**						
		[0.01]						
			0.09					
			[0.37]					
				0.03				
				[0.70]				
					0.01			
					[0.94]			
						0.09		
						[0.38]		
							0.17*	
							[0.08]	
								0.02
								[0.83]
−0.46***	−0.28**	−0.56***	−0.36**	−0.33**	−0.33**	−0.36**	−0.39***	−0.31**
[0.00]	[0.03]	[0.00]	[0.01]	[0.01]	[0.01]	[0.01]	[0.00]	[0.02]
790	808	808	808	802	803	808	808	808
49	49	49	49	49	49	49	49	49

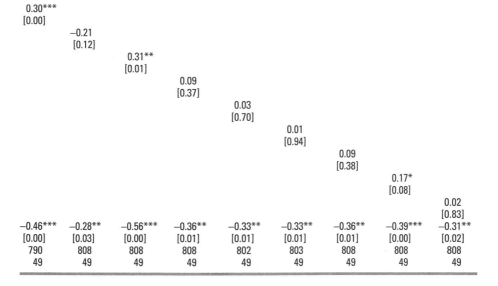

Table A3-4. Results of One-by-One Regressions for Export of Technology-Intensive Products[a]

Independent variable	(1)	(2)	(3)	(4)	(5)	(6)
Size (< 250)	−0.73***	−0.65***	−0.71***	−0.58***	−0.72***	−0.55***
	[0.00]	[0.00]	[0.00]	[0.00]	[0.00]	[0.00]
New private firm	0.32**	0.27*	0.24*	0.28*	0.24*	0.23
	[0.03]	[0.06]	[0.09]	[0.06]	[0.09]	[0.11]
Food	−1.26***	−1.24***	−1.28***	−1.16***	−1.28***	−1.20***
	[0.00]	[0.00]	[0.00]	[0.00]	[0.00]	[0.00]
Textile	−1.42***	−1.38***	−1.39***	−1.27***	−1.42***	−1.37***
	[0.00]	[0.00]	[0.00]	[0.00]	[0.00]	[0.00]
Wood	−0.70***	−0.65***	−0.65***	−0.74***	−0.68***	−0.55**
	[0.00]	[0.01]	[0.01]	[0.00]	[0.00]	[0.02]
Chemicals	−0.06	−0.08	−0.1	−0.1	−0.06	−0.1
	[0.76]	[0.68]	[0.62]	[0.64]	[0.76]	[0.61]
Metallurgy	−0.43**	−0.45**	−0.43**	−0.46**	−0.45**	−0.50**
	[0.03]	[0.02]	[0.03]	[0.02]	[0.02]	[0.01]
Electric	0.05	0.02	0.04	0.02	0.04	−0.08
	[0.79]	[0.92]	[0.80]	[0.89]	[0.80]	[0.65]
Transport	−0.28	−0.31	−0.29	−0.27	−0.29	−0.42**
	[0.16]	[0.12]	[0.14]	[0.18]	[0.13]	[0.04]
Firm holding company	−0.17	−0.13	−0.15	−0.15	−0.16	−0.18
	[0.16]	[0.26]	[0.21]	[0.22]	[0.18]	[0.12]
Foreign owner	0.22	0.29	0.16	0.44	0.26	0.22
	[0.41]	[0.28]	[0.56]	[0.11]	[0.34]	[0.40]
Workforce tertiary education	0					
	[0.81]					
Website		0.57***				
		[0.00]				
Intellectual property			0.54***			
			[0.00]			
R&D expenditure				0.57***		
				[0.00]		
Third-party R&D					−0.05	
					[0.72]	
ISO certification						0.54***
						[0.00]
Financial constraints						
Access to finance						
Macroeconomic instability						
Regulatory constraints						
Infrastructure constraints						
Domestic competitive pressure						
Imports competitive pressure						
Foreign producer competitive pressure						
Constant	−0.05	−0.52***	−0.08	−0.27*	−0.01	−0.28*
	[0.77]	[0.01]	[0.54]	[0.06]	[0.96]	[0.06]
Observations	787	802	808	770	808	790
Number of region code	49	48	49	48	49	49

Source: LME Survey (2005).

a. All regressions include a constant and sectoral dummies and use a random effects model. Significance is given by robust standard errors clustered by regions. P values are in brackets. *Significant at 10 percent; **significant at 5 percent; ***significant at 1 percent.

(7)	(8)	(9)	(10)	(11)	(12)	(13)	(14)
−0.65***	−0.71***	−0.72***	−0.73***	−0.67***	−0.71***	−0.67***	−0.71***
[0.00]	[0.00]	[0.00]	[0.00]	[0.00]	[0.00]	[0.00]	[0.00]
0.25*	0.24*	0.25*	0.24*	0.26*	0.24*	0.25*	0.25*
[0.08]	[0.08]	[0.08]	[0.08]	[0.07]	[0.09]	[0.07]	[0.08]
−1.27***	−1.26***	−1.27***	−1.27***	−1.29***	−1.25***	−1.21***	−1.29***
[0.00]	[0.00]	[0.00]	[0.00]	[0.00]	[0.00]	[0.00]	[0.00]
−1.38***	−1.43***	−1.41***	−1.42***	−1.39***	−1.41***	−1.47***	−1.43***
[0.00]	[0.00]	[0.00]	[0.00]	[0.00]	[0.00]	[0.00]	[0.00]
−0.68***	−0.66***	−0.66***	−0.67***	−0.70***	−0.66***	−0.63***	−0.68***
[0.00]	[0.00]	[0.00]	[0.00]	[0.00]	[0.00]	[0.01]	[0.00]
−0.07	−0.05	−0.06	−0.06	−0.07	−0.05	−0.11	−0.1
[0.72]	[0.79]	[0.77]	[0.76]	[0.73]	[0.81]	[0.59]	[0.63]
−0.43**	−0.46**	−0.47**	−0.48**	−0.48**	−0.44**	−0.41**	−0.44**
[0.03]	[0.02]	[0.02]	[0.02]	[0.01]	[0.02]	[0.04]	[0.02]
0.04	0.05	0.05	0.05	0.07	0.04	0.05	0.03
[0.84]	[0.76]	[0.78]	[0.78]	[0.67]	[0.79]	[0.77]	[0.84]
−0.3	−0.29	−0.29	−0.29	−0.3	−0.29	−0.24	−0.28
[0.12]	[0.14]	[0.14]	[0.13]	[0.12]	[0.13]	[0.22]	[0.15]
−0.15	−0.16	−0.16	−0.16	−0.12	−0.16	−0.14	−0.16
[0.19]	[0.16]	[0.18]	[0.18]	[0.30]	[0.17]	[0.22]	[0.18]
0.24	0.25	0.26	0.23	0.28	0.24	0.25	0.27
[0.37]	[0.35]	[0.33]	[0.40]	[0.30]	[0.36]	[0.34]	[0.30]
−0.35**							
[0.03]							
				0.32**			
				[0.02]			
	0.13						
	[0.22]						
		0.01					
		[0.90]					
			0.07				
			[0.48]				
					−0.11		
					[0.33]		
						0.35***	
						[0.00]	
							0.15
							[0.20]
0.01	−0.1	−0.02	−0.01	−0.29*	0.05	−0.22	−0.06
[0.92]	[0.50]	[0.88]	[0.92]	[0.09]	[0.76]	[0.13]	[0.65]
808	808	802	803	808	808	808	808
49	49	49	49	49	49	49	49

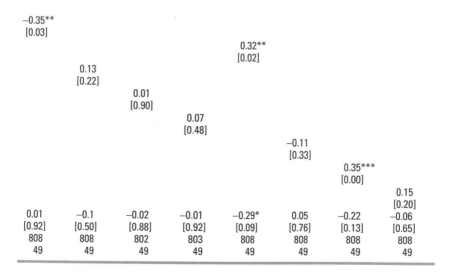

Table A3-5. Regression Results for Full Model of Product and Process Innovation[a]

Independent variable	Introduction of a new or improved product	Introduction of a new or improved technology	Export of technology-intensive products
Size (< 250)	−0.16	0.02	−0.37***
	[0.14]	[0.90]	[0.01]
New private firm	0.16	−0.18	0.36**
	[0.25]	[0.22]	[0.02]
Food	0.11	0.03	−1.05***
	[0.52]	[0.85]	[0.00]
Textile	−0.37*	−0.24	−1.35***
	[0.08]	[0.30]	[0.00]
Wood	−0.40*	0.27	−0.68**
	[0.09]	[0.24]	[0.01]
Chemicals	−0.3	−0.01	−0.21
	[0.16]	[0.98]	[0.35]
Metallurgy	−0.3	−0.13	−0.46**
	[0.13]	[0.53]	[0.04]
Electric	−0.05	−0.15	−0.05
	[0.79]	[0.43]	[0.81]
Transport	0.37*	−0.33	−0.35
	[0.07]	[0.13]	[0.10]
Workforce tertiary education	0.01	0	0
	[0.19]	[0.40]	[0.49]
Firm holding company	−0.06	0.15	−0.13
	[0.58]	[0.19]	[0.31]
Foreign owner	−0.27	−0.39	0.29
	[0.36]	[0.23]	[0.34]
Exporter	0.02	0.16	
	[0.86]	[0.19]	
Website	0.34***	0.29**	0.44**
	[0.01]	[0.04]	[0.01]
Intellectual property	0.47***	0.54***	0.31*
	[0.01]	[0.00]	[0.09]
R&D expenditure	0.41***	0.45***	0.40***
(> 1 million rubles)	[0.00]	[0.00]	[0.00]
Third-party R&D	0.62***	0.43***	−0.11
	[0.00]	[0.00]	[0.44]
ISO certification	0.15	0.19	0.49***
	[0.18]	[0.10]	[0.00]
Financial constraints	−0.03	0.02	−0.32
	[0.86]	[0.91]	[0.12]
Access to finance	0.15	0.28*	0.04
	[0.30]	[0.06]	[0.79]
Macroeconomic instability	−0.20*	0.15	0.15
	[0.07]	[0.20]	[0.24]
Regulatory constraints	0.1	−0.07	−0.03
	[0.30]	[0.49]	[0.79]
Infrastructure constraints	−0.02	−0.03	0.08
	[0.79]	[0.76]	[0.49]
Domestic competitive pressure	0.25**	0.01	−0.13
	[0.02]	[0.91]	[0.30]
Imports competitive pressure	0.13	0.03	0.30**
	[0.29]	[0.84]	[0.03]
Foreign producer competitive	−0.02	−0.06	0.07
pressure	[0.88]	[0.67]	[0.63]
Constant	−0.82***	−1.41***	−0.96***
	[0.00]	[0.00]	[0.00]
Observations	729	729	729
Number of region code	48	48	48

Source: LME Survey (2005).

a. All regressions include a constant and sectoral dummies and use a random effects model. Significance is given by robust standard errors clustered by regions. P values are given in brackets. *Significant at 10 percent; **significant at 5 percent; ***significant at 1 percent.

Table A3-6. Introduction of a New or Improved Product, Cross-Country Comparison[a]

Independent variable	(1)	(2)	(3)	(4)
Size (> 250)	0.147***	0.086*	0.04	0.012
	0.003	0.089	0.454	0.829
Age of firm	0	0	0	0
	0.596	0.542	0.709	0.814
Exporter	0.139***	0.066	0.098*	0.037
	0.002	0.166	0.055	0.484
China	−0.420***	−0.507***	−0.414***	−0.454***
	0	0	0	0
Brazil	0.701***	0.711***	0.769***	0.719***
	0	0	0	0
South Africa	0.704***	0.674***	0.753***	0.704***
	0	0	0	0
ISO certification		0.377***	0.384***	0.328***
		0	0	0
R&D intensity			0	0
			0.783	0.121
R&D non-zero expenditure				0.495***
				0
Constant	−0.268***	−0.350***	−0.431***	−0.589***
	0	0	0	0
Observations	3,724	3,615	3,249	3,248

Source: World Bank (2002–2006) for the comparator countries and BEEPS (2006) for Russia.
a. All regressions include a constant. Significance is given by robust standard errors clustered by regions. P values are in brackets. *Significant at 10 percent; **significant at 5 percent; ***significant at 1 percent.

Table A3-7. Results of One-by-One Regressions for R&D Expenditure[a]

Independent variable	(1)	(2)	(3)	(4)	(5)	(6)
Size (< 250)	−0.68***	−0.58***	−0.61***	−0.69***	−0.67***	−0.58***
	[0.00]	[0.00]	[0.00]	[0.00]	[0.00]	[0.00]
New private firm	−0.09	−0.1	−0.05	−0.12	−0.08	−0.09
	[0.55]	[0.51]	[0.73]	[0.45]	[0.60]	[0.59]
Food	−0.84***	−0.70***	−0.83***	−0.89***	−0.84***	−0.76***
	[0.00]	[0.00]	[0.00]	[0.00]	[0.00]	[0.00]
Textile	−0.84***	−0.79***	−0.89***	−0.85***	−0.81***	−0.89***
	[0.00]	[0.00]	[0.00]	[0.00]	[0.00]	[0.00]
Wood	−0.3	−0.35	−0.35	−0.33	−0.27	−0.23
	[0.24]	[0.15]	[0.16]	[0.18]	[0.27]	[0.36]
Chemicals	0.3	0.23	0.24	0.24	0.27	0.27
	[0.17]	[0.28]	[0.26]	[0.26]	[0.20]	[0.21]
Metallurgy	−0.12	−0.06	−0.04	−0.01	−0.02	0.01
	[0.55]	[0.75]	[0.83]	[0.98]	[0.93]	[0.95]
Electric	0.27	0.35*	0.30*	0.32*	0.31*	0.25
	[0.13]	[0.05]	[0.10]	[0.07]	[0.08]	[0.17]
Transport	0	0.02	0.03	0.05	0.03	−0.05
	[0.99]	[0.94]	[0.90]	[0.80]	[0.89]	[0.82]
Firm holding company	0.11	0.08	0.13	0.1	0.07	0.07
	[0.39]	[0.49]	[0.30]	[0.40]	[0.58]	[0.55]
Foreign owner	−0.25	−0.28	−0.21	−0.37	−0.19	−0.31
	[0.43]	[0.37]	[0.51]	[0.27]	[0.56]	[0.34]
Workforce tertiary education	0.01					
	[0.25]					
Exporter		0.38***				
		[0.00]				
Website			0.84***			
			[0.00]			
Intellectual property				0.67***		
				[0.00]		
Third-party R&D					0.41***	
					[0.00]	
ISO certification						0.49***
						[0.00]
Financial constraints						
Access to finance						
Macroeconomic instability						
Regulatory constraints						
Infrastructure constraints						
Domestic competitive pressure						
Imports competitive pressure						
Foreign producer competitive pressure						
Constant	−0.52***	−0.68***	−1.15***	−0.49***	−0.54***	−0.69***
	[0.00]	[0.00]	[0.00]	[0.00]	[0.00]	[0.00]
Observations	752	770	765	770	770	754
Number of region code	48	48	48	48	48	48

Source: LME Survey (2005).

a. Research and development expenditure > 1 million rubles. All regressions include a constant and sectoral dummies and use a random effects model. Significance is given by robust standard errors clustered by regions. P values are in brackets. *Significant at 10 percent; **significant at 5 percent; ***significant at 1 percent.

(7)	(8)	(9)	(10)	(11)	(12)	(13)	(14)
−0.64***	−0.64***	−0.69***	−0.68***	−0.69***	−0.69***	−0.67***	−0.69***
[0.00]	[0.00]	[0.00]	[0.00]	[0.00]	[0.00]	[0.00]	[0.00]
−0.1	−0.1	−0.09	−0.09	−0.1	−0.09	−0.08	−0.09
[0.52]	[0.51]	[0.54]	[0.55]	[0.52]	[0.56]	[0.62]	[0.55]
−0.89***	−0.91***	−0.86***	−0.87***	−0.87***	−0.88***	−0.82***	−0.86***
[0.00]	[0.00]	[0.00]	[0.00]	[0.00]	[0.00]	[0.00]	[0.00]
−0.84***	−0.87***	−0.87***	−0.88***	−0.88***	−0.87***	−0.92***	−0.87***
[0.00]	[0.00]	[0.00]	[0.00]	[0.00]	[0.00]	[0.00]	[0.00]
−0.38	−0.4	−0.35	−0.35	−0.35	−0.36	−0.32	−0.36
[0.12]	[0.10]	[0.15]	[0.15]	[0.15]	[0.14]	[0.20]	[0.14]
0.25	0.25	0.27	0.25	0.27	0.26	0.24	0.26
[0.24]	[0.22]	[0.20]	[0.23]	[0.20]	[0.22]	[0.26]	[0.22]
−0.03	−0.05	−0.04	−0.04	−0.04	−0.04	0	−0.04
[0.90]	[0.80]	[0.83]	[0.83]	[0.85]	[0.83]	[0.99]	[0.85]
0.31*	0.34*	0.32*	0.33*	0.32*	0.31*	0.33*	0.31*
[0.09]	[0.06]	[0.08]	[0.06]	[0.08]	[0.08]	[0.07]	[0.08]
0.02	0.04	0.03	0.04	0.02	0.03	0.07	0.03
[0.94]	[0.83]	[0.87]	[0.85]	[0.91]	[0.88]	[0.75]	[0.87]
0.09	0.1	0.08	0.06	0.07	0.08	0.08	0.08
[0.46]	[0.39]	[0.52]	[0.61]	[0.57]	[0.50]	[0.50]	[0.51]
−0.2	−0.18	−0.2	−0.24	−0.27	−0.19	−0.22	−0.19
[0.52]	[0.56]	[0.53]	[0.45]	[0.41]	[0.55]	[0.48]	[0.55]
−0.35**							
[0.04]							
	0.52***						
	[0.00]						
		0.04					
		[0.75]					
			0.17*				
			[0.07]				
				0.13			
				[0.19]			
					0.07		
					[0.54]		
						0.28**	
						[0.01]	
							0.04
							[0.75]
−0.37***	−0.87***	−0.43***	−0.41***	−0.40***	−0.46***	−0.57***	−0.42***
[0.01]	[0.00]	[0.01]	[0.00]	[0.01]	[0.00]	[0.00]	[0.00]
770	770	770	764	765	770	770	770
48	48	48	48	48	48	48	48

Table A3-8. Regression Results of Full Model for Soft Innovation and Organizational Changes[a]

Independent variable	Reorganized organizational structure	Hired external consultants	Outsourced to third party	Introduced input quality control	Automated system of inventory management
Size (< 250)	-0.33*** [0.00]	-0.36** [0.01]	-0.35* [0.06]	-0.13 [0.24]	-0.25** [0.03]
New private firm	-0.25* [0.07]	-0.02 [0.91]	0.13 [0.51]	0.06 [0.65]	0.06 [0.69]
Food	-0.39** [0.03]	-0.03 [0.88]	-0.16 [0.52]	0.13 [0.44]	0.17 [0.34]
Textile	-0.02 [0.92]	-0.1 [0.72]	-0.76* [0.09]	0.1 [0.63]	-0.12 [0.60]
Wood	-0.18 [0.42]	0.04 [0.89]	-0.6 [0.11]	-0.03 [0.91]	-0.13 [0.61]
Chemicals	-0.1 [0.63]	0.02 [0.94]	-0.12 [0.68]	0.21 [0.32]	0.1 [0.64]
Metallurgy	0 [0.99]	0.35 [0.14]	-0.12 [0.66]	0.41** [0.05]	0.02 [0.93]
Electric	-0.08 [0.64]	-0.33 [0.18]	-0.32 [0.23]	0.12 [0.51]	0.25 [0.18]
Transport	-0.09 [0.67]	0.21 [0.38]	-0.43 [0.16]	0 [0.99]	0.45** [0.03]
Firm holding company	0.20* [0.06]	0.08 [0.55]	0.44*** [0.00]	0.04 [0.73]	0.14 [0.20]
Foreign owner	0.36 [0.20]	0.67** [0.03]	0.91*** [0.00]	0.26 [0.34]	0.39 [0.15]
Workforce tertiary education	0 [0.75]	0 [0.75]	0 [0.86]	0 [0.95]	0.01*** [0.01]
Exporter	-0.16 [0.22]	-0.13 [0.44]	0.25 [0.22]	-0.06 [0.64]	-0.12 [0.41]
Intellectual property	0.06 [0.74]	0.26 [0.18]	0.36 [0.11]	0.1 [0.57]	0.27 [0.13]
R&D expenditure (> 1 million rubles)	0.18 [0.18]	0.15 [0.35]	0.25 [0.17]	0.12 [0.38]	0.14 [0.32]

	(1)	(2)	(3)	(4)	(5)
ISO certification	-0.16	0.07	0.16	0.17	0.26**
	[0.15]	[0.61]	[0.35]	[0.13]	[0.02]
Financial constraints	-0.21	-0.04	0.07	0.04	-0.19
	[0.18]	[0.84]	[0.79]	[0.79]	[0.27]
Access to finance	0.16	0.81***	0.62*	0.15	0.06
	[0.34]	[0.00]	[0.06]	[0.34]	[0.75]
Domestic competitive pressure	0.1	0.1	0.25	0.11	-0.13
	[0.38]	[0.48]	[0.15]	[0.33]	[0.26]
Imports competitive pressure	0.29**	-0.17	-0.07	-0.05	-0.01
	[0.02]	[0.25]	[0.68]	[0.66]	[0.96]
Foreign producer competitive pressure	0.05	0.22	-0.06	0.06	0.02
	[0.69]	[0.15]	[0.74]	[0.65]	[0.87]
Financed new product	0	0.14	-0.06	0.28***	0.13
	[0.97]	[0.30]	[0.73]	[0.01]	[0.24]
Financed new technology	0.01	0.27*	-0.26	0.18	0.22*
	[0.94]	[0.05]	[0.14]	[0.12]	[0.06]
Exported technology-intensive products	0.33**	-0.08	0.02	0.11	-0.05
	[0.04]	[0.68]	[0.94]	[0.50]	[0.74]
Third-party R&D	0.27**	0.36**	0.25	0.08	0.06
	[0.03]	[0.01]	[0.15]	[0.51]	[0.62]
Machinery and equipment	0.12	0.06	0.13	0.17	0.08
	[0.24]	[0.67]	[0.42]	[0.11]	[0.47]
Macroeconomic instability	-0.14	0.32**	-0.12	0	-0.04
	[0.17]	[0.02]	[0.44]	[0.98]	[0.70]
Regulatory constraints	0.21**	-0.09	0.07	-0.09	-0.01
	[0.03]	[0.44]	[0.61]	[0.31]	[0.95]
Infrastructure constraints	0.1	0.13	-0.18	0.07	0.02
	[0.26]	[0.27]	[0.27]	[0.43]	[0.81]
Constant	-0.04	-2.28***	-2.28***	-0.38	-1.01***
	[0.86]	[0.00]	[0.00]	[0.13]	[0.00]
Observations	731	731	731	731	731
Number of region code	48	48	48	48	48

Source: LME Survey (2005).

a. All regressions include a constant and sectoral dummies and use a random effects model. Significance is given by robust standard errors clustered by regions. P values are given in brackets. *Significant at 10 percent; **significant at 5 percent; ***significant at 1 percent.

Table A3-9. Competitive Pressure and Firm Innovation and Absorption[a]

Independent variable	Introduction of a new or improved product				Introduction of a new or improved technology				Export of technology-intensive products			
	(1)	(2)	(3)	(4)	(1)	(2)	(3)	(4)	(1)	(2)	(3)	(4)
Domestic competitive pressure	0.24** [0.02]	0.17* [0.07]	0.16* [0.09]	0.19** [0.03]	0.07 [0.52]	0.04 [0.67]	0.04 [0.72]	0.06 [0.53]	-0.19 [0.10]	-0.26** [0.01]	-0.18 [0.11]	-0.23** [0.02]
Imports competitive pressure	0.27** [0.01]	0.18* [0.08]	0.14 [0.18]	0.33*** [0.00]	0.20* [0.08]	0.07 [0.52]	0 [0.97]	0.16 [0.12]	0.39*** [0.00]	0.32*** [0.01]	0.29** [0.01]	0.40*** [0.00]
Foreign producer competitive pressure	-0.11 [0.35]	-0.03 [0.76]	-0.03 [0.76]	-0.13 [0.22]	-0.09 [0.47]	0.08 [0.50]	0.09 [0.44]	-0.02 [0.85]	-0.01 [0.94]	-0.01 [0.93]	-0.03 [0.79]	-0.07 [0.55]
Food	-0.06 [0.71]	0.11 [0.44]	0.16 [0.28]	-0.08 [0.53]	-0.26 [0.10]	-0.15 [0.31]	-0.07 [0.64]	-0.28** [0.05]	-1.16*** [0.00]	-1.13*** [0.00]	-1.08*** [0.00]	-1.19*** [0.00]
Textile	-0.70*** [0.00]	-0.47** [0.01]	-0.36* [0.05]	-0.64*** [0.00]	-0.46** [0.03]	-0.3 [0.11]	-0.16 [0.41]	-0.41** [0.02]	-1.48*** [0.00]	-1.35*** [0.00]	-1.20*** [0.00]	-1.37*** [0.00]
Wood	-0.63*** [0.00]	-0.34* [0.07]	-0.28 [0.13]	-0.57*** [0.00]	0.09 [0.65]	0.05 [0.80]	0.09 [0.65]	-0.09 [0.61]	-0.62*** [0.01]	-0.46** [0.03]	-0.50** [0.02]	-0.59*** [0.00]
Chemicals	-0.14 [0.47]	-0.09 [0.61]	-0.12 [0.51]	-0.04 [0.81]	0.13 [0.50]	0.11 [0.55]	0.06 [0.74]	0.2 [0.25]	-0.08 [0.67]	-0.09 [0.60]	-0.08 [0.67]	-0.01 [0.97]
Metallurgy	-0.30* [0.09]	-0.18 [0.28]	-0.18 [0.28]	-0.23 [0.16]	-0.14 [0.45]	-0.04 [0.82]	-0.01 [0.97]	-0.06 [0.72]	-0.41** [0.04]	-0.54*** [0.00]	-0.54*** [0.00]	-0.53*** [0.00]
Electric	0 [0.99]	0.03 [0.84]	0.04 [0.78]	0.08 [0.58]	-0.13 [0.46]	-0.28* [0.08]	-0.30* [0.07]	-0.15 [0.35]	0.05 [0.76]	-0.16 [0.32]	-0.11 [0.50]	0.02 [0.90]
Transport	-0.31* [0.09]	-0.34* [0.06]	-0.40** [0.03]	-0.29* [0.09]	-0.3 [0.12]	-0.32* [0.08]	-0.31 [0.10]	-0.23 [0.20]	-0.24 [0.23]	-0.35* [0.06]	-0.33* [0.09]	-0.2 [0.25]
Size (< 250)	-0.41*** [0.00]				-0.29*** [0.00]				-0.67*** [0.00]			
New private firm	0.19 [0.13]				-0.13 [0.32]				0.24* [0.08]			
Firm holding company	-0.07 [0.47]				0.11 [0.30]				-0.15 [0.22]			

	(1)	(2)	(3)	(4)	(5)	(6)	(7)	(8)	(9)	(10)	(11)
Foreign owner	−0.19 [0.46]				−0.27 [0.33]				0.22 [0.41]		
Exporter		0.15 [0.10]	0.11 [0.27]			0.16* [0.09]	0.14 [0.17]				
Website		0.52*** [0.00]	0.44*** [0.00]			0.34*** [0.00]	0.27** [0.02]			0.52*** [0.00]	0.48*** [0.00]
Intellectual property		0.52*** [0.00]	0.50*** [0.00]			0.44*** [0.00]	0.44*** [0.00]			0.46*** [0.00]	0.36** [0.02]
Third-party R&D		0.55*** [0.00]	0.50*** [0.00]			0.43*** [0.00]	0.38*** [0.00]			−0.09 [0.46]	−0.18 [0.16]
ISO certification		0.21** [0.02]	0.18* [0.06]			0.19* [0.05]	0.14 [0.14]			0.58*** [0.00]	0.54*** [0.00]
R&D expenditure (> 1 million rubles)			0.47*** [0.00]				0.51*** [0.00]				0.45*** [0.00]
Financial constraints				−0.23* [0.06]				−0.05 [0.71]			−0.34** [0.02]
Access to finance				0.12 [0.29]				0.21* [0.07]			0.2 [0.12]
Macroeconomic instability				−0.07 [0.44]				0.1 [0.26]			0.07 [0.51]
Regulatory constraints				0.04 [0.62]				0.01 [0.90]			0.02 [0.83]
Infrastructure constraints				−0.01 [0.88]				−0.05 [0.57]			0.05 [0.58]
Observations	808	978	940	996	808	978	940	996	808	978	940
Number of region code	49	48	48	49	49	48	48	49	49	48	49

Source: LME Survey (2005).

a. All regressions include a constant and sectoral dummies and use a random effects model. Significance is given by robust standard errors clustered by regions. P values are given in brackets.

*Significant at 10 percent; **significant at 5 percent; ***significant at 1 percent.

Table A3-10. Definitions of Independent Variables

Independent variable	Description
Introduction of new or improved product	Dummy that takes a value of 1 for firms that introduced a new or significantly improved product
Introduction of new or improved technology	Dummy that takes a value of 1 for firms that introduced a new or significantly improved production technology
Export of technology-intensive products	Dummy that takes a value of 1 for firms that export technology-intensive products (science-intensive and high-tech products)
Size (< 250)	Dummy that takes a value of 1 for firms with fewer than 250 employees
New private firm	Dummy that takes a value of 1 for firms established after 1992 and with no share of common stock owned by the government
Workforce tertiary education	Percent of workers with graduate education (at least 3 years of university-level studies)
R&D expenditure (> 1 million rubles)	Dummy that takes a value of 1 for firms with R&D expenditure greater than 1 million rubles
ISO certification	Dummy that takes a value of 1 for firms with ISO certification
Website	Dummy that takes a value of 1 for firms with their own website
Competitive pressure from imports	Dummy that takes a value of 1 for firms facing "noticeable" or "considerable" competitive pressure from imported products
Firm holding company	Dummy that takes a value of 1 for firms that belong to a holding company (a group of small companies)
Exporter	Dummy that takes a value of 1 for firms that export directly or through intermediaries
Foreign ownership	Dummy that takes a value of 1 for firms when more than 51 percent of common stock is owned by a foreign individual or company
Intellectual property	Dummy that takes a value of 1 for firms that acquired technological innovation through purchase of patents, licenses, production prototypes, utility models, and general know-how from either Russia or abroad
Third-party R&D	Dummy that takes a value of 1 for firms that acquire technological innovations as a result of third-party research and development
Reorganized organizational structure	Dummy that takes a value of 1 for firms that reorganized their organizational structure in recent years
R&D intensity	Ratio of firm's R&D expenditure to sales
Machinery and equipment	Dummy that takes a value of 1 for firms that acquired technological innovation through purchase of machinery and equipment
Financial constraints	Dummy variable that takes a value of 1 if the firms did not apply for credit due to financial constraints such as high interest rates or unavailable collateral

Table A3-10. Definitions of Independent Variables (*Continued*)

Independent variable	Description
Macroeconomic instability	Dummy that takes a value of 1 for firms that cite macroeconomic instability as an impediment for enterprise's activity and development
Regulatory constraints	Variable generated by conducting a factor analysis when firms cited regulatory constraints such as unpredictability of state regulations, labor regulations, and obtaining licenses as impediments to their development
Infrastructure constraints	Variable generated by conducting a factor analysis when firms cited regulatory constraints such as irregularity of power supply and communications as impediments to their development
Domestic competitive pressure	Dummy that takes a value of 1 for firms facing "noticeable" or "considerable" competitive pressure from domestically produced products
Foreign producer competitive pressure	Dummy that takes a value of 1 for firms facing "noticeable" or "considerable" competitive pressure from products produced by foreign firms operating in Russia.
Hired external consultants	Dummy that takes a value of 1 for firms that hired external management consultants
Outsourced to third-party contractor	Dummy that takes a value of 1 for firms that outsourced to a specialized third-party contractor
Introduced input quality control	Dummy that takes a value of 1 for firms that introduced input quality control for materials and interim quality control for technological parts and components of production
Access to finance	Dummy that takes a value of 1 when firms got loans from banks
Automated system of inventory management	Dummy that takes a value of 1 for firms that introduced automated inventory system
Age	The age of the firm since its establishment
China	Dummy that takes a value of 1 when country is China
Brazil	Dummy that takes a value of 1 when country is Brazil
South Africa	Dummy that takes a value of 1 when country is South Africa
R&D non-zero expenditure	Dummy that takes a value of 1 when a firm spends a positive amount on R&D

Source: LME Survey (2005).

Appendix 4

According to Barro and Lee (2001), in 2001 Russia had one of the most highly educated workforces in the world. With an average of 10.5 years of schooling for the population age 25 and over, Russia ranked seventh in the Barro-Lee sample of countries. In figure A4-1, which compares the educational attainment and GDP per capita of the Barro-Lee countries, Russia is an outlier. It is significantly above the fitted line in the first panel comparing mean years of educational attainment. Russia is ahead of other BRIC and transition countries as well as most OECD countries, leading Germany by 0.7 years, Japan by 0.8 years, and the United Kingdom by 1.1 years; only the United States is ahead of Russia, with an extra 1.8 years of education.

More than half (57 percent) of Russia's population age 25 and over has attained tertiary education, which is 13 percentage points more than in Canada and more than twice that figure in other postsocialist countries. That result is due in part to the very high proportion of the population that attended professional and technical colleges (SSUZ in Russian). However, if only attendance at university-level institutions (VUZ in Russian) is considered, Russia still ranks in the top ten countries, with 21 percent, sharing ninth and tenth place honors with Japan. Russia thus appears on the surface to be well situated to take advantage of knowledge-based economic activities requiring a well-educated workforce and a pool of researchers.

Quality of Education

Its educational achievements notwithstanding, Russia fares less well on international comparisons of education spending, with negative implications for the quality of education. The share of total educational expenditures in GDP (3.7 percent) is lower than that in developed and other transition countries but comparable to educational spending in the BRIC countries (table A4-1). If we look at annual expenditures per student relative to per capita GDP, Russian funding for education is skewed toward tertiary education, with a ratio of 34.9 percent, which is comparable to that of France but behind that of Germany and of Japan. For secondary education, by contrast, the ratio is 9.3 percent, a level comparable to levels in Indonesia, Uruguay, and Peru.

The ratio of students to teachers in Russian educational and training institutions is low by international standards. In primary schools, the ratio is seventeen pupils per teacher, typical for most of the developed and transition countries; the ratio in secondary schools, at 8.5 pupils per teacher, is the

Figure A4-1. Educational Attainment in Russia and Comparators

Panel A: Average years of schooling, total population age 25 and over, 2000[a]

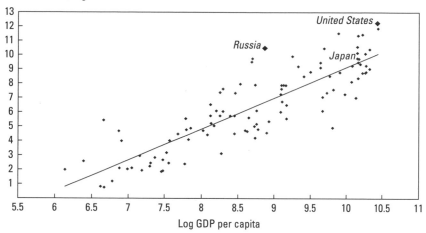

Panel B: Percentage of population age 25–64 that has attained tertiary education, 2003[b]

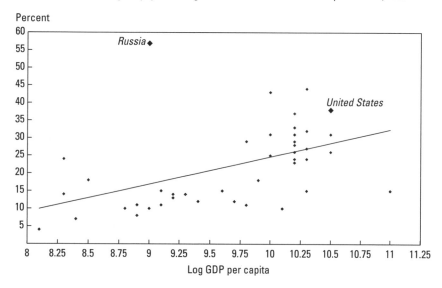

Source: Panel A, Barro and Lee (2001); panel B, OECD (2005a).
a. Purchasing power parity (2000), in constant 2000 international dollars.
b. Purchasing power parity (2003), in constant 2000 international dollars.

Table A4-1. Expenditures on Educational Institutions, 2002

Comparator	Expenditure on education as percent of GDP for all levels of education	Expenditure on education per student as percent of per-capita GDP based on full-time equivalents				
		Primary education	All secondary education	Tertiary professional or technical education	University and advanced research programs	All tertiary education
Developed countries						
France	6.1	18.3	30.8	35.7	33.2	33.8
Germany	5.3	17.0	26.4	21.5	44.5	41.3
Japan	4.7	22.5	25.6	35.2	44.0	43.1
United Kingdom	5.9	17.8	22.5	n.a.	n.a.	40.9
United States	7.2	22.2	25.1	n.a.	n.a.	56.8
Transition countries						
Czech Republic	4.4	12.5	21.9	16.3	40.2	37.6
Hungary	5.6	21.0	22.2	60.5	57.0	57.1
Poland	6.1	23.1	n.a.	n.a.	n.a.	43.2
BRIC countries						
Brazil (2001)	4.0	10.9	12.3	n.a.	n.a.	34.7
India (2001)	4.8	14.6	26.3	n.a.	n.a.	91.7
Russia (2000)	3.7	9.3	16.9	12.6	34.9	26.5

Source: OECD (2005a).

lowest in the world. In universities, the ratio is fifteen students per teacher, also lower than in most developed or transition economies. Low student-teacher ratios in the face of severe underfunding at lower levels of education can be explained by very low pay in the educational sector. In 2004, the average monthly wage in education was only 62 percent of the average wage in the economy as a whole and 53 percent of the average wage in industry (not controlling for individual characteristics). The likely consequences of low relative pay are poor selection of faculty, diminished incentives, and a lower quality of instruction.

Russia's performance on internationally comparable standardized tests supports that conclusion. According to TIMSS (Trends in International Mathematics and Science Study), which is administered to fourth- and eighth-grade students, in 2003 the scores of Russian fourth-grade students in mathematics and science were well above the international average. Russia occupied tenth and eleventh place among the twenty-eight countries that participated but lagged behind the leaders—Singapore, Hong Kong, and Taiwan. Russia continued to perform well at the eighth-grade level, scoring above the international average for the fifty participating countries but slipping to fourteenth and twenty-first place internationally (table A4-2).

Table A4-2. Russian Student Achievement Scores, 1995–2003

Test	1995	1999	2003	International mean score	International ranking
TIMSS (grade 8)					
Mathematics	524	526	508	467	14 in 50
Science	523	529	514	474	21 in 50
		2000	2003		
PISA (15-year-olds)					
Literacy	. . .	462	442	480	32 in 40
Mathematics	. . .	478	468	486	29 in 40
Science	. . .	460	489	488	24 in 40
Problem solving	. . .	. . .	479	486	28 in 40

Source: OECD (2005a).

On PISA (Programme for International Student Assessment), which assesses the quality of education for fifteen-year-old students, in 2003 Russia had an average literacy score of 442, markedly below the international average score of 480. That put Russia in thirty-second place among the forty countries participating and some 90 to 100 points behind the scores of the leaders—Finland, Korea, and Canada. Russia's scores on student assessments in mathematics, science, and problem solving were similarly below the international average. One explanation for Russia's lower scores on PISA is the test's focus (unlike TIMSS) on applied knowledge. The result is consistent with the observation that Russian schools emphasize the acquisition of encyclopedic knowledge over problem solving, innovative thinking, and creativity.[1]

These test scores reveal that the quality of lower secondary education in Russia is poorer than that in other developed and in almost all other transition countries and that many students enter the labor market poorly equipped for work. Furthermore, when one compares Russia's test scores on TIMSS and PISA for several years (table A4-2), it is clear that quality has deteriorated over time.

How about student performance at higher levels of education? The IALS (International Adult Literacy Survey) assesses how well equipped adults of different levels of education are for the demands of the workplace, including by testing their ability to apply knowledge to real-world situations—a core competency highly valued by most employers throughout the world. Russia has not participated in IALS, so no international comparisons can be made of how well Russian schools prepare students for the workplace at the higher levels of education not covered by TIMSS or PISA—including upper secondary schools and vocational, professional, and technical institutes below the university level. The quality and relevance in the workplace of the education and training provided by these institutions are likely to be low, given the fact that, by international standards, they are underfunded (table A4-1). While reforms have taken place, many vocational, professional, and technical institutions continue to operate along pretransition supply-driven lines, teaching narrowly specialized skills that do not meet emerging market needs.

The need for reform of the vocational education system (VET) in Russia is probably greater than the need for reform of either secondary or higher education. The inheritance of a supply-driven, tightly controlled, micromanaged system designed to fit into a planned economy has proven very difficult to reshape to fit Russia's current needs, not least because of stakeholders' resistance to change. With the demise of the majority of state-owned enterprises (SOEs) and of the traditional settings in which vocational education operated in the past, the gap between labor market trends and the qualifications and training provided by vocational schools has widened. The growing mismatch has occurred at the very time that rapid technological development and global competition require a more flexible, learning-ready, and skilled workforce.

Key aspects of the system that need to be reformed include governance, because a large number of different agencies oversee the VET system; rigid professional standards, which slow the adoption of a competency-based qualification system; lack of emphasis on core transferable skills; inadequate funding with which to finance operations and upgrade VET infrastructure and instructor skills; and consolidation of the fragmented VET system.[2]

Restructuring and Human Capital Accumulation

From 1989 to 2002, the proportion of persons with a university-level education (complete and incomplete) increased by 6 percentage points while the proportion with a tertiary-level (SSUV) professional and technical education rose 8 percentage points (table A4-3). The share of persons with primary, vocational, and general secondary education remained unchanged. The share of those with a lower secondary education decreased by 3.5 percentage points, while the share of those with a primary education fell by 4 percentage points and that of those with less than a primary education fell by 5.5 percentage points. Those shifts are even more pronounced if just the employed workforce is considered. The 2002 general census suggests that almost 60 percent of workers had some tertiary education, while the share of low-educated workers (those with less than lower secondary schooling) had fallen below 7 percent.

Table A4-3. Schooling Completion Rates, 1989 and 2002

Percent

Highest level of schooling attained	Total population age 15 years and older		Employed population age 15 years and older	
	1989	2002	1989	2002
Higher complete	11.3	16.2	14.6	23.3
Higher incomplete	1.7	3.1	1.3	3.0
Tertiary (SSUV)	19.2	27.5	24.3	35.7
Secondary vocational	13.0	12.8	17.8	15.3
Upper secondary general	17.9	17.7	20.8	16.2
Lower secondary general	17.5	13.9	13.5	5.6
Primary	12.9	7.8	6.7	0.9
Preprimary	6.5	1.0	1.1	0.1
Total	100	100	100	100

Source: Rosstat (2006).

How much of the increase in educational attainment of the workforce was the result of changes in the industrial and occupational composition of employment that accompanied restructuring, and how much was due to upgrading of education within industries and occupations? A decomposition of the effects of industrial and occupational changes, done separately for 1992–96 and for 1997–2002, suggests the following results:[3]

—In both periods, the largest contribution to the rising educational attainment of the workforce came from educational upgrading within industries and occupations rather than from the reallocation of educated workers across industries and occupations.

—In the initial 1992–96 period, about a quarter of all improvements in educational attainment were associated with shifts between industries, with inter-industry shifts having a slightly positive effect on demand for workers with higher education and stronger effects for those with secondary education and tertiary-level professional and technical training. Inter-occupation shifts contributed 18.5 percent and favored the least-educated group of workers.

—In the more recent 1997–2002 period, virtually all rising educational attainment came from educational upgrading within industries and occupations. The contribution of shifts across industries decreased to 2.6 percent, while that of inter-occupational shifts nearly halved, to 10.6 percent.

The decomposition highlights the fact that while changes in the structure of industry and occupations contributed modestly to the educational upgrading of the workforce in the early 1990s, most of the subsequent educational upgrading was independent of restructuring. That the subse-

Table A4-4. Returns to Schooling in Transition Countries

Percent

Country	Reform starting point	Pre-reform period	Early reform period	Late reform period
China	1979	0.015	0.025	0.061
Czech Republic	1991	0.039	0.070	0.083
Estonia	1992	0.025	0.076	n.a.
Hungary	1990	0.067	0.074	0.098
Poland	1990	0.046	0.067	0.072
Romania	1992	n.a.	0.046	0.056
Russia	1992	0.039	0.075	0.092
Slovak Republic	1991	0.038	0.061	0.097
Slovenia	1991	0.043	0.063	0.070
Ukraine	1992	0.040	n.a.	0.055

Source: Fleisher, Sabirianova Peter, and Wang (2004).

quent upgrading took place within all industries and occupations suggests the presence of a strong skill-biased change process in technological change and in the transformation of organizational and institutional arrangements in the workplace. The demand for education is likely to increase in such an environment, given the comparative advantage that educated workers have in implementing new technology or more generally in responding to disequilibria.[4]

Returns to Education

The rising returns to education in Russia help explain why demand for education was so strong over the transition period. Estimates of the rates of return, based on Mincer-type wage equations, suggest that private returns to an extra year of schooling prior to the transition were 2 to 3 percent, reflecting wage compression resulting from the government-set "wage grid" system. The demise of centralized wage setting led to a rapid increase in the education premium—returns to an extra year of education rose to about 7 to 8 percent in the first five years of transition and by an additional 2 to 3 percent in the later period, stabilizing at 8 to 10 percent by 2000–02.

Similar patterns of post-reform rising returns to education can be observed in other former socialist countries. Table A4-4 reports the returns to education estimated by Fleisher, Sabirianova Peter, and Wang (2004) for several transition countries, for three separate periods: pre-reform, early reform, and late reform. Rates of return to education almost doubled between the pre-reform and late reform period for many CIS countries, while those in Russia more than doubled. For China, increases in the returns to schooling were even more dramatic; it had much lower pre-reform rates of return, about 1.5 percent, and by the late reform period returns to schooling had quadrupled.

The phenomenon of rising returns to schooling is not unique to transition economies. Rates of return to schooling have risen in many countries—in Brazil over 1982–98 and in India over 1993-2004.[5] In these countries, as in the transition economies, economic change brought about by opening up economies to global trade or moving from a centrally planned to a market economy created strong demand for (and rising returns to) more educated and skilled workers.

Ranking of Investment Climate Constraints

Respondents to the Russian Competitiveness and Investment Climate Assessment Surveys (which include the LME Survey and the SE Survey) ranked "Lack of skilled and qualified workforce" as the number 2 investment climate constraint on enterprise growth and development (the number 1 constraint was taxation). Small enterprises with fewer than 100 employees (the SE sample) also ranked the skills constraint as major or severe, though not as significant as regulation or access and cost of finance (figure A4-2).[6]

Characteristics of Firms by Staffing Level

Table A4-5 reports the distribution of staffing levels for the Russia ICS sample according to several firm characteristics. The probability and level of understaffing were highest for firms operating in the textile industry. In that sector, more than 50 percent of respondents reported suboptimal staffing, with the staffing gap averaging 22.6 percent relative to desired levels. New firms established in or after 1992, small enterprises with fewer than 250 employees, firms operating in the metallurgy and machine-building sectors, and government-controlled firms (with more than 25 percent public ownership) also were more likely to report understaffing. Overstaffing was more prevalent among large firms (those with more than 1,000 employees) and firms in the chemical sector.

Staffing levels also are related to how firms rank their competitiveness. Firms rating themselves as having a medium to high level of competitiveness are more likely to have an optimal staffing level (60–61 percent) and less likely to report either understaffing (25–27 percent) or overstaffing (12–15 percent). On the other hand, firms that classified themselves as having "low" competitiveness are less likely to have an optimal staffing level (48 percent) and more likely to be understaffed (35 percent) or overstaffed (17 percent).

Figure A4-2. Enterprises Ranking Investment Climate Constraints as Major or Severe

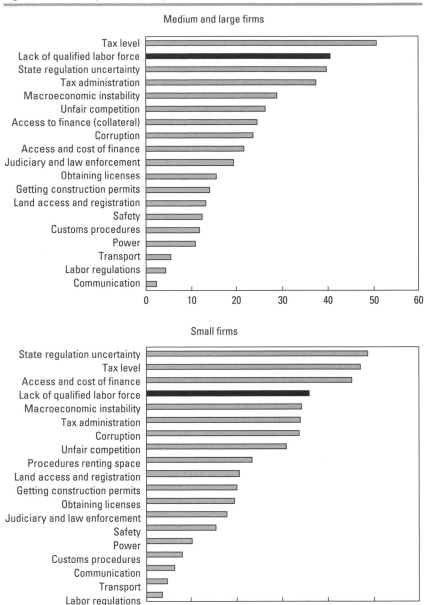

Source: LME Survey (2005) and SE Survey (2005).

Table A4-5. Characteristics of Firms, by Staffing Level

Firm characteristics	Optimal staffing — Percent of firms	Understaffed — Percent of firms	Understaffed — Percent of understaffing	Overstaffed — Percent of firms	Overstaffed — Percent of overstaffing
Industry					
Metallurgy	56.5	29.4	19.5	14.1	13.5
Chemicals	52.4	25	8.9	22.6	13.7
Machinery	57.1	29.6	17.9	13.3	15.3
Wood processing	60.7	25	11.6	14.3	11
Textiles	41.9	50.5	22.6	7.5	12.3
Food	74.3	15.5	13.2	10.2	16.8
Firm size					
Less than 250	62.9	29	22	8.1	13.6
251–500	58.4	28.2	15.2	13.3	16.8
501–1,000	61.4	22.8	8.6	15.8	15
More than 1,000	51.1	25.2	11.7	23.8	13.2
Exporter					
No	62.2	27.6	20	10.2	14.4
Yes	56.9	26.9	13.4	16.2	14.7
R&D spending					
No	63.6	26.8	16.9	9.6	14.4
Yes	56.3	27.7	17.1	16	14.7
New firm (after 1992)					
No	60	26.5	16.5	13.6	14.6
Yes	59.1	30.2	18.6	10.7	14.8
Foreign ownership					
No	61.8	26.8	16.9	11.5	14.3
Yes	53.3	29	17.3	17.8	15.3
Government control					
No	61	26.7	14.9	12.3	14.5
Yes	56.7	28.7	21.8	14.5	14.8
Competitiveness					
High	60.6	24.8	11.6	14.7	15.6
Medium	61.2	26.9	15.6	11.9	14.7
Low	47.9	35	25	17.1	14.7

Source: LME Survey (2005).

Whatever the factors that constrain understaffed firms from employing the personnel that they need or overstaffed firms from discharging redundant staff, nonoptimal staffing levels can adversely affect firms' perceptions of their level of competitiveness.

Major Problems by Unit within the Firm

The extent to which skill shortages are a problem varies across units within firms. Figure A4-3 graphs the percent of firms that ranked several key issues as being a major problem by unit within the firm—operations (or produc-

Figure A4-3. Major Problems, by Unit within the Firm

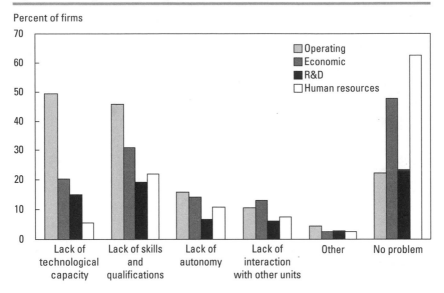

Source: Authors' calculations.

tion), economics (marketing, strategy), research and development (R&D), and human resources (HR). Most firms identified two major problems—lack of technological capacity and lack of skilled and qualified workers—both of which were concentrated in operations, that is, on production lines. A much smaller fraction of firms reported those problems as major constraints in the economics, R&D, or HR units.

Employment Protection Legislation

Table A4-6 reports estimates from an ordered probit model in which the index of difficulty of searching for and hiring skilled labor (based on a scale of 1 to 5, with 5 indicating maximum difficulty) is regressed on an index of employment protection legislation (EPL) as a constraint (determined by the sum of different EPL components that respondents indicate as problematic), wage levels in the firm (to test the Gimpelson hypothesis), and different enterprise characteristics that might shape demand for skills.[7]

In-Service Training

Simple tabulations suggest that about 70 percent of manufacturing enterprises in the LME sample provide employees with in-service training (see figure A4-4).

Table A4-6. Employment Protection Legislation as a Constraint on Hiring Skilled Labor[a]

| | Difficulty in searching for and hiring labor | | |
| | | Skilled workers | |
Dependent variable	Professionals	(1)	(2)
EPL index	.108	.094	...
	(3.03)***	(2.66)***	...
EPL is not a constraint	...	...	−.306
	...	...	(−3.94)***
Log (wages)	−.093	−.199	−.197
	(−1.69)*	(−3.66)***	(−3.63)***
Government controlled	.218	.021	.023
	(2.06)**	(0.20)	(0.21)
Foreign owned	−.153	−.036	−.042
	(−1.33)	(−0.32)	(−0.37)
Small firm (< 250 employees)	−.301	−.166	−.162
	(−3.84)***	(−2.17)**	(−2.11)**
R&D spending indicator	.208	.044	.033
	(2.64)***	(0.56)	(0.42)
New firm (after 1992)	.078	−.115	−.122
	(0.83)	(−1.25)	(−1.32)
Number of observations	896	898	898
Likelihood ratio (chi²)	123.85	181.13	189.56

Source: LME Survey (2005).

a. Industry and regional control variables included; Z values in parentheses. EPL index is the sum of rankings for EPL-related difficulties. *Significant at 10 percent; **significant at 5 percent; ***significant at 1 percent.

That figure is not comparable with figures for other countries because the LME Survey, by design, focuses on medium and large firms with more than 100 employees and larger firms on average tend to train more than small ones. The BEEPS and the SE Survey, in contrast, include smaller firms. To compare the incidence of training in Russia to that of OECD and selected comparator developing countries, we adopted a common weighting scheme based (arbitrarily) on the size distribution of firms in the India ICA survey. The size distribution of micro (15 or fewer workers), small (16–100 workers), medium (101–250 workers), and large firms (more than 250 workers) in India was 40, 44, 7, and 8 percent respectively; the corresponding size distribution for the pooled LME and SE surveys in Russia was 12, 16, 29, and 43 percent respectively. When the weighted figures are used, Russia stands out among the BRIC group with respect to the very small share of its workforce trained within the firm (7.7 percent of skilled and 1.4 percent of unskilled workers) compared with that of Brazil (53 percent and 45 percent) and China (44 and 28 percent) (table A4-7).

Figure A4-4. Incidence of Formal In-Service Training, OECD, Regional, and Country Means

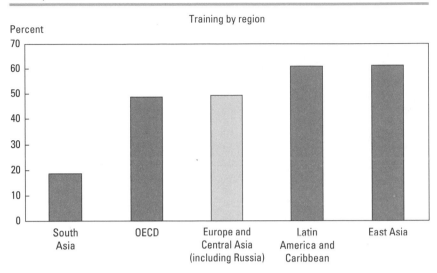

Training by region

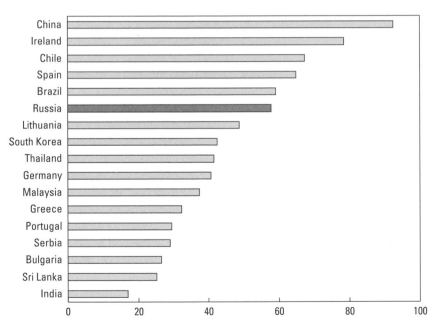

Training by country

Source: BEEPS (2006); World Bank (2002–2006); LME Survey (2005); and SE Survey (2005).

Table A4-7. Percent of Workforce Receiving In-Service Training in Russia and Comparators[a]

Country	Percent of workforce trained	
	Skilled	Unskilled
BRIC		
Russia	7.7	1.4
Brazil	52.8	45.4
China	44.5	28.5
Transition		
Bulgaria	24.0	13.0
Lithuania	11.9	4.0
Serbia	45.2	6.1
OECD		
Germany	37.3	27.2
Greece	53.6	36.8
Ireland	76.0	68.1
Portugal	75.2	50.2
Spain	76.1	56.2
South Korea	65.4	59.2
Developing		
Chile	48.3	36.0
Malaysia	69.6	52.7
Sri Lanka	47.4	34.1

Source: Authors' calculations, based on BEEPS (2006) and World Bank (2002–2006).

a. Country samples are restricted to manufacturing firms, and shares of workers trained are weighted estimates using the firm size distribution of India. WBES = World Bank Enterprise Survey for year indicated.

Training Determinants

The importance of the training correlates can be investigated within a regression framework by using a probit model.[8] The model estimates the probability of in-service training by regressing the "any formal training" variable on a set of explanatory variables, including measures of firm size, the share of workers with higher education, and other firm attributes such as export orientation, R&D spending, foreign or government ownership, and independent assessments of the region's investment climate risk (table A4-8). A corresponding set of regressions were estimated separately for the probability of in-house training and external training.

Training Impact on Firm-Level Productivity

The dependent variable—the logarithm of value added—was regressed on the logarithms of capital (book value of physical plant and equipment assets), alternative measure of training (any formal training, in-house or external

Table A4-8. Determinants of In-Service Training and Training by Source

Dependent variable: training (1,0)	Probit model specification		
	Any formal training	In-house training	External training
Firm size dummies			
Small size (101–250 workers)	0.084	0.108	0.102
	(1.42)	(1.41)	(1.56)
Medium size (251–1,000 workers)	0.219	0.22	0.257
	(3.76)***	(2.90)***	(3.96)***
Large size (> 1,000)	0.273	0.381	0.334
	(4.86)***	(4.58)***	(5.24)***
Percent higher-educated workers	0.003	0.000	0.003
	(2.45)**	(0.03)	(2.37)**
New firm (after 1992)	−0.034	−0.002	−0.068
	(−0.93)	(−0.05)	(−1.72)*
Exporter	0.055	0.065	0.063
	(1.71)	(1.82)*	(1.81)*
Positive R&D spending	0.081	0.074	0.06
	(2.29)**	(1.91)*	(1.59)
R&D sales ration	1.071	0.549	0.283
	(0.99)	(0.66)	(0.32)
Some foreign ownership (> 10 percent)	−0.05	0.037	−0.079
	(−1.06)	(0.74)	(−1.57)
Government control (> 25 percent)	0.059	−0.015	0.115
	(1.40)	(−0.33)	(2.58)**
Moderate IC risk	0.097	0.106	0.058
	(2.70)**	(2.59)**	(1.48)
High IC risk	0.012	0.039	−0.009
	(0.34)	(0.95)	(−0.22)
Missing values	Yes	Yes	Yes
Observations	990	981	986

Source: Pooled LME Survey and SE Survey. *Significant at 10 percent; **significant at 5 percent; ***significant at 1 percent.

training, and combinations of training sources), and a vector of control variables for worker attributes (mean years of education) and for location in moderate– or high–investment risk regions (see table A4-9). The production functions, estimated by ordinary least squares, implicitly treat the different training variables as being exogenously determined. That assumption may be suspect if the firms that train are also more productive and systematically self-select themselves into the training group on the basis of unobserved productivity traits, potentially biasing production function estimates. Qualitatively similar productivity (and wage) results obtain when self-selection into training is taken into account (see the discussion of human capital at the beginning of chapter 4).

Table A4-9. In-Service Training and Productivity[a]

Dependent variable: Log (valued added)	Model specifications		
	(1)	(2)	(3)
Log (capital)	0.197	0.196	0.196
	(6.77)***	(6.68)***	(6.58)***
Log (labor)	0.889	0.876	0.877
	(15.57)***	(15.45)***	(15.28)***
Mean years of education	0.055	0.056	0.057
	(2.69)**	(2.74)**	(2.72)**
Moderate regional IC risk	−0.277	−0.277	−0.272
	(−3.08)***	(−3.01)***	(−3.00)***
High regional IC risk	−0.332	−0.330	−0.333
	(−4.41)***	(−4.39)***	(−4.42)***
Any formal training	0.225		
	(3.48)***		
In-house training		0.092	
		(1.19)	
External training		0.22	
		(3.27)***	
Only in-house training			−0.003
			(−0.03)
Only external training			0.168
			(1.99)*
Both in-house and external training			0.281
			(4.06)***
Constant	8.64	8.695	8.708
	(30.41)***	(30.27)***	(30.21)***
Missing values	Yes	Yes	Yes
Regional cluster	Yes	Yes	Yes
Observations	784	784	784
R^2	0.64	0.64	0.64

Source: Authors' calculations.

a. Value of t statistics in parentheses. *Significant at 10 percent; **significant at 5 percent; ***significant at 1 percent.

Training Impact on Worker Wages

A wage model was estimated both at the firm level, using the logarithm of mean monthly wage and training of the firm, and for the pooled sample of occupations within each firm to exploit the availability of occupation-specific information on wages (see table A4-10). The logarithm of monthly per-worker firm-level or occupation-specific wages was regressed on the training variables, a vector of firm attributes, and average years of education of the workforce. For the occupational wage model, data on up to five occupational groups per firm were pooled and indicator variables included for managers, professionals, skilled workers, and unskilled workers (the omitted category

Table A4-10. Cross-Sectional Wage Models with Training[a]

Dependent variable: log (monthly wage)	Firm-level wage model		Occupation wage model	
	(1)	(2)	(1)	(2)
Constant	10.224	10.205	7.993	7.903
	(46.85)***	(47.58)***	(48.34)***	(49.81)***
Any formal training	0.16		0.091	
	(3.29)***		(1.58)	
In-house training		0.044		0.160
		(0.75)		(3.02)***
External training		0.178		0.096
		(4.21)***		(1.48)
Small enterprise (< 250)	−0.162	−0.147	−0.199	−0.177
	(−3.18)***	(−2.90)***	(−3.60)***	(−3.20)***
Some foreign ownership	−0.109	−0.101	0.084	0.087
	−(1.29)	−(1.21)	(1.17)	(1.23)
Government control	0.059	0.047	−0.06	−0.059
	(0.72)	(0.58)	(−0.84)	(−0.81)
Exporter	0.102	0.095	0.06	0.044
	(2.08)**	(1.84)*	(1.27)	(0.94)
Positive R&D spending	0.054	0.052	0.178	0.168
	(0.94)	(0.91)	(3.07)***	(2.93)***
R&D sales ratio	1.728	1.765	0.069	0.074
	(3.10)***	(3.37)***	(1.03)	(1.09)
New firm (after 1992)	0.018	0.021	−0.199	−0.177
	(0.28)	(0.33)	(−3.60)***	(−3.20)***
Mean years of education	0.061	0.061	n.a.	n.a.
	(3.82)***	(3.87)***		
Occupation dummies	No	No	Yes	Yes
Observations	923	923	3,026	3,026
R^2	0.08	0.09	0.241	0.253

Source: Authors' calculations.

a. Value of t statistics in parentheses. All regressions include control variables for missing values and for regions. *Significant at 10 percent; **significant at 5 percent; ***significant at 1 percent.

being "other white-collar employees") in place of mean years of education, with which occupations are closely correlated. The pooled sample consisted of 3,026 occupations from the 923 firms, and the regression model accounts for the common error structure for all occupations in the same firm.

Bivariate Probit Analysis of Training and Innovating

A bivariate probit model was jointly estimated for the two decision variables—whether or not to innovate and to train. Each equation had some explanatory variables in common but also others that were assumed to affect one decision but not the other.[9] The bivariate regression results for the innovation and training equations are reported in table A4-11. Many of the training results have been reported previously and will not be elaborated on fur-

Table A4-11. Bivariate Probit Regressions of Innovation and Training

Dependent variables: innovation and training	Coefficient	Z score
Innovation equation		
Firm size (101–250)	0.184	0.97
Firm size (251–1,000)	0.492	2.56
Firm size (> 1,000)	1.031	4.65
New equipment dummy[a]	0.264	3.04
Percent workforce with higher education	0.008	2.39
New firm dummy (established after 1992)	−0.019	−0.18
Exporter	0.361	4.05
Foreign ownership (≥ 10 percent)	0.111	0.88
Government control dummy (control ≥ 25 percent)	−0.009	−0.08
Received any government support for R&D	0.047	0.37
Constant	−0.939	−4.82
Training equation		
SME indicator (< 250 workers)	−0.521	−5.73
Percent workforce with higher education	0.010	2.84
New firm (established after 1992)	−0.115	−1.09
Exporter	0.202	2.17
Foreign ownership (≥ 10 percent)	−0.194	−1.45
Government control dummy (control ≥ 25 percent)	0.187	1.48
Difficulty hiring skilled and professional workers[b]	0.108	1.16
Firm overstaffed indicator	0.015	0.15
Firm understaffed indicator	0.460	3.05
Constant	0.403	3.49
Observations	979	
rho	0.1125	
Wald test − *chi*² (24)	170.2	
Log pseudo-likelihood = −1174.4488		
Prob > *chi*²	0	

Source: LME Survey (2005).

a. New equipment = 1 if less than 50 percent of equipment is fully depreciated.

b. Difficulty of hiring skilled and professional workers = 1 if firm gave difficulty for either skill group a 4 or 5 on a scale of 1 to 5 (5 being the most difficult).

ther. The innovation equation, however, is new. The results suggest that innovating firms tend to be larger, to export, to use relatively new machinery and equipment, and to employ a more educated workforce. More pertinent is the estimate of *rho,* which measures the covariance in the errors of the innovation and training equations. Both Wald and likelihood ratio tests reject the null hypothesis that *rho* equals 0; that is, they confirm that the innovation and training decisions were made jointly.

The bivariate probit model also yields estimates of the probabilities that firms choose one investment activity but not the other, both activities together, or neither. To simplify description, let Pr (*ij*) be the joint probability of innovation *i* and training *j*. For the LME sample as a whole, the least

Table A4-12. Predicted Joint Probabilities of Innovation and Training[a]

Firm characteristics	Innovate (0) Train (0)	Innovate (0) Train (1)	Innovate (1) Train (0)	Innovate (1) Train (1)
Total sample	0.19	0.34	0.11	0.36
Small enterprise (< 250)				
No	0.11	0.33	0.10	0.46
Yes	0.30	0.36	0.13	0.22
Exporter				
No	0.25	0.38	0.11	0.26
Yes	0.11	0.30	0.11	0.47
Staffing				
Optimal	0.20	0.33	0.12	0.34
Understaffed	0.20	0.35	0.11	0.34
Overstaffed	0.09	0.37	0.06	0.47

Source: LME Survey (2005).
a. Predicted probabilities from bivariate probit model; see table 4A-11.

likely probabilities are Pr (10)—firms innovate but do not train (10 percent)—and Pr (00), firms engage in neither activity (11 percent). It is much more common for firms to train but not innovate, Pr (01) of 36 percent, or invest in both innovation and training at the same time, Pr (11) of 22 percent. The model also yields estimates of the probability of one investment activity conditional on the other taking place. Denote these as Pr $(i|j)$ and Pr $(j|i)$. The conditional probability of innovating given training is not high, Pr $(i|j)$ of 43 percent, suggesting that firms have many reasons for training besides supporting innovation. In contrast, the conditional probability of training given innovation is much higher, Pr $(j|i)$ of 73 percent, supporting the maintained hypothesis that skills and training are needed to complement investments in the innovative activities of the firm.

Table A4-12 reports the predicted joint probabilities of innovation and training disaggregated by several firm attributes. The tabulations reported here are restricted to firm characteristics that are able to discriminate among the different predicted joint probabilities. First, they suggest that larger firms are more likely to invest in both innovation and training (46 percent) or training alone (33 percent) than small firms, which are more likely just to train (36 percent) than to invest in both innovation and training (22 percent). Similarly, exporting firms are more likely to both innovate and train (47 percent) than to invest in training alone (30 percent), while nonexporters are more likely just to train (38 percent). Finally, overstaffed firms are more likely to invest in both innovation and training

Table A4-13. Production Functions and Wage Models Estimated with Exogenous or Predicted Innovation and Training[a]

Dependent variables	Log (value added)		Log (wages)	
	(1)	(2)	(1)	(2)
Predicted joint probabilities				
Innovate (0); train (1)	−0.186		1.437	
	(−0.23)		(2.31)*	
Innovate (1); train (0)	0.712		2.490	
	(0.50)		(2.66)**	
Innovate (1); train (1)	1.199		1.889	
	(2.66)**		(4.32)**	
Exogenous innovation and training				
Innovate (0); train (1)		0.242		0.153
		(2.60)**		(2.63)**
Innovate (1); train (0)		0.139		0.100
		(1.13)		(1.50)
Innovate (1); train (1)		0.303		0.165
		(3.12)***		(2.66)**
Mean years of workforce education	0.036	0.05	0.038	0.054
	(1.82)*	(2.55)**	(2.79)***	(3.39)***
Observations	775	784	911	923
R^2	0.64	0.63	0.13	0.12

Source: LME Survey (2005).

a. Production functions include logarithms of capital, labor, and controls for missing values and region. Wage equations include firm size, ownership, new firm, and controls for missing values, region, and industry. *Significant at 10 percent; **significant at 5 percent; ***significant at 1 percent.

(47 percent) or in training alone (37 percent) than are optimally staffed or understaffed firms, which are equally likely to do both or to invest in training alone (about 33–35 percent).

Table A4-13 reports estimates of production functions and wage equations that include predicted joint probabilities of innovation and training, with the omitted category being the prediction of investing in neither innovation nor training. By construction, these predicted joint probabilities are uncorrelated with the error terms of the model, yielding unbiased (but inefficient) estimates of the innovation and training variables.

For comparison, the same models are estimated using indicator variables of innovation and training, both treated as being exogenously determined outside the model, to characterize firms as just innovating, just training, or doing both. The production function results indicate that only joint investments in innovation and training improve firm-level productivity. That may be contrasted with the alternative "exogenous" model, wherein both "just training" and "both training and innovating" are associated with productivity increases, but not "just innovating." The wage regression using predicted values suggests that all three states—just training, just innovating, and investing in both activities—are associated with positive wage gains. Curiously, just innovating but not training has the largest coefficient. The alternative "exogenous" wage model also yields different results, namely that both "just training" and "investing in both" show wage gains, but "just innovating" does not.

Notes

1. Fretwell and Wheeler (2001).

2. Canning and others (2004).

3. A shift-share approach is used to decompose changes over time in educational attainment attributable to different components: one that measures the results of shifts in the industry and occupational composition of employment, holding education constant; another that measures the contribution of rising education, holding industry and occupation mix constant; and a third interaction term. The 1992–96 decomposition uses six education, fifty occupation, and fifteen industry groups, while the 1997–2002 decomposition relies on seven education, thirty-two occupation, and nineteen industrial groups.

4. Schultz (1975); Bartel and Lichtenberg (1987); Tan (2005).

5. Blom, Holm-Nielsen, and Verner (2001); Riboud, Tan, and Savchenko (2006).

6. In addition to ranking each constraint on a scale of 1 to 5, with 5 being a severe constraint, enterprises in the LME and SE surveys also were asked to identify the most severe constraint on the previous list. That alternative ranking yielded broadly similar findings, with lack of a qualified workforce being ranked number 3 by medium and large enterprises and number 2 by small enterprises.

7. Gimpelson (2004) hypothesized that understaffing may be the result of low-efficiency firms being unable to pay competitive wages.

8. The advantage of regression analysis over tabular information is that the independent effects of each variable (or set of variables) can be analyzed holding constant the effects of other hypothesized correlates.

9. Each equation must be identified by having one or more instruments that affect (or are highly correlated with) that choice variable but not the other. For the innovation equation, the instruments were indicators for having newer equipment and having received government support for R&D. For the training equation, the corresponding instruments were an index of difficulty of searching for and hiring professionals and skilled workers and whether the enterprise was understaffed or overstaffed.

Appendix 5

Survey data show that firms facing more intense competitive pressures from domestic producers, from foreign producers operating domestically, or from imported goods also tend to be more innovative. Table A5-1 examines the effects of such competitive pressures, first on the sum total of innovation activities (from introducing new products and technologies to initiating training programs) and second on the likelihood that firms introduce fundamentally new product lines. Firms that face greater competitive pressures are more likely to do both. On the other hand, firms that enjoy a monopolist position or other forms of protection not only innovate less than firms facing greater competitive pressures, but they also contribute to an unpredictable and uncertain regulatory environment. Monopolistic firms tend to obtain more favorable treatment from government authorities: they tend to suffer less from any given investment climate constraint than other firms, pay less in bribes to secure government contracts, suffer less from nonpayment by customers, and spend less on protection payments. It is likely that their differential treatment is due to loopholes, exemptions, or special exceptions in existing legislation as well as to the discretionary interpretation and application of regulations by public authorities.

There is evidence, moreover, that firms facing the greatest competitive pressures (from domestic and foreign manufacturers) also face the severest investment climate impediments, yet they are the most innovative companies in the Russian economy. Table A5-2 shows the relationship between the competitive pressures that firms face and the severity of various investment climate constraints. The constraints were generated by using principal component weightings of the individual impediments, generating normally distributed, continuous variables with mean 0. The results also control for firm size, whether or not the firm is a member of a holding company or financial-industrial group, and a firm-specific, systemic "optimism" or favorable bias toward the investment climate. Sectoral dummies also are included. The within-region effects shown in table A5-2 indicate that when systemic biases toward the investment climate in general were controlled for, firms facing competitive pressures were more likely to face harsher governance constraints (poorly functioning legal system, policy uncertainty, crime, and unfair competition), less access to and higher costs of finance, higher taxes and weak tax administration, more problems with labor (skills and regulations), and steeper administrative barriers (customs and licensing barriers). Table A5-3 outlines the impact of competitive pressures on the costs of doing business.

Table A5-1. Competitive Pressures and Innovation[a]

Independent variable	Innovative activities	Introduction of new product
Competitive pressures	0.0206***	0.0669***
	(0.0072)	(0.0255)
External consultant	0.2513***	0.4342**
	(0.0475)	(0.1896)
FIG dummy	−0.0681*	−0.1076
	(0.0410)	(0.1463)
Log (size)	0.1962***	0.2867***
	(0.0204)	(0.0755)
Newly private	0.0246	0.2528
	(0.0572)	(0.2048)
Age	−0.0020***	0.0002
	(0.0006)	(0.0021)
Major city	0.0963**	0.1628
	(0.0456)	(0.1647)
Observations	988	985
Number of regions	46	45
Log likelihood	−1930.97	−559.79
chi^2	58.52	58.52
Probability	(0.0000)	(0.0000)

Source: LME Survey (2005).

a. The dependent variable in model 1 estimates the number of innovative activities in which a firm is engaged. Estimation is by conditional Poisson with regional fixed effects. The dependent variable in model 2 is coded 1 if a firm introduced a new product line during 2003–04, and estimation is by conditional logit regression with regional fixed effects. Competitive pressures is an index based on firms' scoring the impact of competition with 1 (other domestic manufacturers), 2 (imported products), or 3 (foreign producers operating in Russia). FIG dummy is coded 1 if the firm is a group-member of a holding company, 0 otherwise. Size is number of permanent employees in 2004. Newly private is coded 1 if the firm began operations as a private firm after 1992, 0 otherwise. Age is the number of years a firm has been in continuous operation. Major city is coded 1 if the firm is located in a major urban area.

***$p < 0.01$; **$p < 0.05$; *$p < 0.10$.

Table A5-2. Competitive Pressures and Investment Climate Constraints[a]

Independent variable	Governance	Finance	Land	Taxation	Labor	Infrastructure	Administrative barriers
Log (size)	0.0001	0.0799*	-0.0611	-0.0930**	0.0749*	-0.0094	0.1451***
	(0.0577)	(0.0459)	(0.0454)	(0.0427)	(0.0406)	(0.0468)	(0.0403)
Competitive pressures	0.0701***	0.0419***	0.0207	0.0555***	0.0553***	0.0158	0.0420***
	(0.0194)	(0.0152)	(0.0152)	(0.0143)	(0.0136)	(0.0157)	(0.0136)
FIG	-0.2522**	-0.0106	-0.1537*	-0.1892**	0.2390***	0.1311	-0.0794
	(0.1111)	(0.0872)	(0.0873)	(0.0821)	(0.0782)	(0.0901)	(0.0775)
Bias	-1.6816***	-0.1315	-0.8513*	-1.4076***	-1.1044**	-0.8737*	-1.2183***
	(0.6356)	(0.5007)	(0.4997)	(0.4703)	(0.4477)	(0.5158)	(0.4445)
Observations	985	961	982	987	988	987	985
Regions	49	49	49	49	49	49	49
R^2	0.0399	0.0207	0.0276	0.0540	0.0552	0.0257	0.0660

Source: LME Survey (2005).

a. Estimation is by OLS regression using within-region fixed effects. Sectoral dummies and intercepts are included in regressions but are not reported. Standard errors are in parentheses. Dependent variables are principal components groupings of various investment climate constraints. Size is the number of permanent employees in 2004. Competitive pressures is an index based on firms' scoring the "impact of competition" with 1 (other domestic manufacturers), 2 (imported products), or 3 (foreign producers operating in Russia). FIG dummy is coded 1 if the firm is a group-member of a holding company, 0 otherwise. Bias is a valence variable intended to serve as a proxy for firm-specific biases toward the investment climate in general. Higher levels of "bias" mean that the firm is more favorably disposed (less likely to complain about) investment climate constraints.

***p < 0.01; **p < 0.05; *p < 0.10.

Table A5-3. Competitive Pressures and Business Costs[a]

Independent variable	Bribes for government contracts (percent value)	Excess employment (percent of staff)	Sales on credit (percent of sales)	Nonpayment
Competitive pressures	0.1397**	0.5963*	1.0108**	0.1524***
	(0.0571)	(0.3376)	(0.4920)	(0.0292)
Former state-owned	0.2873	3.1864	−5.3956	−0.1708
enterprise	(0.3782)	(2.2147)	(3.7059)	(0.1900)
Age	0.0037	−0.0942	−0.0260	0.0158**
	(0.0125)	(0.0726)	(0.1204)	(0.0076)
Medium	0.3280	−7.9645***	2.5916	0.5545***
	(0.3606)	(2.1213)	(3.1119)	(0.1821)
Large	−0.1707	−10.2951***	0.7585	0.3727
	(0.5021)	(2.9171)	(4.4591)	(0.2513)
Observations	875	955	524	972
R^2	0.0452	0.0478	0.0348	0.0691

Source: LME Survey (2005).

a. Estimations for the first three columns are by OLS regression and for the fourth column by logistic regression (pseudo R^2 is reported). Dummies for city type (village, town, minor city, major city) and intercepts are included in regressions but are not reported. Standard errors are in parentheses.

***$p < 0.01$; **$p < 0.05$; *$p < 0.10$.

Table A5-4. Business Association Membership and Innovative Activities[a]

Independent variable	Introduced new product	Introduced new technology	Outsourced production	Obtained quality certification	Agreed to new JV
Business association	0.7161***	0.5212**	1.0996***	1.4806***	1.8093***
member	(0.2345)	(0.2374)	(0.3698)	(0.3332)	(0.6122)
Former state-owned	−0.1720	−0.0700	−0.3738	−0.2077	0.4645
enterprise	(0.2836)	(0.2752)	(0.4877)	(0.4348)	(0.9836)
Age	−0.0018	0.0016	−0.0028	0.0071	0.0099
	(0.0091)	(0.0089)	(0.0173)	(0.0115)	(0.0295)
Medium	0.2219	0.0809	0.7382*	0.4904	0.0503
	(0.2413)	(0.2369)	(0.3917)	(0.3700)	(0.7130)
Large	0.6651**	0.3162	−0.7605	0.4910	0.3921
	(0.3372)	(0.3394)	(0.7447)	(0.5080)	(0.8295)
Percent foreign	0.0001	0.0037	−0.0056	−0.0004	−0.0217***
owned	(0.0038)	(0.0037)	(0.0057)	(0.0061)	(0.0079)
Percent state	0.0252	0.0195	0.0433	0.0354	−0.0315
owned	(0.0289)	(0.0276)	(0.0279)	(0.0277)	(0.0723)
Observations	539	539	539	539	472
R^2	0.0347	0.0246	0.0910	0.1112	0.1888
chi^2	24.50	18.38	25.48	38.53	23.80
Probability < chi	(0.0108)	(0.0731)	(0.0077)	(0.0001)	(0.0081)

Source: BEEPS (2006).

a. Estimation is by logistic regression. Dummies for city type (village, town, minor city, major city) and intercepts are included in regressions but are not reported. Standard errors are in parentheses.

***$p < 0.01$; **$p < 0.05$; *$p < 0.10$.

Table A5-5. Business Association Membership and Investment Climate[a]

Independent variable	Excess employment	Regulatory burden (percent of management time)	Predictability of regulations	Bribe payments for government contracts
Competitive pressures	0.9276**	0.1873	−0.1101***	0.2223***
	(0.3815)	(0.2248)	(0.0289)	(0.0406)
Business association membership	5.7940	10.3745***	−0.7855*	1.5297***
	(5.9636)	(3.5304)	(0.4522)	(0.5720)
Competitive pressures × business association membership	−1.3731*	−0.7884*	0.1074*	−0.1715**
	(0.7918)	(0.4667)	(0.0589)	(0.0731)
Former state-owned enterprise	2.8933	−0.0989	0.1507	0.5541***
	(2.2126)	(1.3062)	(0.1617)	(0.2146)
Age	−0.0908	−0.0399	−0.0131**	0.0158**
	(0.0725)	(0.0427)	(0.0057)	(0.0062)
Medium	−7.3537***	−1.1862	0.2866*	0.3478*
	(2.1409)	(1.2552)	(0.1568)	(0.1876)
Large	−8.8897***	−1.6304	0.5503**	0.2484
	(2.9730)	(1.7881)	(0.2156)	(0.2540)
Observations	955	966	943	824
R^2	0.0545	0.0287	0.0124	0.0402

Source: BEEPS (2006).

a. Estimations for the first and second columns are by OLS regression and for the third and fourth columns by ordered-logit regression (pseudo R^2 is reported). Dummies for city type (village, town, minor city, major city) and intercepts are included in regressions but are not reported. Standard errors are in parentheses.

***$p < 0.01$; **$p < 0.05$; *$p < 0.10$.

References

Abramovitz, Moses. 1956. "Resources and Output Trends in the United States since 1870." *American Economic Review* 46 (2): 5–23.

Acemoglu, Daron, and Jorn-Steffen Pischke. 1998. "Why Do Firms Train? Theory and Evidence." *Quarterly Journal of Economics* 113 (1): 79–119.

Acs, Zoltan J., and David B. Audretsch. 1988. "Innovation and Firm Size in Manufacturing." *Technovation* 7 (3): 197–210.

Aghion, Philippe, and others. 2002. "Competition and Innovation: An Inverted U Relationship." Working Paper 9269. Cambridge, Mass.: National Bureau of Economic Research.

Aidis, Ruta, and Yuko Adachi. 2007. "Russia: Firm Entry and Survival Barriers." *Economic Systems* 31 (4): 391–411.

Ark, Bart van, and Marcin Piatkovski. 2004. "Productivity, Innovation, and Investment Climate Surveys in Old and New Europe." *International Economics and Economics Policy* 1 (2–3): 215–46.

Barro, Robert J., and Jong-Wha Lee. 2001. "International Data on Education Attainment: Updates and Implications." *Oxford Economic Papers* 53 (3): 541–63.

Bartel, Anne, and Frank Lichtenberg. 1987. "The Comparative Advantage of Educated Workers in Implementing New Technology." *Review of Economics and Statistics* 69 (1): 1–11.

Batra, Geeta, Daniel Kaufmann, and Andrew H. W. Stone. 2003. "The Firms Speak: What the World Business Environment Survey Tells Us about Constraints on Private Sector Development." Washington: World Bank.

Becker, Gary S. "Human Capital." 2002. In *The Concise Encyclopedia of Economics,* edited by David R. Henderson. Indianapolis: Liberty Fund.

BEEPS (Business Environment and Enterprise Performance Surveys). 2006. European Bank for Reconstruction and Development and World Bank (http://info.worldbank.org/governance/beeps).

Bell, Martin, and Keith Pavitt. 1992. "National Capacities for Technological Accumulation: Evidence and Implications for Developing Countries." Annual Bank Conference on Development Economics (ABCDE). Washington: World Bank.

Bhojwani, Hiro. 2006. "Report on the Indian Public Research and Development System." Washington: World Bank.

Blanchflower, David G., and Simon M. Burgess. 1996. "Job Creation and Job Destruction in Great Britain in the 1980s." *Industrial and Labor Relations Review* 50 (1): 17–38.

Blom, Andreas, Lauritz Holm-Nielsen, and Dorte Verner. 2001. "Education, Earnings, and Inequality in Brazil: 1982–1998: Implications for Education Policy." World Bank Policy Research Working Paper 2686. Washington: World Bank.

Bortnik, Ivan. 2004. "Desiat' let razvitia malogo innovatsionnogo predprinematel'stva v Rossii" [Ten Years of the Development of Innovative Small Entrepreneurship in Russia]. Moscow: Foundation for Assistance to Small Innovative Enterprises.

Broadman, Harry. 2006. "From Disintegration to Integration." Washington: World Bank.

Canning, Mary, and others. 2004. *The Modernization of Education in Russia.* Moscow: World Bank.

Carlin, Wendy, Mark Schaffer, and Paul Seabright. 2004. "A Minimum of Rivalry: Evidence from Transition Economies on the Importance of Competition for Innovation and Growth." William Davidson Institute Working Paper 670. University of Michigan, Stephen M. Ross Business School.

Carlin, Wendy, and others. 2001. "Competition and Enterprise Performance in Transition Economies: Evidence from a Cross-Country Survey." William Davidson Institute Working Paper 376. University of Michigan, Stephen M. Ross Business School.

CEFIR (Center for Economic and Financial Research at the New Economic School). 2005. *Monitoring the Administrative Barriers to Small Business Development in Russia: The Fifth Round.* CEFIR Policy Paper Series. Moscow: New Economic School.

CEFIR and IET. 2006. "Survey of Corporate Governance in Russian Companies in 2005 and 2006." Unpublished. Moscow.

Coe, David T., Elhanan Helpman, and Alexander W. Hoffmaister. 1995. "North-South R&D Spillovers." *Economic Journal* 107 (440): 134–49.

CSRS (Center for Science Research and Statistics). 2005. "Science in Russia at a Glance." In *2005 Statistical Yearbook.* Moscow.

Dossani, Rafiq, and Martin Kenney. 2001. "Creating an Environment: Developing Venture Capital in India." Stanford University, Asia/Pacific Research Center (A/PARC).

Enos, John L. 1962. *Petroleum Progress and Profits: A History of Process Innovation.* MIT Press.

Eurostat (Statistical Office of the European Communities). Various years. *Europe in Figures.* Luxembourg: Office for Official Publications of the European Communities.

Expert Rating Agency. 2006. *Investment Rating for Russia's Regions, 2005–2006.* Moscow (www.raexpert.org/ratings/regions/2006).

FIAS (Foreign Investment Advisory Service). 2004a. *Administrative Barriers to Investment.* Washington: World Bank.

———. 2004b. *Russia's Runaway Investors.* Washington: World Bank.

Fleisher, Belton, Klara Sabirianova Peter, and Xiaojun Wang. 2004. "Returns to Skills and the Speed of Reforms: Evidence from Central and Eastern Europe, China, and Russia." William Davidson Institute Working Paper 703. University of Michigan, Stephen M. Ross Business School.

Fretwell, David, and Anthony Wheeler. 2001. "Russian Secondary Education and Training." World Bank Secondary Education Series. Washington: World Bank.

Frye, Timothy. 2002. "Capture or Exchange: Business Lobbying in Russia." *Europe-Asia Studies* 54 (7): 1017–1036.

Gill, Indermit, Fred Fluitman, and Amit Dar. 2000. *Vocational Education and Training Reform: Matching Skills to Markets and Budgets.* Oxford University Press.

Gimpelson, Vladimir. 2004. "Defitsit Kvalifikatsii i Navykov na Rynke Truda: Nedostatok Predlozhenia, Ogranichenie Sprosa, ili Lozhnie Signaly Roboto-datelei?" [Qualifications and Skill Deficiency in the Labor Market: Lack of Supply, Demand Constraints, or False Signals of Employers?]. Working Paper 3/2004/01. Moscow: Higher School of Economics.

Goskomstat (State Committee for Statistics, Russian Federation). 1995. *Natsional'nye Scheta Rossii v 1989–1994 Godakh* [National Accounts of Russia, 1989–1994]. Moscow.

Griliches, Zvi. 1986. "Productivity, R&D, and Basic Research at the Firm Level in the 1970s." Working Paper W1547. Cambridge, Mass.: National Bureau of Economic Research.

———. 1994. "R&D, Patents, and Productivity." In *NBER Conference Proceedings.* University of Chicago Press.

———. 1998. *R&D and Productivity: The Econometric Evidence.* University of Chicago Press.

Haltiwanger, John, and Helena Schweiger. 2004. "Firm Performance and the Business Climate: Where Does ICA Fit In?" University of Maryland.

Hare, Paul, Mark Schaffer, and Anna Shabunina. 2004. "The Great Transformation: Russia's Return to the World Economy." CERT Discussion Papers 0401. Edinburgh: Heriot-Watt University, Centre for Economic Reform and Transformation.

Helpman, Elhanan, and Manuel Trajtenberg. 1996. "Diffusion of General Purpose Technologies." Working Paper 5773. Cambridge, Mass.: National Bureau of Economic Research.

Hoekman, Bernard, and Beata Smarzynska Javorcik. 2006. *Global Integration and Technology Transfer.* Washington: Palgrave Macmillan and World Bank.

HSE (Higher School of Economics). 2005. *Nauka v Rossyiskoy Federatsii: Statistichesky sbornik* [Science in the Russian Federation: Statistical Handbook]. Moscow.

ILO (International Labor Organization). 2005. *The Key Indicators of the Labor Database.* Geneva.

IMEMO (Institute of World Economy and International Relations). *Russian Economic Barometer (REB) Surveys: 1991 to the Present.* Moscow (www.imemo.ru/eng/barom/survey.htm).

Jaffe, Adam B., and Manuel Trajtenberg. 2002. *Patents, Citations, and Innovations: A Window on the Knowledge Economy.* MIT Press.

Javorcik, Beata Smarzynska. 2004. "Does Foreign Direct Investment Increase the Productivity of Domestic Firms? In Search of Spillovers through Backward Linkages." *American Economic Review* 94 (3): 605–27.

Kee, Hiau Looi, Alessandro Nicita, and Marcelo Olarreaga. 2006. "Estimating Trade Restrictiveness Indices." World Bank Policy Research Paper 3840. Washington: World Bank.

Keller, Wolfgang. 2002. "Trade and Transmission of Technology." *Journal of Economic Growth* 7 (1): 5–24.

———. 2004. "International Technology Diffusion." *Journal of Economic Literature* 42 (3): 752–82.

Kikeri, Sunita, Thomas Kenyon, and Vincent Palmade. 2006. *Reforming the Investment Climate: Lessons for Practitioners.* Washington: International Finance Corporation.

Kraay, Aart. 1999. "Exportations et Performances Economique: Etude d'un Panel d'Enterprises Chinoises" [Exports and Economic Performance: Study of a Sample of Chinese Enterprises]. *Revue d'Economie du Developpement* [Review of Development Economics] 1 (2): 183–207.

Krueger, Alan, and Mikael Lindahl. 2001. "Education for Growth: Why and for Whom?" *Journal of Economic Literature* 39 (4): 1101–36.

Lazareva, Olga, Irina Denisova, and Sergei Tsukhlo. 2006. "Hiring or Retraining: Russian Firms' Experience." Working Paper 3/2006/11. Moscow: Higher School of Economics.

Lederman, Daniel, and William F. Maloney. 2003a. "Innovation in Mexico: NAFTA Is Not Enough." Washington: World Bank, Office of the Chief Economist.

———. 2003b. "R&D and Development." Policy Research Working Paper 3024. Washington: World Bank.

Litwack, John. 2005. "Achieving Diversified Growth in Russia." Washington: World Bank.

LME Survey (Russian Competitiveness and Investment Climate Assessment Surveys: Large and Medium Enterprise Survey). 2005. Washington: World Bank.

Middleton, John, Adrian Ziderman, and Arvil van Adams. 1993. *Skills for Productivity.* Oxford University Press.

Ministry of Education and Science, Russian Federation. 2006. *Strategiya Razvitiya Nauki i Innovatsii v Rossiiskoi Federatsii na Period do 2015* [Research and Development Strategy of the Russian Federation to 2015]. Moscow.

Ministry of Industry, Science, and Technology, Russian Federation. 2001. "Role of the State in Creating a Favorable Innovation Climate in Russia: Background Report." OECD Helsinki Seminar, March 1–2.

OECD (Organization for Economic Cooperation and Development). 1994. *Science, Technology, and Innovation Policies: Federation of Russia.* Vol. 1. Paris: Centre for Co-Operation with the Economies in Transition.

———. 2004a. ANBERD (Analytical Business Enterprise Research and Development) Database. Paris.

————. 2004b. *Science, Technology, and Industry Outlook 2004: Multinational Enterprises and Productivity Growth: Insight at the Firm Level*. Paris.

————. 2004c. STructural ANalysis (STAN) Indicators Database. Paris (www.oecd.org/sti/stan/indicators).

————. 2005. *Science, Technology and Industry Scoreboard 2005*. Paris.

————. 2005a. Patent Database. Paris (www.oecd.org/sti/ipr-statistics).

————. 2005b. *Fostering Public-Private Partnership for Innovation in Russia*. Paris.

————. 2006. *Investment Policy Review of the Russian Federation*. Paris.

Peter, Klara Sabirianova. 2001. "The Great Human Capital Reallocation: A Study of Occupational Mobility in Transitional Russia." EERC Working Paper Series. Moscow: EERC (Economic Education and Research Consortium) Russia and CIS.

Reynolds, Sarah. 2004. "Competition Law and Policy in Russia." *OECD Journal of Competition Law and Policy* 6 (3): 7–83.

Riboud, Michelle, Hong Tan, and Yevgeniya Savchenko. 2006. "Globalization and Education and Training in South Asia." Washington: World Bank.

Rodrik, Dani. 2006a. "Industrial Development: Stylized Facts and Policies." Unpublished. Harvard University, John F. Kennedy School of Government.

————. 2006b. "What Is So Special about China's Exports?" Faculty Research Working Paper Series RWP06-001. Harvard University, Kennedy School of Government.

Rosstat (State Statistics Service, Russian Federation). 2004. *Indicators of Science*. Moscow: Rosstat Information and Publishing Center.

————. 2006. *Statistical Register of Enterprises and Establishments*. Moscow: Rosstat Information and Publishing Center.

————. 2006a. *Statistics of Russia*. Moscow.

Rutherford, Thomas, and David Tarr. 2006. "Regional Impact of Russia's Accession to the WTO." Policy Research Working Paper 4015. Washington: World Bank.

Rutkowski, Jan, and Stefano Scarpetta. 2005. *Enhancing Job Opportunities in Eastern Europe and the Former Soviet Union*. Washington: World Bank.

Saggi, Kamal. 2006. "Foreign Direct Investment, Linkages, and Technology Spillovers." In *Global Integration and Technology Transfer*, edited by Bernard Hoekman and Beata Smarzynska Javorcik. Washington: Palgrave Macmillan and World Bank.

Saltykov, Boris. 2001. "Is Russian Science a Cherry Orchard?" *Nezavisimaya Gazeta*, February 16, 2001.

Scarpetta, Stefano, and others. 2002. "The Role of Policy and Institutions for Productivity and Firm Dynamics: Evidence from Micro and Industry Data." Economics Department Working Paper 329. Paris: OECD.

Schultz, Theodore. 1975. "The Value of the Ability to Deal with Disequilibria." *Journal of Economic Literature* 13 (3): 827–46.

Schweitzer, Glenn E., and Rita S. Guenther. 2005. "Basic Principles of the Russian Federation Policy on the Development of Science and Technology for the Period to 2010 and Beyond." In *Innovating for Profit in Russia: Summary of a Workshop.* Washington: National Academies Press.

SE Survey (Russian Competitiveness and Investment Climate Assessment Surveys: Small Enterprise Survey). 2005. Washington: World Bank.

Slinko, Irina, Evgeny Yakovlev, and Ekaterina Zhuravskaya. 2003. "Laws for Sale: Evidence from Russia." Working Paper W0031. Moscow: CEFIR (Center for Economic and Financial Research).

Tan, Hong. 1980. *Human Capital and Technological Change: A Study of Japanese Wage Differentials in Manufacturing.* Ph.D. dissertation, Yale University.

———. 2000. *Malaysia Skill Needs Study.* Washington: World Bank Institute.

———. 2005. *The Skills Challenge of New Technology.* Washington: World Bank.

Tan, Hong, and Geeta Batra. 1995. *Enterprise Training in Developing Countries: Incidence, Productivity Effects, and Policy Implications.* PSD Department Monograph. Washington: World Bank.

UNCTAD (United Nations Conference on Trade and Development). 2006a. Commodity Trade Statistics (COMTRADE) Database. Geneva (http://comtrade. un.org).

———. 2006b. *World Investment Report: The Shift Towards Services.* Geneva.

UNESCO. 2006. *Education Statistics.* Montreal: UNESCO Institute for Statistics (http://stats.uis.unesco.org).

UNESCO (United Nations Educational, Scientific, and Cultural Organization). Various years. *Statistical Yearbook.* Montreal: UNESCO Institute for Statistics.

U.S. PTO (U.S. Patent and Trademark Office). Various years. *All Technologies (Utility Patents) Report.* Washington (ftp://ftp.uspto.gov/pub/taf/all_tech.htm).

Watkins, Al. 2003. "From Knowledge to Wealth: Transforming Russian Science and Technology for a Modern Knowledge Economy." World Bank Policy Research Working Paper 2974. Washington: World Bank.

Weisner, Robert. 2005. "Research and Development Productivity and Spillovers: Empirical Evidence at the Firm Level." *Journal of Economic Surveys* 19 (4): 587–621.

Whalley, John., and X. Xin. 2006. "China's FDI and Non-FDI Economies and the Sustainability of Future Growth." Working Paper 12249. Cambridge, Mass.: National Bureau of Economic Research.

WITSA (World Information Technology and Services Alliance). *Enhanced Digital Planet 2006.* Arlington, Va.

World Bank. 1997. *Malaysia: Enterprise Training, Technology, and Productivity.* Country Study. Washington.

———. 2002–2006. *Enterprise Surveys,* various countries. Washington.

———. 2004. *World Development Report 2005: A Better Investment Climate for Everyone.* Oxford University Press.

———. 2005a. "Achieving Diversified Growth in Russia." Russian Economic Report 10. Washington.

————. 2005b. "From Disintegration to Reintegration: Eastern Europe and the Former Soviet Union in International Trade." Washington.

————. 2005c. "Malaysia: Firm Competitiveness, Investment Climate, and Growth." Report 26841-MA. Poverty Reduction, Economic Management, and Financial Sector Unit, East Asia and Pacific Region. Washington.

————. 2005d. "Russian Federation—From Transition to Development: A Country Economic Memorandum for the Russian Federation." Report Number 32308. Washington.

————. 2006a. *Doing Business 2006: Creating Jobs.* Washington.

————. 2006b. *Russian Federation: Country Partnership Strategy.* Washington.

————. 2006c. "Public Financial Support for Commercial Innovation: Europe and Central Asia Knowledge Economy Study." Part 1. Chief Economist's Regional Working Paper Series 1 (1). Washington.

————. 2006d. "Russian Economic Report." Working Paper 38402. Washington.

————. 2006e. *World Development Indicators 2006.* Washington.

Yakovlev, Andrei. 2006. "State Support Measures in Industry: Coverage, Recipients, Efficiency." Unpublished. Moscow: Higher School of Economics.

Yakovlev, Andrei, and Ekaterina Zhuravskaya. 2005. "State Capture: From Yeltsin to Putin." CEFIR Working Paper. Moscow: CEFIR.

Yermakov, Viktor P., and Veniamin S. Kaganov. 2000. "Razvitie malogo predprini-matel'stva v Rossii: glavnye napravleniya (po materialam II Vserossiyskogo s"ezda malykh predpriyatiy)" [Strategies for Small and Medium Enterprise Development in Russia]. Proceedings of the Second All-Russian Conference on SME Development, March 19.

Contributors

Enrique Blanco-Armas is an economist in the Jakarta Country Office of the World Bank.

Raj M. Desai is associate professor of international development at the Edmund A. Walsh School of Foreign Service at Georgetown University and a visiting fellow at the Wolfensohn Center for Development at the Brookings Institution.

Vladimir Gimpelson is director of the Center for Labor Market Studies at the Higher School of Economics at Moscow State University and a research fellow at the Institute for the Study of Labor (Bonn).

John Gabriel Goddard is an economist in the Private and Financial Sector Development Department for the Europe and Central Asia Region at the World Bank.

Itzhak Goldberg is senior adviser for policy and strategy in the Private and Financial Sector Development Department for the Europe and Central Asia Region at the World Bank.

Smita Kuriakose is a private sector development specialist in the Private and Financial Sector Development Department for the Europe and Central Asia Region at the World Bank.

Boris Kuznetsov is a chief researcher in the Interdepartmental Analytical Center and senior researcher in the Institute for Industrial and Market Studies at the Higher School of Economics at Moscow State University.

Yevgeniya Savchenko is a Ph.D. candidate in the Department of Economics at Georgetown University and a consultant to the Human Development Division for the South Asia Region at the World Bank.

Mark Schaffer is director of the Center for Economic Reform and Transformation and a professor in the Department of Economics at the School of Management and Languages at Heriot-Watt University and a research fellow at the Center for Economic Policy Research (London), the William Davidson Institute at the University of Michigan, and the Institute for the Study of Labor (Bonn).

Hong Tan is a consultant to the World Bank and former lead economist in the Human Development Division for the South Asia Region at the World Bank and the Investment Climate Enhancement Unit of the World Bank Institute.

Index

177